Environmental Health Risks

Environmental health involves the assessment and control of environmental factors that can potentially affect human health, such as radiation, toxic chemicals and other hazardous agents. It is often assumed that the assessment part is just a matter of scientific research, and the control part is only a matter of implementing standards which would unambiguously follow from that research. It is less commonly understood that environmental health also requires addressing questions of an ethical nature.

Bringing together work from experts across a range of sub-disciplines of environmental health, this collection of essays discusses the ethical implications of environmental health research and its application in practice. In doing so, it builds upon the insights and ideas put forward in the first volume of *Ethics of Environmental Health*, published by Routledge in early 2017.

This volume will be of great interest to students and scholars of environmental health, applied ethics, environmental ethics, medical ethics and bioethics, as well as those concerned with public health, environmental studies, toxicology and radiation.

Friedo Zölzer is Head of the Department of Radiology, Toxicology and Civil Protection at the University of South Bohemia, Czech Republic.

Gaston Meskens works part-time with the Centre for Ethics and Value Inquiry of the Faculty of Arts and Philosophy at the University of Ghent, Belgium and with the Science and Technology Studies group of the Belgian Nuclear Research Centre SCK-CEN, Belgium.

Routledge Studies in Environment and Health

The study of the impact of environmental change on human health has rapidly gained momentum in recent years, and an increasing number of scholars are now turning their attention to this issue. Reflecting the development of this emerging body of work, the *Routledge Studies in Environment and Health* series is dedicated to supporting this growing area with cutting edge interdisciplinary research targeted at a global audience. The books in this series cover key issues such as climate change, urbanisation, waste management, water quality, environmental degradation and pollution, and examine the ways in which these factors impact human health from a social, economic and political perspective.

Comprising edited collections, co-authored volumes and single author monographs, this innovative series provides an invaluable resource for advanced undergraduate and postgraduate students, scholars, policy makers and practitioners with an interest in this new and important field of study.

Ethics of Environmental Health
Edited by Friedo Zölzer and Gaston Meskens

Healthy Urban Environments
More-than-Human Theories
Cecily Maller

Climate Information for Public Health Action
Edited by Madeleine C. Thomson and Simon J. Mason

Environmental Health Risks
Ethical Aspects
Edited by Friedo Zölzer and Gaston Meskens

For more information about this series, please visit: www.routledge.com/Routledge-Studies-in-Environment-and-Health/book-series/RSEH

Environmental Health Risks

Ethical Aspects

Edited by Friedo Zölzer and Gaston Meskens

LONDON AND NEW YORK

from Routledge

First published 2019
by Routledge
2 Park Square, Milton Park, Abingdon, Oxon OX14 4RN

and by Routledge
711 Third Avenue, New York, NY 10017

Routledge is an imprint of the Taylor & Francis Group, an informa business

British Library Cataloguing-in-Publication Data
A catalogue record for this book is available from the British Library

Library of Congress Cataloging-in-Publication Data
A catalog record for this book has been requested

ISBN: 978-1-138-57470-0 (hbk)
ISBN: 978-1-351-27336-7 (ebk)

Typeset in Goudy
by Apex CoVantage, LLC

Contents

Figures

Tables

Contributors

Elisabeth Cardis is research professor in radiation epidemiology and head of the Radiation Programme at ISGlobal, Barcelona, Spain. Her main research area is epidemiology of radiation.

Carl F. Cranor is distinguished professor of philosophy and faculty member of the Environmental Toxicology Graduate Program at the University of California, Riverside. His publications include *Legally Poisoned: How the Law Puts Us at Risk from Toxicants* (Harvard, 2011).

Jessica Nihlén Fahlquist is a senior lecturer in biomedical ethics at the Centre for Research Ethics and Bioethics at Uppsala University, Sweden. Her research focuses on notions of moral responsibility, and generally on ethical aspects of risk in the context of public health, environment and technology.

Chris J. Kalman is a Consultant Occupational Physician, working in the National Health Service in Scotland. He has a specialist interest in support to radiation workers, and has previously worked as Chief Medical Officer of a Nuclear Power Utility.

Michiel Korthals is emeritus professor of applied philosophy at Wageningen University, Netherlands, and guest professor at Free University Amsterdam and University of Gastronomic Sciences, Pollenzo, Italy. His publications include *Before Dinner: Philosophy and Ethics of Food* (Dodrecht, 2004).

Liudmila Liutsko is postdoctoral fellow in the Radiation Programme at ISGlobal, Barcelona, Spain. Her specialisations are in mathematics, radioecology and psychology. She holds an MSc in Environmental Science & Policy and a Ph.D. in Psychology.

Leslie London is a professor of public health medicine and head of the Health and Human Rights programme in the School of Public Health and Family Medicine at the University of Cape Town, South Africa. His research include examining the intersection of human rights with public health policy.

Gaston Meskens is a scientist, philosopher and artist. He works part-time with the Centre for Ethics and Value Inquiry of the Faculty of Arts and Philosophy of the University of Ghent, Belgium, and with the Science and Technology Studies group of the Belgian Nuclear Research Centre SCK•CEN.

Takashi Ohba is assistant professor of radiation health management of the Fukushima Medical University, Fukushima, Japan. He is working on health physics aspects of nuclear accidents.

Deborah Oughton is research director of the Centre for Environmental Radioactivity (CERAD) at the Norwegian University of Life Sciences. She has worked extensively on ethical and social aspects of radiation risk management.

David B. Resnik is a bioethicist and Institutional Review Board chair at the National Institute for Environmental Health Sciences, National Institutes of Health. He is also associate editor of the journal Accountability in Research and a Fellow of the American Association for the Advancement of Science.

Sabine Roeser is professor of ethics and head of Ethics and Philosophy of Technology at TU Delft, Netherlands. Her research concerns moral knowledge, intuitions, emotions and evaluative aspects of risk. She has served on various Dutch governmental advisory boards concerning risky technologies.

Thierry Schneider is director of CEPN (Nuclear Evaluation Protection Centre) in Fontenay-aux-Roses, France. His main research area is health economics applied to radiation protection.

Peter Schröder-Bäck is Associate Professor in the Department of International Health of Maastricht University, Netherlands. He is also president of the section *Ethics in Public Health* of the European Public Health Association (EUPHA).

Colin L. Soskolne is professor emeritus at the University of Alberta, Edmonton, Canada. Before, he was professor of epidemiology in the School of Public Health at that university. He is also adjunct professor in the Faculty of Health at the University of Canberra, Australia.

Husseim Stuck earned a bachelor's degree in Environmental Engineering from Brandenburg University of Technology, Cottbus, Germany, where his final project was on value judgments in environmental economics.

Behnam Taebi is Associate Professor in ethics of technology at Delft University of Technology. He is the coordinating editor of a volume on *The Ethics of Nuclear Energy* (Cambridge, 2015). He is also a member of The Young Academy of the Netherlands Royal Academy of Arts and Sciences.

Joanne Vincenten is an independent consultant for strategy development and implementation with UNICEF and WHO, and a Research Associate with the Department of International Health of Maastricht University, Netherlands.

Friedo Zölzer is professor of environmental sciences at the Faculty of Health and Social Sciences of the University of South Bohemia, Ceske Budejovice, Czech Republic. His main research area is radiobiology. He was a member of the ICRP task group on *Ethics of Radiological Protection*.

Foreword

The consistent application of ethical principles provides a firm and defensible basis for a civilised society. It is often the case that scientific findings are numerous and deep, but a fundamental challenge remains – how to use this information to make good decisions that will support and sustain the environment and human health. What exactly is a "good decision"? What or whose values form the foundations of a "good decision"? Ethical principles provide a foundation and common language to understand personal and social values, to encourage an interconnection between the scientific and social disciplines and to help discuss what makes a "good" decision.

Biomedical ethical constructs have focused on protecting the individual and have sometimes served as a framework for ethics as applied to environmental health issues. The Beauchamp and Childress approach to biomedical ethics has four principles: respect for autonomy, nonmaleficence (do no harm), beneficence (do good) and justice (be fair). This framework has served the medical community well and provides minimal safe guards for individuals. However, it has been suggested that the environmental health community needs an additional and broader focus. The ethical principles to guide decision and activities around environmental health issues should be expanded to include, among others, solidarity, precaution, dignity, veracity, responsibility and sustainability.

New branches of science, such as epigenetics, have deepened our understanding of the environment, but with these new approaches and information there is also a need to expand the ethical constructs. Epigenetic changes (exposures that may change genetic expression) may occur at very low levels of exposure not only to environmental chemicals but also from diet and stress. This moves us beyond the passive biomedical ethical construct of "do no harm" to a more positive frame of "do good". For example, adults and society in general have a responsibility to provide children with quality nutrition, and a clean, healthy and relatively stress-free environment in which they can reach and maintain their full genetic and epigenetic potential.

Who is better to take on the task of integrating the sticky issues around personal and social values when they intersect with the structure and often-unwavering data from scientific pursuits than two physicists with interests in radiobiology, toxicology, moral philosophy, intelligent decision technologies, art and ethics?

Friedo Zölzer, Professor of Environmental Sciences, Faculty of Health and Social Studies at the University of South Bohemia, Czech Republic, and Gaston Meskens, Faculty Member of Arts and Philosophy, Centre for Ethics and Value Inquiry, Ghent University, Belgium, have pulled together an interesting and thought-provoking collection of writers to explore some of the issues facing scientists, students, policymakers and the public as we all try to understand and address challenges facing the world.

In this volume, Zölzer and Meskens work with subject authors to explore important and timely scientific issues that require the application of ethical principles. The volume is divided into four parts: perceptions of risk, philosophical approaches, vested interests and tools for decision-making.

Risk perception, risk assessment and risk communication have not often been linked with ethical principles, making Part I of the book a notable and useful contribution to any discussion of environmental issues. Toxicology and risk assessment have primarily focused on summarising the scientific data and applying models, often unfettered by the acknowledgement of personal biases or points of view. Adding ethical constructs to these efforts is an important and essential addition. Risk assessment and risk communication have benefited from integration into the broader goal of health assessment; however, ethics also needs to be integrated into the health assessments of chemical compounds or policies around their use. Ethics should be no longer focused on protecting the just individual, but also ethics have a strong role to play when decisions are made that impact the community in general.

In Part II of the book, authors explore the macro-level challenges to the social acceptance and integration of ethical constructs and include an examination of the ethical hypothesis and how to design the ethically based study. Part III of the book adds the highly important exploration of vested interests in science. For too long, corporate influence and personal biases that cannot help but influence interpretation of scientific findings have gone unacknowledged and unreported. This lack of transparency, and even lack of personal insight among scientists, has contributed to public cynicism with regard to science and scientific endeavours. The inclusion of ethical principles in the design and conduct of scientific investigation, discussion of scientific findings and the application of the results of scientific projects will help us all do a better job of developing supportable and sustainable policies that truly protect the public.

It is critically important to use existing tools and develop new ones to incorporate ethical principles into our decision-making, whether it is corporate, public or personal policy issues. Part IV of the book addresses the tools specifically designed to enhance the inclusion of ethics into decision-making. Many of these decisions necessitate that businesses, academics, non-profits and the public work together and take joint responsibility for addressing the pertinent problems. Ethical principles provide the common language, the structure and the framework to have fruitful and longer-lasting solutions to the world's many current and future problems. This book is a must-read for environmental scientists, policymakers or anyone interested in applying scientific findings to environmental problems with a defensible ethical approach to better help their community or country.

Steven G. Gilbert
Director and Founder of the Institute of Neurotoxicology and Neurological Disorders, and Affiliate Professor at the University of Washington's School of Public Health, Seattle, USA

Preface

Environmental health encompasses the assessment and control of those environmental factors that can potentially affect human health, such as radiation, toxic chemicals and other hazardous agents. It is often assumed that the assessment part is just a matter of scientific research, and the control part is only a matter of implementing standards which would unambiguously follow from that research. But it is less commonly understood that environmental health also primarily requires addressing questions of an ethical nature. How can we determine what is an "acceptable" risk for the general population or for certain groups? How can different types of risks – for instance, economic and health risks – be compared? How should we deal with uneven distributions of risks and benefits? How do we communicate about risks with the stakeholders? What should science do when confronted with factual uncertainties about risks that cannot be cleared out? What is the role of emotions such as sympathy, empathy and feelings or responsibility in environmental health governance? How to counter vested interests of the powerful and to restore deprived rights of the vulnerable

The questions raised above show the complexity of each of the environmental health issues at stake as well as the wide variety of challenges that need ethical scrutiny. For all of them, the ethical concepts tacitly assumed in environmental health need to be made explicit, critically reviewed and, to some extent at least, developed further. These are the objectives of the authors contributing to this book. They are scholars and practitioners coming from the whole range of environmental health research and practice, and their writings result from a series of presentations and discussions that made up the *Third International Symposium on Ethics of Environmental Health* held at České Budějovice, Czech Republic, in August 2016. As with the preceding symposium, financial support was again kindly provided by OPERRA, the "Open Project for the European Research Area", which included a subtask aimed at "identifying issues and relevant institutions in the fields of risk communication, risk perception and ethics of radiation protection". Nevertheless, the papers included in this selection represent a mix of radiation-related and radiation-unrelated issues, and we trust they are of interest and relevance to those involved in environmental health research and practice independent of their respective subdisciplines. This book can be seen as a follow-up on a first volume – entitled "Ethics of Environmental Health" published by

Routledge in early 2017 – that came into being through a similar dynamic. Similar to that publication, we hope readers will find this book once again inspiring in a general ethical-philosophical sense as well as useful in their daily professional activity.

Gaston Meskens
Friedo Zölzer
July 2018

Part I

Perception of environmental health risks and ethics

1 Environmental health risks, moral emotions and responsible risk communication[1]

Jessica Nihlén Fahlquist and Sabine Roeser

1 Introduction

Environmental health risks give rise to intense and emotional debates, which pose a great challenge for risk communication. The effectiveness of risk communication is a well-debated and well-researched area. However, effective risk communication can give rise to ethical questions, which have not yet been extensively discussed in the literature on risk communication, with some exceptions (cf. Morgan and Lave 1990; Valenti and Wilkins 1995; Johnson 1999). In this paper, we focus on how to 'communicate responsibly' about risk, an activity that requires ethical analysis. We develop a three-level framework of morally responsible risk communication, focusing on the procedure, the message and the effects of risk communication. These levels provide a basis for three conditions for ethical risk communication: ethical risk communication requires an ethically legitimate procedure, an ethically justified message and concern about the effects of risk communication. We specifically address the role of emotions as a key to addressing and explicating moral values at these three levels of risk communication. We then discuss several cases related to environmental health risks to see what implications our framework has for risk communication.

2 Moral emotions and risk

Emotions play an important role in public risk perception (Slovic 2010). However, emotions are usually seen as an obstacle to sound decision-making and communication about risks (Sunstein 2005). At most, emotions are seen as a potential tool for manipulation, which is why emotions are often endorsed by marketing experts and eschewed by those who are looking for criteria for responsible risk communication. These views are based on the idea that emotions are irrational gut reactions, i.e. suggesting a dichotomy between rationality and emotions (e.g. Haidt 2001). However, developments in emotion research show that this is a false dilemma, based on an overly simplistic conception of emotions. Emotion scholars from philosophy and psychology have shown that emotions are not opposed to rationality, knowledge and cognition, but they are a form of practical, moral rationality and that they have cognitive and affective aspects

(Scherer 1984; Frijda 1987; Lazarus 1991; Solomon 1993; Nussbaum 2001; Roberts 2003; Zagzebski 2003). Neuropsychological research by Damasio shows that people without emotions but intact rationality have impaired capacities for decision-making when it comes to concrete practical and moral judgements, and concerning judgements about acceptable risk (Damasio 1994). Decision-making about technological risks is not only a matter of technical, scientific expertise but also involves an ethical assessment (Shrader-Frechette 1991; Hansson 2004; Asveld and Roeser 2009). Technologies and risks are inherently value laden (Verbeek 2011; Möller 2012). Emotions such as sympathy, compassion and feelings of responsibility help to draw our attention to moral aspects of risks such as justice, fairness and autonomy (Roeser 2006, 2009, 2010a, 2010b). Including moral values, virtues and emotions does not threaten the objectivity of risk; rather, they are required for a proper appreciation of risk (Roeser 2006; Athanassoulis and Ross 2010; Hansson 2010; Hermansson 2012). These ideas can shed important new light on morally responsible risk communication (Roeser 2012b; Roeser and Nihlén Fahlquist 2013). In the following sections, we will explore how moral emotions can contribute to ethically responsible communication about environmental health risks.

3 Three conditions for ethical risk communication

According to Leiss and Powell (2004), the practice of risk communication has developed through three phases. In the first phase, risk communication was seen as a form of education whereby the public should be informed about risk estimates. The underlying idea was that people in general did not understand science well enough and needed to be educated. The second phase transformed risk communication into a marketing practice with the aim to persuade people to adopt a certain message. In the current, third phase risk communication is viewed as a participatory practice with which the gap between experts and lay people can be bridged (Leiss and Powell 2004). Trust plays an important role in bridging this gap and making risk communication effective (e.g. Persensky et al. 2004). However, it should be emphasized that trust is not merely important in order to achieve effective risk communication. Trust is a moral emotion that requires trustworthiness and ethically responsible risk communication. When a government, a powerful agency or corporation aims to affect people's attitudes and behaviour in accordance with a certain goal, this entails moral responsibility. If this responsibility is taken seriously, this can create trust. It is important to see the difference between building trust in order to communicate effectively and building trust because one acknowledges one's power and takes responsibility accordingly. Thus, ethical risk communication is not merely required for instrumental reasons, but first and foremost for normative reasons.

We will now discuss three levels of risk communication and how feelings of moral responsibility, trust and other moral emotions can and should play a role at these levels in order to achieve responsible risk communication.

Risk communication consists of a message concerning risk and a procedure through which the message is designed and communicated, which can be an iterative process. Needless to say, there will also be effects of the risk communicative process and the message communicated. Risk assessors and risk managers are likely to have intended effects with the process and their message, i.e. their assessment and description of the risk, but it is also conceivable that the procedure and message have unintended effects. Consequently, risk communication can be analyzed at three levels: the procedure, the message and the effects.

These three levels provide a conceptual model that can be used for ethical analysis. Moral emotions are relevant in relation to all of these stages. In common approaches to risk communication and stakeholder participation, emotions do not play an explicit role. However, given the research illustrating the importance of moral emotions in relation to risk (Slovic 2010), stakeholders should be explicitly encouraged to express moral emotions concerning risks, as this will help to clarify moral concerns, thereby facilitating ethical reflection (Roeser 2018). In a similar vein, we see that messages about risk usually either consist of callous numbers or attempts to appeal to superficial gut reactions in a manipulative way. However, risk messages are inherently value laden. These values can be expressed through moral emotions like care, empathy and respect. Such emotions are not primitive gut reactions, but have cognitive content and a focus on moral values. This way, they can contribute to critical reflection (Roeser 2018).

In addition to the procedure and the message, the effects of risk communication should also be analyzed from an ethical perspective. Interestingly, evaluation of risk communication is under-theorized and seldom undertaken in practice (Fischoff, Brewer, and Downes 2011). However, Downs distinguishes between three types of evaluation which should be undertaken. First, there is the formative evaluation during the planning phase. Second, there is the process evaluation, evaluating the implementation of, for example, a campaign. Finally, there should be an outcome evaluation, analyzing whether the goals of, for example the campaign, were met (Downs 2011). Our suggestion is that the evaluation should take emotions into account: those of recipients or stakeholders. This could be done by assessing whether they have been emotionally affected in a morally acceptable way. In addition, the evaluation could also address the emotions of risk communicators, for example care, empathy and feelings of responsibility which contribute to designing a morally responsible risk message and procedure.

Evaluating the intended and unintended effects of risk communication is needed to evaluate whether the procedure and message are ethically justified and whether they address all relevant actors, moral emotions and values.

Against the background of the three-level framework presented previously, risk communication should fulfil three conditions. Ethically responsible risk communication has a legitimate procedure, an ethically justified risk message, and concern for and evaluation of the effects of the message and procedure. We will now go through these conditions in more detail in turn.

4 A responsible risk communication procedure and the role of moral emotions

The first condition for responsible risk communication requires a legitimate procedure. The dominant view in the social science literature is that a legitimate procedure of decision-making about risk should be a form of participatory technology assessment. Participation can take place at different stages of risk analysis, i.e. in risk assessment, risk management and risk communication. Many scholars argue that if relevant stakeholders are involved in political discussions and decisions about risk, it increases the likelihood of achieving acceptance (Skitka, Winquist, and Hutchinson 2003). People may accept a decision that they think has been reached fairly, even when they disagree with the actual outcome.

It is worth emphasizing that regardless of the efficacy of participatory approaches, it is ethically imperative in a democratic society that the public is included and allowed to participate in decision-making and communication about risk. However, including stakeholders in risk communication and regulation entails numerous challenges (cf. e.g. Bijker, Bal, and Hendriks 2009; Lofstedt et al. 2010). First, how should fairness and legitimacy be achieved within the participatory context? Second, who should be represented, by whom and how should the representation be implemented? Jamieson and Briggs (2009), discussing so-called stakeholder partnerships as a promising way to make risk communication more inclusive, argue that some of the challenges involve deciding how to achieve properly balanced and representative partnerships and how to make sure the representatives actually speak for their stakeholder groups (Jamieson and Briggs 2009). It has been argued that even if risk communication becomes more inclusive and participatory, it is essentially a 'relationship between unequal parties' and there will always be an asymmetry in communicative initiative, informational privilege, and risk influence between experts and lay people (Hayenhjelm 2006). The party that initiates communication naturally has the privilege to set the agenda and decide with whom to communicate (Hayenhjelm 2006). An additional problem is the fact that experts often disagree, because contemporary risk issues are often ambiguous and value laden and experts can be biased due to conflicts of interest. However, that does not necessarily imply a relativistic argument for abandoning the role of experts and to leave all risk decisions to lay people. As Munnichs argues, experts do have specific cognitive skills and enjoy public authority for this reason. However, their dominance may be questioned in an adequate procedure of expert contestation (Munnichs 2004). The latter entails a view, inspired by Popper, according to which scientific claims should be exposed to a free competition of thought, where as many different expert views as possible are represented in a debate. Some experts are likely to share the same worries as the public, which means that those worries are represented in scientifically informed debates about risk. Although this may be part of the solution to make the procedure more legitimate, a morally responsible risk communication procedure also requires that the public actively participate in the debate. Lay people can add important perspectives, as they have a broader conception of risk that comprises moral values (Slovic 2000) that are also emphasized by philosophers who study risk (Hansson

2004; Roeser 2007; Asveld and Roeser 2009). As emotions are important in lay people's risk perceptions and could draw our attention to moral aspects of risk issues, they should be explicitly discussed and reflected upon (Roeser 2010b). This allows for a fair dialogue in which all the affected parties and their emotions are heard and seriously considered (Roeser and Pesch 2016).

5 Responsible risk communication: the risk message and the role of moral emotions

In addition to a legitimate procedure for communicating risks, the second condition for ethically responsible risk communication requires that the risk message should be formulated and presented in a way that is ethically justified. It has been illustrated by social scientific research on risk that different framings of risk messages have different results on people's perceptions and behaviour (Tversky and Kahneman 1974; Thaler and Sunstein 2008). Since there are no neutral ways to design a message, it is crucial to analyze the moral values expressed by different framings. This entails two tasks, a formal and a content-related task. First, moral values and emotional appeals expressed by risk messages should be made explicit (formal task). Second, a debate on relevant moral emotions should result in a deliberated and morally reasonable risk message (content-related task). As mentioned previously, a risk message contains scientific data, but it is also inherently value laden. Risk messages usually concern the effects of human activity on health, safety and the environment, which touch upon important moral values such as the well-being of humans, nature and future generations. Furthermore, since it is impossible to communicate all risks, a selection has to be made, and this selection is not a purely scientific issue (cf. Slovic 2000), but also a normative decision with ethical implications. How the risks are presented or framed in messages has direct implications on how the audience is affected, which can involve moral emotions such as sympathy, empathy, care and feelings of responsibility. Are possibly existing scientific uncertainties or controversies presented, and if so, how? One decision to be made is whether the message should aim at convincing people to behave in a specific way, or whether it should present various options for action with a list of pros and cons. Depending on the urgency, the former or latter option might be chosen. For example, in the case of a text message alert to an explosion with life-threatening gas formation, the message might be simple and unambiguous: 'close all windows due to dangerous gas' (cf. e.g. Jagtman 2010). On the other hand, in the case of long-term health effects of a certain activity, the pros and cons of alternatives may be presented in a balanced and nuanced way to leave more room for the decisions of recipients (Nihlén Fahlquist and Roeser 2011; Roeser and Nihlén Fahlquist 2013).

6 Responsible risk communication: assessing the effects on people and their emotions from a moral perspective

Finally, the third condition for ethically responsible risk communication requires that, when the message has been communicated on a larger scale in society, an outcome evaluation should assess how it is perceived and experienced. Evaluating risk communication is important for reasons of effectiveness and efficiency (Downs 2011). For example, if a public health authority has spent a substantial amount of money on an anti-smoking campaign, the outcome evaluation will ask whether the campaign actually led to a decrease in smoking. However, ethically justified risk communication should also be concerned with the effects in a wider context. For example, one could ask whether people experience that their moral concerns were adequately addressed in the procedure and risk message. The importance of including the effects becomes clear if we consider public health risks. For example, the current infant feeding information lacks concern for certain groups of stakeholders, i.e. non-breastfeeding mothers. The latter are oftentimes negatively affected by the framing of the message, i.e. whereas breastfeeding is portrayed as risk-free, bottle-feeding is portrayed as risky (Nihlén Fahlquist and Roeser 2011; Nihlén Fahlquist 2016). It is possible that a risk communication is effective, but ethically problematic due to other types of outcomes. It may be effective and efficient in that intended effects were achieved within the budgetary limits, but it can at the same time have unintended effects which are ethically questionable. For example, a vaccination programme may lead to herd immunity and be in that sense effective, but at the same time it can lead to a lack of trust because it was carried out in a morally irresponsible way, for example by presenting information in a lopsided, manipulative way.

Hence, evaluating the effects of risk communication should entail assessing whether the effects on the emotions and values of recipients are legitimate. This in turn requires an emotionally sensitive attitude of risk communicators. They should use emotions such as care, empathy, compassion and feelings of responsibility and respect when designing a risk communication strategy.

7 Environmental health risks and the three conditions of ethical risk communication

In this section, we will discuss how the three conditions of ethical risk communication can be applied to environmental health risks and what role moral emotions can play in these three stages.

Condition 1: environmental health risks and a legitimate risk communication procedure

The Fukushima accident in 2011 illustrates the need for a legitimate risk communication procedure. Nuclear risk communication in Japan prior to Fukushima appears far from participatory and transparent. There were close ties between government and industry, and the approach to risk communication was top-down, leading to public distrust. Despite public concern, nuclear plants were sited in local communities and when there were lawsuits, courts ruled in favour of government and industry (Figueroa 2013).

Environmental health risks are complex issues, technically as well as politically and ethically, and nuclear energy is a case in point. The lack of a concise and consistent message in the case of nuclear energy puts the procedure to the fore, as this involves societal decisions with potentially great impact. The most important lesson from recent studies and arguments in social science and philosophy is that questions like to what extent, if at all, we should use nuclear energy, will not be answered by conventional methods, e.g. risk analysis. There are moral values at stake, which means that decisions have to be made in a democratic way, after serious debate about values and not merely about numbers. This also holds for other environmental health risks, for example related to other energy sources such as natural gas extraction (including shale gas).

A crucial question in relation to both procedure and risk message is how to delineate the so-called 'decision horizon'. The problem of an 'indeterminate decision horizon' concerns the lack of clarity concerning what the decision is about, for example when there is no agreement on the scope of the decision or what problem it is supposed to solve. In cases of societal decision-making under uncertainty, a line has to be drawn to demarcate the horizon for the decision (Hansson 1996). There is no one 'right' horizon, but depending on the perspectives of stakeholders, the horizon will be different. Different stakeholders are likely to have different views on what the risk decision is about, and hence what to communicate. For example, nuclear energy producers might think that the relevant risk decisions are about acceptable risks in the context of already existing power plants. Greenpeace, on the other hand, might argue that the major decision to make is whether nuclear energy should be allowed. It should be acknowledged that the choice of a decision horizon and the fact that different stakeholders have different views on this is ethically relevant, because different decision horizons reflect different moral values of different stakeholders, indicating the morally crucial role of a fair procedure. Furthermore, a transparent and open procedure should enable and facilitate moral emotions to be explicitly addressed and the public to be treated with respect and care (Roeser and Pesch 2016). This is currently not the case in many risk debates. Emotions either get ignored or are seen as endpoints of debates (the technocratic and populist pitfalls respectively, Roeser 2011). Even though there are currently many forms of participatory technology assessment (Van Asselt and Rijkens-Klomp 2002), such approaches do not include emotions (Harvey 2009). However, based on the view that emotions provide us with insight into moral values, emotions should be seen as the starting point of public debate and they should play an explicit role in deliberation. This can be done by moderators of public debates and deliberations, by asking people explicitly about their emotions, for example with the following questions:

- What are you afraid of?
- What do you think could happen?
- Why does that worry you?
- Do you find the provided information clear? Transparent? Trustworthy? If not, why not?

- Under what conditions would you be less worried?
- Can you understand the viewpoint of the person from the other group? If not, can you try to place yourself in their shoes by listening to their story?
- What do you think the problem is for which this technology has been developed? Do you think there is a simple solution to this problem? Can we solve the problem by not using this technology? Or does that give rise to other problems? Can you try to imagine scenarios with and without this and/or other technologies?
- If you were in charge, how would you solve this problem?

These questions can be geared towards different kinds of risks. In the case of nuclear risks, one can include references to specific morally relevant aspects of nuclear energy such as the potential for catastrophic risks on the one hand vs. the low probability on the other hand, the long-time horizon of nuclear waste disposal, the problems of climate change, energy consumption and how to design a responsible energy mix.

Questions such as these can entice people to use reflection and deliberation, however, not in a detached, purely analytical way, but by drawing on emotional capacities such as imagination, compassion and empathy. They stimulate people to think further, listen to each other in a respectful way and try to take on different points of view, thereby facilitating ethical reflection. At the same time, a procedure in which questions like the ones above are asked can prevent stalemates that often occur in public debates, which are probably partially due to the way these debates are usually conducted. Even in methods of participatory technology assessment, emotions are not explicitly addressed. However, such methods can be made more fruitful by drawing on emotions and imaginative and empathetic capacities by asking questions such as the ones suggested here. Questions such as these enable people to feel that they have something to contribute, that they are agents, not merely passive pawns in the hands of powerful companies and governments.

What has been argued so far points to the conclusion that it is highly important to include stakeholders and their moral emotions and considerations in an ethically justified procedure of communication about environmental health risks.

Condition 2: environmental health risks and legitimate risk messages

It could be argued that the procedure is the most important, or only, important thing in order to achieve ethically justified risk communication: if communication is democratic and inclusive, the result will be legitimate. However, even if the procedure is legitimate, risk decisions and risk messages will not automatically be ethically acceptable. A possible pitfall is that a procedure taking all possible viewpoints into consideration might result in a lack of leadership and a 'risk information vacuum' if no decisions are reached and the discussion continues (Leiss and Powell 2004). A lack of message is thus also a message and it is not only ineffective, but in some cases unethical to refrain from communicating risks. From an ethical perspective, a risk information vacuum is disrespectful and shows a lack of care and concern for other people. Furthermore, the procedure and the message are intertwined and co-shape each other.

Environmental health risks can manifest themselves in various ways. First, there are safety risks relating to accidents and the immediate repercussions in terms of e.g. people's health. Second, there are long-term environmental risks. Risks can be caused by technology or human error. Materialized risks can affect human beings and the environment, now and in the future.

Regardless if the message concerning a technology is that 'It is safe' or 'It is not safe', values are expressed, as the messages are based both on probability calculations and views on moral acceptability. The notion 'safety' suggests that a risk is acceptable, but acceptability is a normative notion and requires normative reflection next to empirical data (cf. Möller 2012 who argues that safety is a 'thick concept', i.e. a concept that is descriptive and normative at the same time). As has been argued by social scientists and philosophers, quantitative information is not sufficient to decide whether a risk is acceptable or not (Shrader-Frechette 1991; Krimsky and Golding 1992). For example, a certain activity is always safe or risky in relation to something else, and what we choose to compare it to is a normative choice. After the Fukushima accident, several countries revised their main official risk message concerning nuclear energy. In Germany, the previous message that nuclear energy was safe enough was replaced by a message stating that nuclear power is not safe enough and should be banned. For example, within a few days the German Chancellor, Angela Merkel, decreed to immediately shut down nine reactors (Ionescu 2012). Messages such as these, concerning the risks and safety of a technology, contain values. A complex range of issues can be included in messages which all reflect values. For example, stating that nuclear energy is needed in order to mitigate climate change may express values concerning the need to reduce anthropogenic CO2 emissions, but could also be seen as expressing a lack of concern for the ability of future generations to deal with nuclear waste. Other relevant values include intergenerational justice, rights not to be harmed, and environmental and social sustainability. These values should be made explicit and discussed when deliberating and deciding what the message ought to be.

Borrowing a concept used in ethics of technology, we could say that a risk message should be designed in a 'value-sensitive' way in order to be ethical (see e.g. Friedman 2004; Flanagan, Howe, and Nissenbaum 2005; Van den Hoven 2005; Manders-Huits 2011).

Values in risk messages can be made more explicit by appealing to moral emotions, i.e. care about the lives of people who live in other places or in a remote future. Fear, care and feelings of responsibility, for example, could help us to morally reflect about whether we are justified to expose other people to the risks of climate change or about how acceptable the risks and benefits of various energy technologies are. Of course this is challenging, since emotions can be abused in communication, for example, by appealing to instinctive responses, in order to manipulate people to engage in certain behaviour, as marketing experts are very well aware (cf. e.g. Ross and Davis 2010). However, by appealing to potentially reflective emotions such as sympathy, compassion and feelings of responsibility, risk communication can stimulate critical, ethical thinking. When communicating about values involved in for example energy technologies, one could include pictures and stories of victims of climate change and coal mining on the one hand, and victims of disasters of nuclear energy, fracking and scenarios of future generations dealing with nuclear waste on the other. One could also include visualizations of our ecological footprint and energy consumption to increase awareness of our wasteful lifestyle. Additionally, one could include pictures of more or less successful siting of alternative energy sources such as windmills, solar panels and water dams. By showing the multifaceted nature of energy policy one could increase awareness for the complexity of this issue. Such a risk message could communicate that decisions about the acceptability of an energy technology might not be all or nothing decisions, but rather concern possible ingredients in a future energy mix about which we all have to make up our minds and in which we all have a responsibility. Such a risk message would explicate the values involved, thereby facilitating sound and moral decision-making concerning messages about environmental health risks.

Condition 3: environmental health risks and the effects of risk communication

The third condition of ethical risk communication requires a moral evaluation of the effects of risk communication. If we consider risk communication concerning the Fukushima accident in Japan, there were a number of ethically problematic features before, during and after the accident, which led to a (justified) lack of trust. As the Fukushima accident occurred in a time when information is accessible on the Internet in real time, it might seem as though this ensures adequate risk communication. However, experts did not themselves have access to all information, resulting in confusing and contradictory messages. According to some studies, the Japanese government did not reveal key aspects of the accident and its associated risks. The government understated the risks and wrongly sent the message that nuclear power is safe (Shrader-Frechette 2011; Figueroa 2013). The government's attempts to convince the public that it was in control backfired, since the events revealed that the government was not in control (Figueroa 2013). Thus, the ethically flawed risk communication procedure and message led to anger, frustration and distrust. Arguably, these are justified moral emotions in this case.

This illustrates that risk communication strategies can have different results in terms of effectiveness as much as in terms of trust and moral responsibility. This could also provide invaluable information for future decisions on messages and procedures concerning risk. Assessing the effects of risk communication should be an iterative process where the message and procedure can be reassessed and reevaluated in the light of the possible effects. Emotions can play a key role in assessing, evaluating and reflecting on how to possibly improve the effects of risk communication. People could be asked how they experienced a certain risk communication campaign. This should also involve asking them about their emotions and moral views: have they been affected by the risk communication? If not, why do they think they have not, and what could be done differently? If they were affected, one should ask in what ways they were affected. It should be asked whether people experienced it as helpful, providing further insights. Furthermore, it should be asked whether the risk communication has made them feel uncomfortable and if so, how. There is important information to be gained if we understand why risk communication made people feel uncomfortable. Was it because it made them aware of their own responsibilities, or was it because it provoked a sense of hopelessness, making them passive? As Hulme (2009) has pointed out, this is a possible pitfall in communication about climate change, and we can extend this to communication about environmental health risks. From an ethical point of view, it would be desirable to practice forms of risk communication that encourage people to be actively engaged, to see a possible role for a contribution of one's own rather than seeing oneself as a victim of inevitable circumstances or higher powers that are ignorant or dismissive of people's views. Assessing effects on emotions is a currently underdeveloped possibility that can provide potentially huge effects in creating awareness about climate change and critical reflection about technologies that may give rise to environmental health risks.

Against the background of the third condition of responsible risk communication, there are desirable and less desirable outcomes. If the effect of a certain risk communication effort is emotional reflection and a willingness to take responsibility for energy-related issues that is a desirable effect. If the outcome is a lack of trust or a sense of hopelessness and passivity, arguably, risk communication should be reconsidered and reformed.

8 Conclusion

We have argued that risk communication should not only be effective, but also ethical, which requires taking moral emotions into consideration. Current approaches to risk communication either dismiss emotions or take them as inevitable and irrational. In direct contrast, we have argued that emotions are a source of practical rationality and moral knowledge, and are hence crucial for responsible risk communication. We have argued that there are three levels of risk communication, implying three conditions for ethically responsible risk communication. First, the procedure should be legitimate. Second, the message should be ethically justified. Third, the effects should be adequately addressed. All of these should involve moral emotions. This means that ethical risk communication requires a legitimate procedure for discussing the moral values and emotions associated with a technology. Furthermore, it requires ethical deliberation about the values and emotions involved in different messages. Finally, it requires that proper attention is paid to the effects of risk communicative efforts, for example in terms of a sense of responsibility or a lack of trust between lay people and experts.

Taking emotions seriously in risk communication provides for huge potential, as it enables people to develop and articulate more nuanced points of views, to overcome stalemates and to be more respectful and understanding of diverging points of views due to increased awareness of the problems and due to an atmosphere in which people treat each other in a respectful and open minded way. This is especially important in the case of communication about environmental health risks, given the high stakes and current stalemates, to which this approach can provide a promising, constructive and morally legitimate way out.

Note

1 This is an adapted version of the following article: Jessica Nihlén Fahlquist and Sabine Roeser (2015), 'Nuclear Energy, Responsible Risk Communication and Moral Emotions: A Three Level Framework', *Journal of Risk Research* Vol. 18, Issue 3: 333–46. With kind permission by the *Journal of Risk Research*.

References

Asveld L., Roeser S. (2009) *The Ethics of Technological Risk*. London: Earthscan.

Athanassoulis N., Ross A. (2010) 'A Virtue Ethical Account of Making Decisions About Risk', *Journal of Risk Research*, 13(2), 217–30.

Bijker W., Bal R., Hendriks R. (2009) *The Paradox of Scientific Authority: The Role of Scientific Advice in Democracies*. Cambridge, MA: MIT Press.

Damasio A. (1994) *Descartes' Error*. New York, NY: Putnam.

Downs J. S. (2011) 'Chapter 3: Evaluations', in: *Communicating Risks and Benefits: An Evidence-based User's Guide, New Hampshire: US Food and Drug Administration (FDA)*, 11–18. Silver Spring, MD: U.S. Department of Health and Human Services.

Figueroa P. M. (2013) 'Risk Communication Surrounding the Fukushima Nuclear Disaster: An Anthropological Approach', *Asia Europe Journal*, 11, 53–64.

Fischoff B., Brewer N. T., Downes J. S. (2011) *Communicating Risks and Benefits: An Evidence-based User's Guide*. Silver Spring, MD: US Food and Drug Administration (FDA), U.S. Department of Health and Human Services.

Flanagan M., Howe D., Nissenbaum H. (2005) 'Values at Play: Design Tradeoffs in Socially-oriented Game Design', in: *Proceedings of the CHI 2005 Conference on Human Factors in Computing Systems*. CHI 2005, April 2–7, Portland, OR, 751–60. New York, NY: ACM Press.

Friedman B. (2004) 'Value Sensitive Design', in: *Berkshire Encyclopedia of Human-computer Interaction*, 769–74. Great Barrington, MA: Berkshire Publishing Group.

Frijda N. (1987) *The Emotions*. Cambridge: Cambridge University Press.

Haidt J. (2001) 'The Emotional Dog and Its Rational Tail: A Social Intuitionist Approach to Moral Judgment', *Psychological Review*, 108, 814–34.

Hansson S. O. (1996) 'Decision Making Under Great Uncertainty', *Philosophy of the Social Sciences*, 26, 369–86.

Hansson S. O. (2004) 'Philosophical Perspectives on Risk', *Techné*, 8, 10–35.

Hansson S. O. (2010) 'Risk: Objective or Subjective, Facts or Values', *Journal of Risk Research*, 13(2), 231–8.

Harvey M. (2009) 'Drama, Talk, and Emotion: Omitted Aspects of Public Participation', *Science, Technology and Human Values*, 34, 139–61.
Hayenhjelm M. (2006) 'Asymmetries in Risk Communication', *Risk Management*, 8(1), 1–15.
Hermansson H. (2012) 'Defending the Conception of "Objective Risk"', *Risk Analysis*, 32(1), 16–24.
Hulme M. (2009) *Why We Disagree About Climate Change*. Cambridge: Cambridge University Press.
Ionescu T. B. (2012) 'Communicating in Germany about the Fukushima Accident: How Direct Encounter Beat Media Representations', *Environmental Communication*, 6(2), 260–7.
Jagtman H. M. (2010) 'Cell Broadcast Trials in the Netherlands: Using Mobile Phone Technology for Citizens' Alarming', *Reliability Engineering & System Safety*, 95(1), 18–28.
Jamieson I. A., Briggs D. J. (2009) 'Towards Effective Risk Discourse: The Role of Stakeholder Partnerships', *International Journal of Risk Assessment and Management*, 13(3–4), 276–92.
Johnson B. (1999) 'Ethical Issues in Risk Communication: Continuing the Discussion', *Risk Analysis*, 19(3), 335–48.
Krimsky S., Golding D. (eds.) (1992) *Social Theories of Risk*. Westport, CT: Praeger.
Lazarus R. (1991) *Emotion and Adaptation*. New York, NY: Oxford University Press.
Leiss A., Powell D. (2004) *Mad Cows and Mother's Milk: The Perils of Poor Risk Communication*. Montreal: McGill-Queen's University Press.
Lofstedt R., Bouder F., Wardman J., Chakraborty S. (2010) 'The Changing Nature of Communication and Regulation of Risk in Europe', *Journal of Risk Research*, 14(4), 409–29.
Manders-Huits N. (2011) 'What Values in Design? The Challenge of Incorporating Moral Values Into Design', *Science and Engineering Ethics*, 17, 271–87.
Möller N. (2012) 'The Concepts of Risk and Safety', in: *Handbook of Risk Theory: Epistemology, Decision Theory, Ethics and Social Implications of Risk*, edited by Roeser S., Hillerbrand R., Sandin P., Peterson M., 55–85. Dordrecht: Springer.
Morgan M. G., Lave L. (1990) 'Ethical Considerations in Risk Communication Practice and Research', *Risk Analysis*, 10, 355–8.
Munnichs G. (2004) 'Whom to Trust? Public Concerns, Late Modern Risks, and Expert Trustworthinesss', *Journal of Agricultural and Environmental Ethics*, 17, 113–30.
Nihlén Fahlquist J. (2016) 'Experience of Non-breastfeeding Mothers: Norms and Ethically Responsible Risk Communication', *Nursing Ethics*, 23, 231–41.
Nihlén Fahlquist J., Roeser S. (2011) 'Ethical Problems With Information on Infant Feeding in Developed Countries', *Public Health Ethics*, 4, 192–202.
Nussbaum M. (2001) *Upheavals of Thought*. Cambridge: Cambridge University Press.
Persensky J., Browde S. A., Szabo A., Peterson L., Specht E., Wight E. (2004) *Effective Risk Communication: The Nuclear Regulatory Commission's Guideline for External Risk*'. '*Communication (NUREG/BR-0308)*. Washington, DC: Division of Systems Analysis and Regulatory Effectiveness: Office of Nuclear Regulatory Research.
Roberts R. C. (2003) *Emotions: An Essay in Aid of Moral Psychology*. Cambridge: Cambridge University Press.
Roeser S. (2006) 'The Role of Emotions in Judging the Moral Acceptability of Risks', *Safety Science*, 44, 689–700.
Roeser S. (2007) 'Ethical Intuitions About Risks', *Safety Science Monitor*, 11, 1–30.

Roeser S. (2009) 'The Relation Between Cognition and Affect in Moral Judgments About Risk', in: *The Ethics of Technological Risks*, edited by Asveld L., Roeser S., 182–201. London: Earthscan.

Roeser S. (ed.) (2010a) *Emotions and Risky Technologies*. Dordrecht: Springer.

Roeser S. (2010b) 'Intuitions, Emotions and Gut Feelings in Decisions About Risks: Towards a Different Interpretation of "Neuroethics"', *Journal of Risk Research*, 13, 175–90.

Roeser S. (2011) 'Nuclear Energy, Risk, and Emotions', *Philosophy & Technology*, 24, 197–201.

Roeser S. (2012b) 'Risk Communication, Public Engagement, and Climate Change: A Role for Emotions', *Risk Analysis*, 32, 1033–40.

Roeser S. (2018) *Risk, Technology, and Moral Emotions*. London: Routledge.

Roeser S., Nihlén Fahlquist J. (2013) 'Moral Emotions and Risk Communication', in: *Effective Risk Communication*, edited by Arvai J., Rivers L. London: Earthscan.

Roeser S., Pesch U. (2016) 'An Emotional Deliberation Approach to Risk', *Science, Technology & Human Values*, 41, 274–97.

Ross B., Davis W. (2010) 'Marketing Risks: The Mindless Acceptance of Risks Is Promoted by Emotional Appeals', in: *Emotions and Risky Technologies*, edited by Roeser S., 61–80. Dordrecht: Springer.

Scherer K. R. (1984) 'On the Nature and Function of Emotion: A Component Process Approach', in: *Approaches to Emotion*, edited by Scherer K. R., Ekman P., 293–317. Hillsdale, NJ: Lawrence Erlbaum Associates.

Shrader-Frechette K. (1991) *Risk and Rationality*. Berkeley, CA: University of California Press.

Shrader-Frechette K. (2011) 'Fukushima, Flawed Epistemology, and Black-swan Events', *Ethics, Policy and Environment*, 14(3), 267–72.

Skitka L. J., Winquist J., Hutchinson S. (2003) 'Are Outcome Fairness and Outcome Favorability Distinguishable Psychological Constructs? A Meta-analytic Review', *Social Justice Research*, 16, 309–41.

Slovic P. (2000) *The Perception of Risk*. London: Earthscan.

Slovic P. (2010) *The Feeling of Risk: New Perspectives on Risk Perception*. London: Earthscan.

Solomon R. (1993) *The Passions: Emotions and the Meaning of Life*. Indianapolis, IN: Hackett.

Sunstein C. R. (2005) *Laws of Fear*. Cambridge: Cambridge University Press.

Thaler R., Sunstein C. (2008) *Improving Decisions About Health, Wealth, and Happiness*. New Haven, CT: Yale University Press.

Tversky A., Kahneman D. (1974) 'Judgment Under Uncertainty: Heuristics and Biases', *Science*, 185(4157), 1124–31.

Valenti J., Wilkins L. (1995) 'An Ethical Risk Communication Protocol for Science and Mass Communication', *Public Understanding of Science*, 4, 177–94.

Van Asselt M., Rijkens-Klomp N. (2002) 'A Look in the Mirror: Reflection on Participation in Integrated Assessment From a Methodological Perspective', *Global Environmental Change*, 12, 167–84.

Van den Hoven M. J. (2005) 'Design for Values and Values for Design', *Journal of the Australian Computer Society*, 7(2), 4–7.

Verbeek P. (2011) *Moralizing Technology*. Chicago, IL: University of Chicago Press.

Zagzebski L. (2003) 'Emotion and Moral Judgment', *Philosophy and Phenomenological Research*, 66, 104–24.

2 Discourses on environment, public health and values

The case of obesity

Michiel Korthals

1 Introduction

The relationship between the environment and public health has many aspects. Pollution of water, air and soil harm public health severely. On the other hand, green areas, fresh air and water improve public health. Due to the fact that most humans now live in cities, the environment is often the physical environment; the way houses, infrastructure, green areas, industrial and commercial areas and public spaces are structured determine the public health of the majority. However, the environment can also be the food and drinks offered. In particular, the relationship between the environment and public health in the case of food and agricultural production is more controversial than ever. Increasingly more people are obese; large companies are criticized by NGOs because of the low quality of their produced food and social environments are seen as encouraging obesity (Poston and Foreyt 1999; WHO 2003). An important factor of this environment is how food production, distribution and preparation are organized. Healthy or unhealthy food affects public health in opposing ways. In many developed countries, food production, distribution and preparation is done by specialized sectors: most consumers do not produce, share and prepare their own food, but large industries have taken over these activities, often by producing 'fast food' (Vandevijvere et al. 2015). This specialization has an enormous impact on the quality of the food that is finally eaten. Most industrially prepared food is too salty, sugary and fatty due to the fact that short-term profit rather than long-term public health is the main objective. This food system, together with the physical environment with its focus on driveways, elevators and escalators, doesn't stimulate physical exercise, and shapes an obesogenic environment. When the environment is obesogenic (with an emphasis on driving cars and fast food), obesity flourishes.

This contribution consists of four sections, treating four ethical issues at stake. First, a controversial issue concerns the *identification* of what type of problem obesity is, where the problem is located and to what extent environmental factors, such as fast food and other environmental factors, are causing the problem. Second, *responsibility* for managing and increasing environmental health is in need of ethical attention. This means that fast food producers and land use planners should accept responsibility for obesity, because continuing in the same vein with producing fast food and obesogenic structures will aggravate the problem in the future. What should producers do to prevent negative impacts on the health of consumers and what are they permitted to do? Third, there is the *ethics of doing research* into the factors that produce environmental hazards. There are good reasons to believe that research paid for by the fast food industry is often one-sided (concentrating on the positive aspects of sweet and fatty foodstuffs) or even not done in an integral way. Fourth, *the right to intervene* to reduce unhealthy factors and the type of intervention in the behaviour of consumers and producers requires ethical analysis; not everything helps and not everything is permitted to prevent a person from becoming overweight. For example, nudging people towards healthy food choices and attitudes, and promoting urban design that facilitates physical activity, are acceptable only under certain ethical conditions.

In all these issues of the relationship between the environment and public health, normative values are intrinsically connected with research, decisions and activities. I will argue that studying and managing environmental risks require value decisions; the common definition of a risk (chance of a big future loss), enables us to quantify the risk, and presupposes value decisions about what type of problem the risk is.

2 The relationship between the environment and public health in the case of obesity

The benign or harmful effect of environmental factors on human health is a very complex question. As such it cannot be solved by scientific research alone. Therefore, the identification of these effects in itself raises ethical questions. Exposure to potentially hazardous substances and processes is often difficult to identify and document, not only because of the complexity of their interactions and their long-term risks, but also because individuals can experience differing susceptibilities to their harmful effects (Sharp 2001; Paulson 2006). Moreover, the environment is dynamic and consists of many interacting (micro-, meso- and macro-) levels. The widespread presence of obesity is a very negative public health problem, along with increased instances of concomitant diseases such as type-two diabetes, cancer of the intestines and cardiovascular diseases (Roth et al. 2004).

In general, one can discern three (inevitable normative) approaches to obesity: one that emphasizes the individual behaviour, one that emphasizes genetic factors and one that emphasizes the influence of environmental factors, like the building environment and the workplace, but also the easy access to unhealthy food. In some clinical cases it is proven that clients have a genetic disposal to being obese (Loos and Bouchard 2003). As a type of genetically caused disease, obesity starts in early childhood; the *genetization* of obesity can therefore not be generalized to the total population. However, many see obesity as the result of an individual's choice and behaviour. This ethical position has important implications for the ascription of responsibility for this disease. *Individualization* means that obesity is

Table 2.1 Different levels of interaction between genetic susceptibility and the environment

Levels of genetic susceptibility	*Body size in a non-obesogenic environment*	*Body size in an obesogenic environment*
Genetic	High risk to become massively obese	High risk to become massively obese
Strong predisposition	Normal weight/overweight	High risk to become obese
Slight predisposition	Normal weight/overweight	High risk to become overweight/obese
Genetically resistant	Normal weight	Normal weight

only caused by individual characteristics, and no other social actor can be held accountable. For example, Coca Cola, one of the most powerful food companies, thinks and acts in this way (Jong 2013). On the other hand, obesity is clearly correlated with fast food, processed food and the urban environment, which is emphasized in the *socialization* approach. Therefore, many think that when on-street eateries such as McDonald's, KFC, Fish'n'chips, and Ben and Jerry's, are tolerated not only in cities but also in mass media advertising and sponsorship, it should not be surprising that the numbers of obese persons are greatly increasing (as they still are in Europe). Moreover, just as with most environmental risks to health, the risk of obesity is for the most part not equally distributed. Rich people tend to live in healthier, less obesogenic environments than poor people and are therefore less obese. One can assume that the three approaches, individual behaviour, genes and the environment, work together to determine an individual's risk to obesity, as is shown in Table 2.1.

Only in an obesogenic environment (with fast and processed food dominantly present and little emphasis on the importance of physical exercise) can something like an epidemic of obesity occur, and one can say this is currently the case in many developed countries. This means that, ethically and scientifically, the influence of the fast food industry and the lack of physical exercise can be seen as important causal factors in determining the risks of obesity. With the previous considerations, we have delineated what type of problem obesity is, where the problem is located and which factors, such as fast food and environmental factors, are causing the problem.

3 Responsibilities for reducing obesity

When a causal relationship between certain environmental factors and obesity is established, the issue of responsibilities emerges. In addition, not only casual factors determine responsibilities, but also future possibilities of actors to change a harmful situation. Even when many causal factors can be discerned (ethicists, in these cases, speak of the problem of 'many hands'; Van de Poel et al. 2012), some actors are able to do more to prevent unhealthy situations than others. In other words, at stake are the *responsibilities* different people and organizations

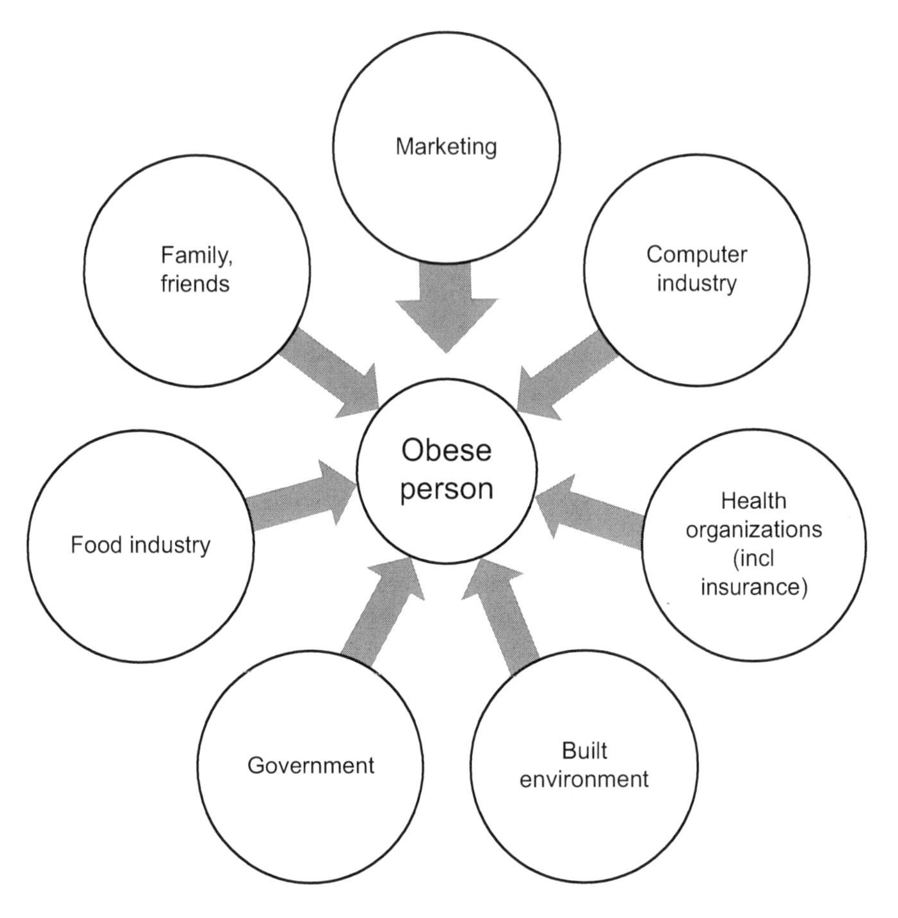

Figure 2.1 Main actors and their relationships in determining obesity

had in the past and have today and in the future, vis-à-vis adverse effects of the environment on human health (FEC 2005; Minkler 2000). To what extent can the actors involved be held accountable, and to what extent can they, from an ethical point of view, be prevented in one way or another from continuing similar actions that contribute to those adverse effects? As already alluded to, from an environmental point of view, many very different actors are involved, as can be seen in Figure 2.1.

These complicated problems in confused contexts, so characteristic of obesity, give rise to the issue of many hands, and that of the diffusion of responsibility: when too many people are involved, the individuals involved can easily deny their responsibility. However, even in the most complicated cases, one can always identify more powerful and less powerful people. It is said that children are more vulnerable than adults, implying that parents are solely responsible for their health. However, how can a parent be held responsible when children are directly addressed by unhealthy food marketing campaigns? Often, new technologies and practices (such as genomics) create new public responsibilities and new distributions of responsibility, but also new types of responsibility for food professionals (Kraak et al. 2016). How can obese persons (adults, children and their caretakers) move on in this jungle of new responsibilities? Who is held responsible/accountable for the causes of obesity, and for its remedies? Is the current distribution of responsibilities adequate in the new circumstances created by the introduction of genomics?

Currently, most people blame the obese, in accordance with the individualization approach. The famous ethicist Peter Singer states: 'Others just eat too much and should show more restraint. Along with the old-fashioned virtue of frugality, the idea that it is wrong to be a glutton is in urgent need of revival' (Singer 2006). However, moralizing to the obese should be restricted by one important condition (Korthals 2004): individuals can only be held responsible for their own weight when they are adequately informed about their food and are able to act accordingly (Kant 1983). Otherwise, their choices are not autonomous, in the sense that they are not free but manipulated. Living in an obesogenic environment has this effect (COS 2008). It implies that obese persons do not have enough resources to rid themselves of their obesity; they can be seen as addicted to fast food (Lerma-Cabrera et al. 2016).

However, ethically and scientifically, the fast food industry and the physical environment with its lack of stimuli for physical exercise, are more important in changing the obesogenic environment than the goodwill of individuals. This means that fast food producers and land use planners should acknowledge responsibility for obesity, in particular towards children. Even when it can be shown that other causal factors play a role, the effects of consuming their products is a principal factor both in the present and in the future. Therefore they should take their responsibility and start to reduce the obesogenic effects on the population. What should producers and policy makers do to prevent negative impacts of the environment on the health of consumers and what are they permitted to do?

4 Ethics of research into the relationship of environment and public health

A third ethical issue comprises the fact that research on the factors that produce environmental hazards has its own ethical problems. The establishment of research agendas selects certain ethical outcomes; identification of a problem and its concomitant outcome sometimes resists powerful entrenched positions and will often encounter many difficulties. Research into policy measures aiming to deal with environmental factors responsible for a decline in public health confronts policy makers with the adverse outcome of their decisions. For example, when researchers identify environmental toxicants like dioxin in waste locations and step up research about their effects, ethics come to the fore, because the decision to pursue research in certain areas can interfere with power relations, people's concerns about safety and other expectations. This is also the case with obesity; research paid by the fast food industry on the effect of fast food (too much salt, sugar and fat) is often done concentrating only on the positive effects and sometimes is not even done in an integral way (CSPI 2003; Katan 2007; Nestle 2002). There is evidence that the World Health Organization received less governmental contributions due to lobbying by the sugar industry that became angry because of its critical report on sugar.

Second, data that are indeterminate due to their complexity and dynamics often result in different and opposing interpretations upheld by rival groups. Data can be interpreted in multiple ways, depending on theoretical assumptions and normative perspectives. Sometimes, an answer is found by initiating very detailed and large-scale research, which often means that more animal testing is required (here one stumbles upon an ethical dilemma again). But although scientific evidence is often indeterminate due to uncertainty, it is still clear that certain conclusions can be established. An ethics of dealing with uncertainties is lacking to date; it should enable researchers, policy makers and stakeholders to identify distinct important major uncertainties and separate them from minor unimportant ones. New types of research also challenge traditional research methods, applications and practices. For example, genomics (scientific research into the relationship between genes and their environment) can have an important role to play in improving public and environmental health (Brand et al. 2008; Darnton-Hill et al. 2004; Khoury and Mensah 2005). However, often hype and easy promises (like the rumour of an anti-obesity pill) are loudly applauded in the mass media. Mostly, these turn out to be totally wrong (Korthals 2011).

To tackle the issue of easy expectations and hype, it is necessary to establish independent gatekeepers to safeguard the independence of testing, marketing, communicating and providing the services of nutrigenomics.

To tackle the influence of large corporations and their research strategies aimed at supporting their own interests, private money should go to an independent body, which, in turn, distributes the money to scientific programmes according to clear and ethical acceptable criteria. Public means or public ways of distribution of private financing for this type of research are advisable.

With respect to *ethics for scientists*, scientists are in need of codes of practice that would guide them in setting up ethically acceptable research agendas and in validating scientific claims with respect to environmental health hazards. Here again it is clear that research agendas are not neutral but value laden. Values determine what type of questions and claims are relevant to study. Only recently has interest in research on the healthiness of foodstuffs been rising, due inter alia to the growing concern of the public about health.

5 Interventions improving the relationship between environment and public health

Finally, new ethical issues are raised by the *type of interventions* that should follow once decisions have been taken on the basis of ethical considerations, taking into account research results related to the environmental effects on the health of particular groups. It is necessary to distinguish between the more personal types of intervention and more collective social regulations, as well as between more expert or community-based interventions. Estimates of cost and effectiveness on the basis of value perspectives do play an important role here. Identification of susceptible sub-populations can lead to a discriminating attitude when ineffective precautions are taken – a question also related to the issue of responsibility.

The right to intervene to reduce unhealthy factors and the type of intervention in the behaviour of consumers and stakeholders requires ethical analysis. In other words, in the case of obesity, not everything is permitted to prevent extreme overweight, and even justified interventions require justification of their application in a particular situation.

Different stakeholders can take recourse to several strategies to implement food and health governance. However, from an ethical point of view not all are allowed. In Table 2.2 some examples are given. Governments have quite strong legitimate strategies, such as laws and fiscal regulations, to prohibit or stimulate particular environmental measures in order to curb obesity. Even when some of these strategies are legitimate, their proportionality is at stake: harsh laws can make a situation worse (think about anti-prostitution laws or the alcohol prohibition laws in the US of 1920–1933). However, governments can also take recourse to softer strategies, such as giving information and advice and defining what should be standard practice. Without necessarily wanting to prohibit fast food or processed food, promoting healthy food would make an enormous difference. Dependent on proportionality and feasibility, governments can use one of these strategies. Private partners cannot use compulsory strategies, but generally they use lots of nudging strategies (i.e. marketing and advertisements) to promote the selling of their products. Although misleading strategies are officially forbidden, they are quite common. Nudging strategies, favouring healthy food choices, can also be stimulated. Putting healthy products at eye-height in the supermarkets, instead of chips and other highly processed food, would make an enormous difference in sales.

Nudging people towards healthy food choices and attitudes, and promoting urban design that facilitates physical activity, for example, are acceptable only under certain ethical conditions. The complex interaction of food production, consumption and the environment, determining class-dependent obesity, has various components. However, there is not one effective treatment for obesity. Moreover, identifying individuals or groups of individuals who show higher risks of certain vulnerability for environmentally induced diseases can produce discrimination.

Often, all the emphasis of health and food experts (in both personal and collective programmes of intervention) is put on dietary intake and the importance and necessity of special diets. For example, in Japan, national law instructs Japanese citizens between the ages of 40 and 74 to measure their waistlines. If they exceed a certain limit, they will receive dietary education (Onishi 2008). This looks like a rather forceful intervention into personal life, and is rather dubious when viewed from the standpoint of autonomy. Moreover, as we have seen, eating

Table 2.2 Various strategies of implementation by actors of food and health governance

	Formal: laws; governments	*Formal: fiscal regulations; governments*	*Informal: via information and advice; governments and others*	*Informal: default context; government and others*	*Informal: nudging; government and others*	*Manipulation; private partners*
Mechanism	Obligations, prohibitions	Punishments	Communication	Facilitation	Context framing	Misleading; threats
Degree of freedom	No freedom	Limited freedom	Choice	Choice	Choice	No freedom
Examples	Fines, prison	Taxation on unhealthy food items	Health and Food Information Centre	Subsidies for self organization, web-platform etc.	Descriptive norms for fair trade buying	Many health claims; children ad.

(partly from House of Lords 2011)

is an 'institution', comprising various activities (one of which is 'eating together'), having a huge social impact and contributing in high measure to the improvement of the informal ties of society. Dieting is often connected with fear, with feeling humiliated and guilty; feelings and emotions that obviously do not contribute well to a healthy life. To discourage eating is therefore a very tricky affair, and is moreover ineffective in the main because people always have to eat. Also, dieting often goes together with temporary but strong cravings, or even binge eating. Many interventions incorporate the idea that obese persons are somehow immoral (Prose 2003). Therefore, many strategies directed at reducing personal food intake or increasing energy output are one-sided; they should be complemented by social and medical strategies directed at energy input, such as radical changes in the supply chain to produce healthier foods, and in the physical environment. Free bicycle lanes, biking and hiking trails, easy accessible stairs, pleasant walking pathways, and discouraging car use could be some of these actions. Plans of action to prevent obesity should cover a broad portfolio of promising interventions. More than one billion people are overweight and obese, and the number is growing, which implies that more investment in health is needed to manage their health problems.

6 Conclusion

Environmental factors determine public health in several ways. The cheap and easy availability of fast and processed food and the built-up environment play a dominant role in causing obesity. The risk of becoming obese is high for those living in such an environment. Analyzing these risks requires a conscious decision to approach obesity as a problem of body, environment and genes. Obesity is a serious epidemic, and the cause of many other diseases, such as cardiovascular diseases, type-two diabetes and cancer. The complexity of the interactions and the 'many hands' that are responsible for this epidemic cannot be used as a legitimation of the existing situation. Although other actors also have a causal role, the responsibility of the food industry and building agencies is dominant. Research into the relationship between the environment and obesity, and into the effect and efficacy of strategies that aim at reducing the number of obese people should be supported and carried out unhampered by commercial considerations. The risks of becoming obese will be neglected when research takes the normative approach of focussing on the individual. However, when the other approaches are taken into account, a broader perspective of risks allows for a better-informed analysis and intervention. Public means or public ways of distributing private financing of this type of research is advisable. Interventions in the physical environment and food supply are some of the strategies that are recommendable. One strategy considered ethically acceptable is making healthy food easily accessible, for instance, by presenting it more prominently in supermarkets and in marketing and advertising campaigns. 'Nudging', as this is called, can have a positive contribution in reducing the number of obese people.

References

Brand A., Brand H., den Baumen T. S. (2008) 'The Impact of Genetics and Genomics on Public Health', *European Journal of Human Genetics*, 16(1), 5–13.

CoS (Council of the Obesity Society, Chair: D.B. Allison) (2008) 'Obesity as a Disease: A White Paper on Evidence and Arguments Commissioned by the Obesity Society', *Nature*, 16(6), 1161–77.

CSPI (Center for Science in the Public Interest) (2003) *Lifting the Veil of Secrecy: Corporate Support for Health and Environmental Professional Associations, Charities, and Industry Front Groups*. Washington, DC: CSPI.

Darnton-Hill I., Margetts B., Deckelbaum R. (2004) 'Public Health Nutrition and Genetics: Implications for Nutrition Policy and Promotion', *Proceedings of the Nutrition Society*, 63(1), 173–85.

FEC (Food Ethics Council) (2005) *Getting Personal: Shifting Responsibilities for Health*. Brighton: FEC.

House of Lords (2011) *Behaviour Change*. London: The Stationery Office Limited.

Jong de H. (2013) 'Interview With Benelux CEO of Coca-Cola', *NRC Handelsblad*, August 10.

Kant I. (1983) 'The Metaphysics of Morals', in: *Ethical Philosophy*, edited by Kant I., translated by Ellington J. W. Indianapolis, IN: Hackett.

Katan M. B. (2007) 'Does Industry Sponsorship Undermine the Integrity of Nutrition Research?', *PLoS Medicine*, 4(1), e6.

Khoury M. J., Mensah G. A. (2005) 'Genomics and the Prevention and Control of Common Chronic Diseases: Emerging Priorities for Public Health Action', *Preventing Chronic Disease* (serial online). Available at www.cdc.gov/pcd/issues/2005/apr/05_0011.htm. Date Accessed: 17 November 2017.

Korthals M. (2004) *Before Dinner*. Dordrecht: Springer.

Korthals M. (ed.) (2011) *Genomics, Obesity and the Struggle Over Responsibilities*. Dordrecht: Springer.

Kraak V. et al. (2016) *Bulletin of the World Health Organization 2016*, 94, 540–8. Available at http://dx.doi.org/10.2471/BLT.15.158667.

Lerma-Cabrera J. M., Carvajal F., Lopez-Legarrea P. (2016) 'Food Addiction as a New Piece of the Obesity Framework', *Nutrition Journal*, 15, 5.

Loos R. J., Bouchard C. (2003) 'Obesity – Is It a Genetic Disorder?', *Journal of Internal Medicine*, 254, 401–25.

Minkler M. (2000) 'Personal Responsibility for Health: Contexts and Controversies', in: *Promoting Healthy Behavior*, edited by Callahan D., 1–22. Washington, DC: Georgetown University Press.

Nestle M. (2002) *Food Politics: How the Food Industry Influences Nutrition and Health*. Berkeley, CA: University of California Press.

Onishi N. (2008) 'Japan, Seeking Trim Waists, Measures Millions', *New York Times*, June 13.

Paulson J. A. (2006) 'An Exploration of Ethical Issues in Research in Children's Health and the Environment', *Environmental Health Perspectives*, 114(10), 1603–9.

Poston II W. S. C., Foreyt J. P. (1999) 'Obesity Is an Environmental Issue', *Atherosclerosis*, 146(2), 201–9.

Prose F. (2003) *Gluttony: The Seven Deadly Sins*. New York, NY: Oxford University Press.

Roth J., Qian X., Marbán S. L., Redelt H., Lowell B. C. (2004) 'The Obesity Pandemic: Where Have We Been and Where Are We Going?', *Obesity Research*, 12, 88S–100S.

Sharp R. (2001) 'Ethical Issues in Environmental Health Research', *Environmental Health Perspectives*, 111(14), 1786–8.

Singer P. (2006) *Eating*. London: Penguin Press, 178.

Van de Poel I., Fahlquist J. N., Doorn N., Zwart S., Royakkers L. (2012) 'The Problem of Many Hands: Climate Change as an Example', *Science and Engineering Ethics*, 18(1), 49–67.

Vandevijvere A. et al. (2015) 'Increased Food Energy Supply as a Major Driver of the Obesity Epidemic: A Global Analysis', *Bull World Health Organ*, 93, 446–56.

WHO (World Health Organization) (2003) *Diet, Nutrition and the Prevention of Chronic Diseases*. Geneva: WHO.

3 Socio-economic, historical and cultural background

Implications for behaviour after radiation accidents and better resilience

Liudmila Liutsko, Takashi Ohba, Elisabeth Cardis, Thierry Schneider and Deborah Oughton

1 Introduction

Naturally occurring radionuclides have always existed on earth, but it is only relatively recently (at the end of the 19th century) that humans became aware of their existence. At the time that Marie and Pierre Curie and their colleagues first carried out research into the properties of radioactive elements, nobody was aware of the possible harmful health effects of radiation exposure, and Marie, who had been in close contact with radioactive sources, eventually died of radiation-induced leukaemia as per her own beliefs (Carl 2004; Curie 1939; Rollyson 2004). Since then, various medical applications of radioactivity and X-rays were discovered and implemented: Marie Curie equipped ambulances with X-ray equipment as part of her service in World War I (WWI). During that time, applications expanded to the military context – including the first nuclear weapon test towards the end of WWII, closely followed by the use of atomic bombs at Hiroshima and Nagasaki. With an estimated 130 000 deaths, these events had devastating consequences and created negative emotions related to nuclear technology among Japanese citizens until the present day. Later, radiation applications also extended further to peaceful uses, in particular in the medical context and for energy production.

Increasing awareness of the potential risks of radiation led to the emergence of radiation protection (RP) policies and practices in the first part of the 20th century – the first international recommendation of the International Commission on Radiation Protection (ICRP) was issued in 1928, marking the official "birth" of the System of Radiation Protection (Clarke and Valentin 2009). Initially the aim was to reduce possible harmful effects that could occur in medical workers (working with X-rays and radium) in nuclear medicine. That scope was later expanded to protection of other categories (such as patients, the public and non-human species).

Although technical RP development and knowledge has improved since the first uses of radiation for medical purposes, the risk of nuclear accidents and the challenge to deal with their consequences remains (TMI, Windscale accident, Chernobyl, Fukushima, etc.). To meet these challenges, RP needs to recognise the importance of the socio-historical context in which affected populations were living at the time of the accident, and to take into account the knowledge and experiences available then.

Over time, scientific knowledge of effects of accidents has also increased through practical experience, and RP implementation programmes are evolving. In this context, the EC funded the SHAMISEN project ('Nuclear Emergency Situations: Improvement of Medical and Health Surveillance'). The project conducted a critical review and analysis of lessons learned from past nuclear accidents, with the aim to make recommendations to optimise emergency preparedness and response in the case of a nuclear accident. In doing so, the project paid special attention to the empowerment of populations in order to enable them to participate in decision-making.

The uniqueness of SHAMISEN is due to the fact that it not only considers purely scientific and technical RP issues but also socio-economical, psychological and ethical issues, all with the purpose to maximise the well-being of affected populations. Lessons learned, as formulated in the project, were mainly based on the Chernobyl and Fukushima experiences, since the populations affected by these accidents still suffer from their consequences (in particular long-lasting contamination of their day-to-day environment inducing notably psycho-social effects). The recommendations concern both the long-term surveillance and well-being of those populations, as well as the emergency preparedness and response anticipating a possible future accident, which, it is hoped, will not occur.

2 Methods

In order to study the experiences from past major nuclear accidents, a review of available scientific publications on the topic (mainly based on the Chernobyl accident) was carried out. In addition, regulations and recommendations in place at the time of the accidents and thereafter were studied, as well as various reports, books and newspaper and magazine articles related to the topic. Last but not least, the project also devoted attention to the analysis of testimonies of affected populations. In particular with respect to the Chernobyl and Fukushima accidents, lessons learned are also based on exchanges with Ukrainian, Belarusian, Russian, Norwegian and Japanese colleagues directly involved in the management of the consequences of the accident and on various stakeholder workshops organised in the aftermath of the accident.

3 Results and analysis of observations

> And a great star . . . fell from the sky on a third of the rivers . . . The name of the star is Wormwood. A third of the waters turned bitter, and many people died from the waters that had become bitter.
>
> (The Bible, Rev 8:10–11)

> Lexically the meaning of the word "CHERNO-BYL" consists of two words: "cherno" – *black* and "byl" – a *real story, fact.*

The Wormwood star is another name for Halley's Comet, and the bitter wormwood herb (also cited in the Bible) is also called "chernobyl" and "chernobylnik" in Russian. With this in mind, the appearance of Halley's Comet in 1986 (which passed closest to the Earth between the 10th of March and the 25th of April), were seen by people as a possible "sign from the sky" or warning about the Chernobyl accident. This interpretation spread quickly to the West with the New York Times publication "Chernobyl Fallout: Apocalyptic Tale" by Serge Schmemann on 25 July 1986 (Schmemann 1986). The main author of this chapter has also met people who saw Halley's Comet and who interpreted both its appearance and the Chernobyl accident as a sign to stop the nuclear weapons race between the US and the USSR that had reached its peak by that year. In October 1986, Gorbachev and Reagan met in Rekiavick, a meeting that is now considered as the first step towards the ending of the Cold War (Sokolov 2007).[1]

Other events for the dates nearest to the Chernobyl accident (On This Day, 2000–2018)[2] include a nuclear test performed in Nevada on the 22nd of April and another, performed by France, on the date of the Chernobyl catastrophe, 26th of April 1986 (Table 3.1).

After the Chernobyl catastrophe, President Gorbachev's anti-nuclear feelings intensified and the event is said to have stimulated his will to bring the arms race to a halt and to start nuclear disarmament talks (among them, the October summit in Rekiavick, 1986).

3.1 *Socio-historical moment at the time of the Chernobyl accident*

The Cold War between the US and the USSR, the main producers of nuclear weapons, was part of the socio-historical period just before the Chernobyl accident. Initially these nuclear tests were performed above ground, with the release of radioactive contamination to the environment as a consequence. Later, the tests were held underground. Though the Three Mile Island accident had occurred in the US in 1979 (with a score of 5 out of 7 according to the International

Table 3.1 Some calendar events dated by April 1986

Apr 26	Firestone World Bowling Tournament of Champions won by Marshall Holman
Apr 26	**France performs nuclear test**
Apr 26	Game between Angels and Twins delayed for 9 minutes by strong winds
Apr 26	**World's worst nuclear disaster: 4th reactor at Chernobyl nuclear power station in USSR explodes, 31 die, radioactive contamination reaches much of Western Europe**

Data taken from the Historical events calendar, available at www.onthisday.com/events/date/1986/april

Nuclear Event Scale INES), little information was available about it in Eastern European countries. Other accidents related to weapons production, e.g. at the Mayak plant, were also kept secret at that time (Komarova 2000).

Referring to the Chernobyl case, neither the Soviet government nor the general population expected that the use of the "peaceful atom" (as the use of radioactivity for the production of energy in nuclear power plants was called in the USSR) could result in an accident, let alone one of such magnitude. As in many other countries, the Cold War and memories of the bombing of Hiroshima and Nagasaki meant that the Soviet people were more informed and prepared for "a sudden nuclear attack or war" than they were for an industrial accident. At the time, many professionals provided testimonies about their very first reaction to the news of the Chernobyl accident: "It was a shock, nobody could believe that it had happened and nobody knew what the consequences would be". Some even thought of a possible "enemy's sabotage" (as per interviewed testimonies cited in the book "Voices of Chernobyl", Alexievich 1997). It was hard to believe and understand what had happened and everything about the accident was shrouded in secrecy. In order not to create panic and chaos, and because of the fear that the outside world might learn about it (the cultural approach was that one should not "wash one's dirty linen in public"), the Soviet government minimised the information about the Chernobyl accident, and gave updates on the event in the form of brief news, using key words such as "fire", "accident", while stressing that "everything is under control". The official speech by Gorbachev about the Chernobyl accident was not given on TV or in the mass media until about two weeks later (Figure 3.1, the publication in the central newspaper Izvestia).

ИЗВЕСТИЯ

СОВЕТОВ НАРОДНЫХ ДЕПУТАТОВ СССР

Выступление М. С. ГОРБАЧЕВА
по советскому телевидению

Figure 3.1 The first extended communication on TV of Gorbachev after the Chernobyl accident, 15 May 1986

In that speech, Gorbachev highlighted the importance of nuclear security, and declared that the one-sided moratorium of the USSR on nuclear weapon testing would be prolonged until the 6th of August (the date on which, 41 years before, the first nuclear bomb was detonated over Hiroshima). He invited the US president, Ronald Reagan, to meet at any European capital or in Hiroshima to discuss and agree on the banning of nuclear testing.

3.2 *Complexity of decision-making processes with regards to radiation risky behaviour*

The analysis of the information collected, including results from stakeholder workshops, testimonies of citizens and the main author's personal communications and experiences while growing up in Belarus, suggests that the behaviour of affected populations in case of an unexpected accident depends on the information on RP (including prevention) and the accident that they receive from:

- the government (local and central),
- professionals (specialists in RP, medical and educational workers etc.),
- their own local environment and education.

Human behaviour, however, is a complex process, driven not only by cognitive processes such as scientific or logical thinking based on knowledge and information but also on emotions, feelings and personal preferences (related, for example, to the economic situation and daily survival needs).

In situations of risk, behaviour has been shown to be influenced by two parallel processes, applied in parallel ways: the logical (slow, effortful and with conscious control) and the emotional (fast and automatic), both of which will be influenced by the individual's own limitations and bias. It is expected that people, like robots, should follow a strictly logical way of thinking when assessing risks. However, it has been suggested that "cold" analytic reasoning that blindly follows the norms and rules without considering other aspects of life is not a "real" one and cannot be effective unless it is guided by emotion and affect (Slovic et al. 2004). A number of examples (in the form of narratives of testimonies) of how people really behaved after the Chernobyl accident are provided below:

- A feeling of curiosity motivated some of the residents of Pripyat town and nearby areas (e.g. fishermen who were fishing during the night when the Chernobyl accident occurred) to go and see what had happened at the nuclear power plant (NPP). They approached the plant (without knowing or thinking about radiation exposure) in time to observe the striking aureole of the fire at night. Many people from Pripyat city also went out on their balconies to better see the "amazingly coloured" fire at the station, as reported by testimonies (Alexievich 1997).

- Once the seriousness of the situation was realised and evacuations conducted, the painful grief and frustration due to loss of their native environment (houses, villages, schools and all social contacts and lifestyles considered stable before the accident) were combined with fear and uncertainty about what was happening and with worries about the future. Separation from family members during the evacuation (due to prioritisation of pregnant women and children) was also experienced as painful, and it provoked more uncertainty during the transitional phase of evacuation.
- The most affected first responders (namely those suffering from acute radiation syndrome) were transported by helicopter to hospitals in Moscow and their families were not allowed to follow or stay nearby. However, some wives/mothers wanted to stay near their husbands/sons despite the risks to themselves (eventually expressed by medical personnel as: "You should understand that now in front of you is not the body of your husband, but . . . a reactor"). Affective and emotional feelings were at odds with standard RP behaviour: "I wanted to be near to him [her husband] until the last day he lived on the Earth" (Alexievich 1997).
- The impossibility to take domestic animals from the zones nearest to the NPP due to high contamination caused additional negative emotional states: "Also we were instructed to take only the necessary things for evacuation and were prohibited to take our pets with us; we couldn't leave them there; our dog/cat/cow/etc. . . . was a part of our family" (the evacuees' voices, Alexievich 1997). Moreover, for others, their domestic animals (cows, goats, geese, chickens) provided the basis of their daily alimentation (eggs, milk and meat).
- Many people who resided in contaminated areas or who worked on the liquidation of the consequences of the accident (often without adequate training or equipment) were not aware of radiation and its possible negative effects. In one testimony, (from the book "Voices of Chernobyl/Chernobyl Prayer" (Alexievich 1997)) a "liquidator" said: "When I returned home, my small son was very happy and honoured to see me" (at that time the liquidators were seen and presented in the mass media as heroes). "He took my forage-cap and wore it almost all the time. . . . Later he had a brain tumour".

State decision makers were also in "shock" and hesitated on how to best manage the situation. Faced with a lack of experience on the one hand, and fear of "giving food for external critics" on the other, they tried to minimise the panic. However, the general public later felt frustration and mistrust towards the government due to the delayed, partial and unclear information received.

Many people also could not appreciate the actual magnitude of the disaster (testimonies from those nearest to the Chernobyl regions, Alexievich 1997):

> My dear, why are you sunbathing? Remember the accident that happened at the Chernobyl station!
>
> Mam, but that is 40 km from us!

Other voices from the testimonies:

> The emotions we had the first days were fear and anger that we were not informed . . .
>
> We didn't believe the information that was given to us officially. We only observed the behaviour of those who knew what to do then and reacted to it and tried to do what they did.

Due to a lack of official information during the very first days after the accident (when preventive measures such as sheltering and thyroid protection with stable iodine were particularly important to reduce exposure), unfounded rumours about personal protective measures started circulating, for example "you should add 2–3 drops of iodine to milk", (personal communications from testimonies).

In order to perceive and interpret the information adequately, risk communication and information related to radiation and radiation protection should be done using clear language, understandable by each population group (professionals vs. non-professionals, adults vs. children etc.). Moreover, people's efforts are needed to be good "receivers" and practitioners of what they hear and learn. Analysis performed by the first author of mass media related to people's worries after the Chernobyl accident shows that they asked for practical day-to-day "life recommendations", based on science and experience, but translated into simple and clear indications of "what to do". Although the mass media can be an important source of information, it should be taken into account that "sensational news" in mass media publications can play a role of magnifier of stress and anxiety. Mass media publications have been linked to the development of post-Chernobyl mental stress in the population (Lazarev 1999). At the 20th Anniversary Forum of the Chernobyl nuclear power plant accident, the direct and non-direct effects of the consequences of the nuclear accident led to the declaration that psychological and mental health issues were the most significant for public health (Bromet, Havenaar, and Guey 2011).

Such anxiety-driven increases in stress have been reported with other accidents. For example, a study of anticipatory stress effects (Brazil, Goiania, 3.5 years after an accident involving ^{137}Cs radioactive contamination) found that the presence of chronic stress, measured by psychological, behavioural and neuroendocrine indices, in the group exposed to ionising radiation was comparable to that of those who were not exposed (Collins and de Carvalho 1993).

Other decision-making processes in post-accidental situations, such as the one related to the question of whether or not to go or return to affected areas were also influenced by factors not related to the accident. Some people escaped from other more dangerous risks to their life or that of their family members: testimonies to the main author related that refugees from areas of ethnic conflicts or local wars or escaped prisoners sought shelter by "hiding" in the restricted contaminated areas in the Chernobyl zone.

Especially for elderly people, emotional "attachment" to the home place (own house and goods or environment) and an inability to adapt in a new environment was crucial, and, after the accident, many old people from the Chernobyl rural areas returned to their home, finding it impossible to live in another place than their own. They had been living there for the whole of their life and "to live at home gives them energy to live further".

A similar sense of "belonging" to their homes was observed in Fukushima: During one interview, a woman in her late 80s expressed no worry with respect to the radiation but only had one concern: "For generations, my family has lived in a close relationship with this land. I will feel accursed if I lost the lands that my ancestors passed down to me" (Sugimoto et al. 2012).

In contrast to Chernobyl, where the populations largely experienced permanent relocation, in Fukushima, the government has promoted the ideal that populations will be able to return home once the order of evacuation is lifted, although people have the right to decide to return or not. The Japanese government implemented decontamination work in evacuation areas and prepared infrastructures to facilitate the return home. In the Chernobyl case, instead of reopening evacuated zones after the accident, additional relocations were adopted. It is however difficult to compare both cases, given that the level of contamination was higher in Chernobyl while, at the same time, the economic situation was worse there (a situation that also has consequences for food measures).

In the Chernobyl experience, we could also observe how the emotional "attachment" of people to the belongings they took with them when evacuated (as important memories of their lives or as things with "heredity values") can also lead to imprudent behaviour in terms of radiation protection: when resettled to a new place, people often took with them radioactively contaminated things or pets from their old houses.

The poor economical situation was another reason leading to the use of radioactive goods or food products from the Chernobyl zone. One can think of the stealing of goods from the abandoned houses or other buildings, and/or the growing or picking of products in the contaminated zones, either for personal consumption or to sell them to others.

The differences in behaviour also depend on the level of economic development. While in Japan the need to refrain from picking wild mushrooms and berries and from individual fishing and farming means that people lose their hobbies and favourite leisure time activities, for people in the rural region around the Chernobyl zone, these activities provide a main part of their daily food. This situation became obviously worse with the economic crisis that occurred after the collapse of the USSR.

3.3 *Ambiguous approach of the affected populations to medical examinations or health surveillance*

The Chernobyl experience shows that affected populations that received low doses of radiation had mixed feelings related to medical examinations and health surveillance, mainly due to a lack of trust in the proposed measures and a lack of direct involvement in the design and follow-up of these medical examinations.

People undergoing medical examinations were reluctant to participate ("We are like laboratory animals"), believing that the main purpose of the health programme was not to monitor and improve their health but rather scientific research (testimonies from personal communications). The examinations also resulted in the stigmatisation of participants seen as "contaminated" (this was observed also in the case of the Fukushima accident), but also in resentment of those who were not included in the surveillance programmes. Moreover, even those initially reluctant to participate felt abandoned when medical programmes had to be discontinued due to economic or other reasons, leading to reactions such as "first we were needed, and now nobody cares about us anymore".

The issues raised above illustrate the importance of providing adequate information when medical and health surveillance programmes are organised, making sure that the objectives and limitations are well understood and avoiding the generation of false expectations. Unless the situation is critical, participation in surveillance programmes should be voluntary, and appropriate support and explanations should be given to the participants. Wherever possible, the affected population should be involved in the design and evaluation of the programmes, to ensure that relevant social aspects are taken into account and that the programmes answer their concerns.

An important issue in planning health and medical surveillance programmes relates to the definitions of the populations to be followed, taking into account radiation levels, specific concerns of the population (including uncertainties, stigma and worries), the dignity of individuals and other ethical aspects, and often difficult economic situations.

It is noted that economic considerations are important not just in terms of post-accident health surveillance but also in the handling of the accident itself (in Chernobyl, participation by civilians in the post-accidental decontamination or emergency work was done on a voluntary basis. In exchange, the authorities promised future socio-economic benefits. For example, the poor economical situation stimulated some liquidators to be "more" ill or "not to recover" as the disability allowed them to obtain financial compensation from the state health programme (Dr Malova, in a personal communication with the author, 2014).

4 Education and best practices in adaptation to new conditions

> We cannot change the past: we can accept it and understand it to derive lessons to go further and find the optimal way for it, and thus modify our present and future.
> (Liutsko's personal communication with Dr. Malova, 2014)

Human behaviour is complex and, as also mentioned earlier, depends on knowledge, emotions and preferences in different moments of a person's life. It also reflects habits and social behaviour incrusted by the specific cultural and sociohistorical environment as well as the psycho-socio-economic situation. Decision-making processes depend on a complex or multilayered construction of one's self (Figure 3.2), the formation of which will depend on the nearest and further

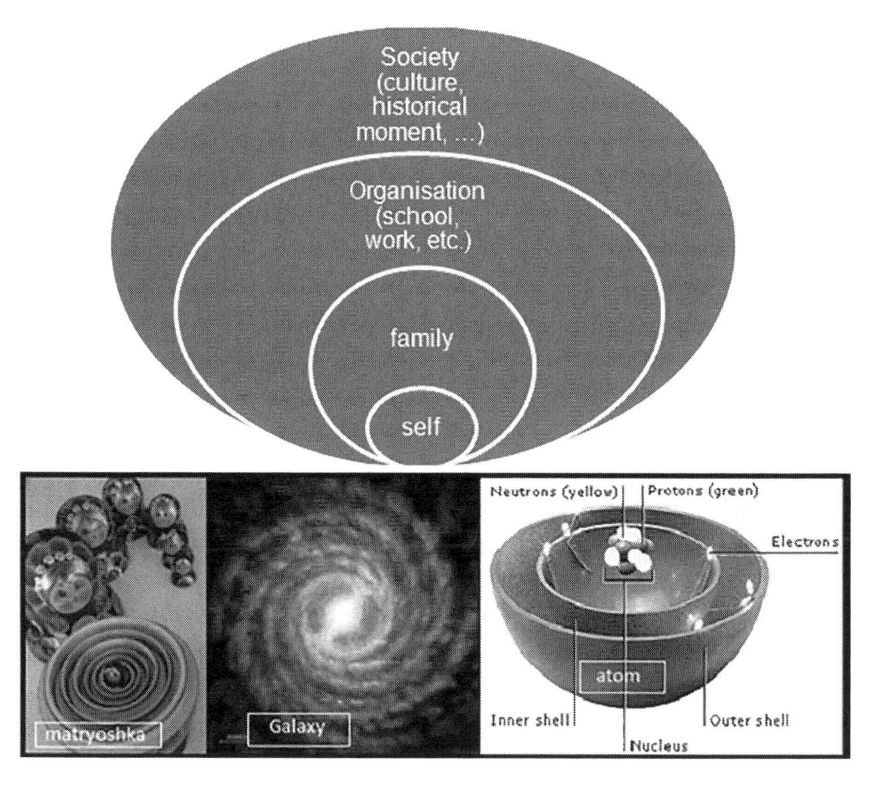

Figure 3.2 Multilevel structure of a personality, a galaxy and an atom: the complex structure of "self" construction

(adapted from Liutsko 2013)

social environments (where the person has been formed and educated and lives) (Liutsko 2013; Liutsko and Cardis 2016).

To help foster resilience and adaptation for affected persons, we therefore need to understand and interpret the events, experiences and solutions and the cultural and historical context that have forged their behaviour and knowledge/comprehension.

Individuals grow and evolve together and within societies, which in their turn change with time. The rapid changes in the 20th and 21st centuries have resulted in the development of new technologies and new knowledge that, together with practical experience, can be useful in providing information and knowledge and enhance health and environmental protection. Though specific cultural patterns can affect and differentiate the behaviour of affected populations after a nuclear accident, the knowledge and experience of the past can, with the use of new communication and the engagement of local actors, be adapted in an optimal way to support and enhance the resilience and adaptation of affected populations whatever their culture and history.

4.1 *Process of resilience after a nuclear accident*

> Individuals experiencing surviving exhibited anxiety about their personal and family members' health, expressed mistrust, and felt a stigma associated with being a survivor. For those who were thriving, peace activism, overcoming and forgiveness were typically displayed.
>
> (Knowles 2011)

Kübler-Ross described stages of the general grieving process (or remedy of the "loss") (Kübler-Ross 2009; Kübler-Ross and Kessler 2005) as follows:

- *Denial* – The first reaction is denial (mistake, false).
- *Anger* – When the individual recognises that denial cannot continue, they become frustrated.
- *Bargaining* – Hope that a cause of grief can be avoided.
- *Depression* – "I'm so sad, why bother with anything".
- *Acceptance* – "It's going to be okay"; "I can't fight it, I may as well prepare for it".

Similarly to the grieving process cycle, resilience in the post-accidental period can be achieved only after overcoming the first stages:

- No information, little information or misinformation about the scope and consequences of disaster. Shock, denial and/or ignorance.
- Anger, frustration, fear, anxiety and depression. Feelings of guilt.
- Resilience (adaptation to new conditions and lifestyle) – a recovery stage.

In these cases, striving for well-being and health beyond "mere survival" is not possible if a person cannot find ways to recover from the accident and to build resilience. To adapt to a new lifestyle means to try to do the best within given limitations, taking into account that these limitations can persist for years, as is the case with living in contaminated areas.

Unfortunately, even 31 years after the Chernobyl accident, there are people still at the stage of anger and frustration, claiming the Chernobyl disaster is responsible for all the bad things that happen in their lives. Some still live in the first stage (denial): some women who emigrated to Israel, for example, did not accept and did not want to "remember" that they came from the "Chernobyl" areas (personal communication of the author with Prof Julie Cwikel). In some cases, their local doctors suggested "to avoid becoming pregnant and having your own children".[3] Those women's reaction of "escape" even if it was not adaptive, was in a way understandable. They wanted to be mothers and to have their own children. They preferred not to mention or think of "Chernobyl" and to erase this part of their history, trying to convince themselves that in a new country they had a new future and the possibility to realise their dream to be a mother (from the author's personal communication with Prof Julie Cwikel).

Persons who, in this way, do not move past the first or second stage, according to the therapeutic process, are not able to progress towards resilience, to adapt to their circumstances and to move on, improving their well-being and health.

4.2 *Good practices after the Chernobyl and Fukushima nuclear accidents*

Some of the more successful initiatives in improving the understanding of radiation and radiation protection and support for practical implementation of dosimetry and food measurements have been carried out at the local level (such as in villages affected by the Chernobyl and Fukushima accidents). Such projects have been run by volunteers, local NGOs and/or international programmes (CORE, ETHOS, ICRP dialogue). They have contributed to empowering people by enabling them to make their own decisions about their lives (Lochard 2000; Lepicard and Dubreuil 2001; Lochard 2007; Liland, Lochard, and Skuterud 2009; Mizuno and Ando 2012; Ando 2016) or by enabling them to make their own measurements of radioactive contamination, thus regaining control of their daily lives in their new conditions (Adachi et al. 2015). The projects have also allowed people to share their worries and to obtain support from professionals, thus reducing their fears and anxiety and improving the understanding of the environment in which they live after the nuclear accident. A common aim is to allow affected populations to develop suitable protection strategies with the support of radiation protection experts.

Another example of the favourable effects of professional support (psychological help and counselling) was the case of liquidators in Chernobyl, as described in Malova (2000) and discussed in personal communications of the author with Prof Malova.

In all cases, the most effective way was to use simple and clear language and to work together, engaging local people in measurements and decisions. In general, one can conclude that the resilience process can be facilitated by access to both

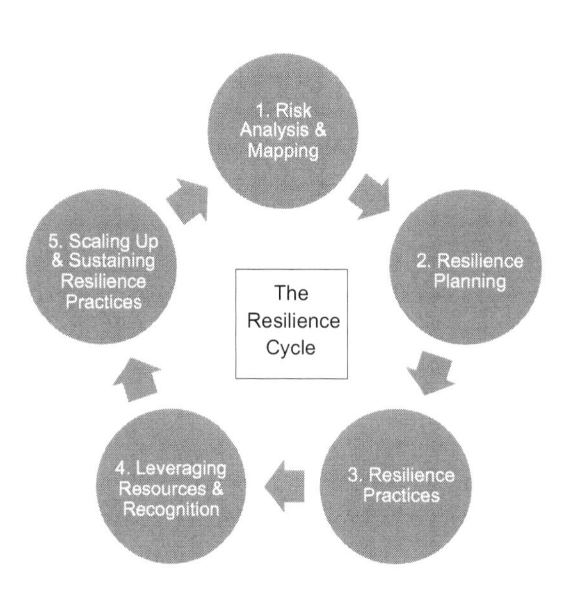

Figure 3.3 The evolution of the Resilience Cycle

knowledge and dialogue about the interpretation of an event (in this case a nuclear accident), as well as by adaptation to new changes.

To conclude, the role of the SHAMISEN project was to review positive and negative experiences from previous post-accident circumstances, in order to identify needs and to make recommendations for a better preparedness and response to nuclear accidents. These recommendations include the design of communication strategies and programmes and of engagement and health surveillance protocols that respond to the needs of affected populations without causing unnecessary anxiety.

"If we only claim the past, we go nowhere", as it is said (Liutsko et al. 2016). Fortunately, the positive resilience aptitudes that have appeared in affected populations after the Chernobyl accident are also relayed by the mass media, as shown in Figure 3.4, where we can see a new growing tree inside of the old trunk as a sign of resilience ('30 Years After Chernobyl' 2016).

Figure 3.4 The front page of the journal "Rodnaia priroda", Minsk, Belarus, N°4, April 2016, dedicated to the 30th anniversary of the Chernobyl accident and entitled "Life after Chernobyl"

Acknowledgements

This work was conducted within the framework of the EC funded SHAMISEN project (Grant 604984 OPERRA, FP7 – Fission – 2013).

Notes

1 See http://www.nti.org/analysis/articles/reykjavik-summit-legacy/
2 www.onthisday.com/date/1986/april (accessed 20th October 2016).
3 Note: not all doctors made such recommendations, and it is considered to have been incorrect advice. But the recommendation, or the reporting of such recommendations, had a clear impact on the women.

References

'30 Years After Chernobyl', (2016, April). *Journal "Rodnaia priroda"* [*Native Nature*]. Belarus: Minsk, 5–15. [In Byelorussian].

Adachi N., Adamovitch V., Adjovi Y., Aida K., Akamatsu H., Akiyama S., Anzai S. (2015) 'Measurement and Comparison of Individual External Doses of High-school Students Living in Japan, France, Poland and Belarus – The "D-shuttle" Project –', *Journal of Radiological Protection*, 36(1), 49.

Alexievich S. (1997) Светлана Алексиевич. Чернобыльская молитва. — М.: Остожье [The Chernobyl Prayer. M: Ostogzie]. ISBN 5-86095-088-8. [in Russian] [The version in English: Alexievich, S. (2005) *Voices From Chernobyl: The Oral History of Nuclear Disaster*. Dalkey Archive Press. ISBN 1-56478-401-0].

Ando R. (2016) 'Measuring, Discussing, and Living Together: Lessons From 4 Years in Suetsugi', *Annals of the ICRP*, 45(1 Suppl), 75–83. Available at https://doi.org/10.1177/0146645315615018.

Ando, R. (2016) 'Measuring, Discussing, and Living Together: Lessons from 4 Years in Suetsugi', *Annals of the ICRP*, 45(1_suppl), 75–83.

Bromet E. J., Havenaar J. M., Guey L. T. (2011) 'A 25 Year Retrospective Review of the Psychological Consequences of the Chernobyl Accident', *Clinical Oncology*, 23(4), 297–305.

Chernobyl and the Bible (2005) Available at http://academickids.com/encyclopedia/index.php/Chernobyl_accident. Date Accessed: 8 August 2017.

Clarke R. H., Valentin J. (2009) 'The History of ICRP and the Evolution of Its Policies', *Annals of the ICRP*, 39(1), 75–110.

Collins D. L., de Carvalho A. B. (1993) 'Chronic Stress From the Goiania 137Cs Radiation Accident', *Behavioral Medicine*, 18(4), 149–57.

Curie, E. (1939) *Madame Curie: A Biography*. Doran: Doubleday.

Gorbachev's speech on soviet TV (1986). *Izvestia*, 15 May 1986.

Knowles A. (2011) 'Resilience Among Japanese Atomic Bomb Survivors', *International Nursing Review*, 58(1), 54–60.

Komarova G. (2000) 'Ethnic Behaviour Under Conditions of High Radiation', *Inner Asia*, 2(1), 63–72.

Kübler-Ross E. (2009) *On Death and Dying: What the Dying Have to Teach Doctors, Nurses, Clergy and Their Own Families*. New York: Scribner.

Kübler-Ross E., Kessler D. (2005) *On Grief and Grieving: Finding the Meaning of Grief Through the Five Stages of Loss*. New York: Scribner.

Lazarev V. S. (1999) 'Contribution of Mass Communication Media to Development of Population Psychological Trouble After the Chernobyl Accident'. *Abstract, International hin.* Wien, Austria: IAEA. Available at www.iaea.org/inis/collection/NCLCollectionStore/_Public/31/043/31043113.pdf [In Russian].

Lepicard S., Dubreuil G. H. (2001) 'Practical Improvement of the Radiological Quality of Milk Produced by Peasant Farmers in the Territories of Belarus Contaminated by the Chernobyl Accident: The ETHOS Project', *Journal of Environmental Radioactivity*, 56(1), 241–53.

Liland A., Lochard J., Skuterud L. (2009) 'How Long Is Long-term? Reflections Based on Over 20 Years of Post-Chernobyl Management in Norway', *Journal of Environmental Radioactivity*, 100(7), 581–4.

Liutsko L. (2013) 'Proprioception as a Basis for Individual Differences', *Psychology in Russia: State of the Art*, 6(3), 107–19.

Liutsko L., Cardis E. (2016, June) Cultural-historical approach in risky and non-adaptive vs. resilient behaviour to negative consequences of radiation effects. *IV Vigotsky Estoril Conference*. Portugal: Estoril (invited oral presentation).

Liutsko L., Ohba T., Cardis E., Schneider T., Oughton, D. (2016, August) Socio-economic, historical and cultural background: implications for behaviour after radiation accidents and better resilience. *ISEEH, III International Symposium of Ethics and Environmental Health; OPERRA workshop on radiation protection*. Check Republic: Budweis (invited oral presentation).

Lochard J. (2000) 'Stakeholder Involvement in the Rehabilitation of Living Conditions in Contaminated Territories Affected by the Chernobyl Accident. The ETHOS Project in Belarus', *Proceedings of an International Symposium on Restoration of Environments With Radioactive Residues. Papers and Discussions*. Wien, Austria: IAEA. Available at https://inis.iaea.org/search/search.aspx?orig_q=RN:32007838

Lochard J. (2007) 'Rehabilitation of Living Conditions in Territories Contaminated by the Chernobyl Accident: The ETHOS Project', *Health Physics*, 93(5), 522–6.

Malova Yu. (2000) 'Psychological Detection and Correction in Rehabilitation of Individuals Who Liquidated the Chernobyl Power Plant Accident', *Journal Medicina Truda I Promishlennaia Ecologia*, 7, 81–9 (In Russian).

Mizuno Y., Ando R. (2012) '"Fukushima-Method" for Local Dissemination of Information to Recover Living Conditions After Nuclear Accident', *Journal of Socio-informatics*, 5(1), 81–9.

On This Day. *Search the World's Largest, Most Accurate Site for Today in History*. (2000–2018). Available at www.onthisday.com/date/1986/april

Rollyson C. (2004). *Marie Curie: Honesty in Science*. Bloomington, IN: iUniverse. p. x. ISBN 978-0-595-34059-0.

Schmemann, S. (1986) 'Chernobyl Fallout: Apocalyptic Tale', *New York Times*, July 25.

Slovic P., Finucane M. L., Peters E., MacGregor D. G. (2004) 'Risk as Analysis and Risk as Feelings: Some Thoughts About Affect, Reason, Risk, and Rationality', *Risk Analysis*, 24(2), 311–22.

Sokolov, N. (2007) *Introduction: The Clear and Present Danger of Nuclear Proliferation Risks*, December 1. Available at www.nti.org/analysis/articles/reykjavik-summit-legacy/

Sugimoto A., Krull S., Nomura S., Morita T., Tsubokura M. (2012) 'The Voice of the Most Vulnerable: Lessons From the Nuclear Crisis in Fukushima, Japan', *Bulletin of the World Health Organization*, 90(8), 629–30.

Part II

Philosophical approaches to environmental health ethics

4 How to bridge the gap between social acceptance and ethical acceptability

A Rawlsian approach[1]

Behnam Taebi

1 Introduction

Introducing new technology into society often brings great benefits, but it can also create new and significant risks. Serious efforts have been made to assess, map, understand and manage these risks. For instance, in the chemical industry, risk assessment methods have been proposed for describing and quantifying "the risks associated with hazardous substances, processes, actions, or events" (Covello and Merkhofer 1993: 3). Perhaps the most notable example is the Probabilistic Risk Assessment, originally developed in order to systematically understand and reduce the risk of melt-down in nuclear reactors (NRC 1975), and to evaluate aviation risks. However, these and other risk assessment methods have been criticized for neglecting social aspects of risk and, more specifically, overlooking the issue of risk acceptance on the part of the public.[2] This in turn has initiated a new yet powerful strand of social science scholarship devoted to developing the concept of "social acceptance" of technological risk (Wynne 1992b; Flynn and Bellaby 2007). During the last three decades, social acceptance studies have gained more relevance for major technologies, most notably large-energy projects such as sizeable wind parks and nuclear energy technologies (Chung 1990; Walker 1995; Sjöberg 2004; Wüstenhagen, Wolsink, and Bürer 2007; Huijts, Molin, and Steg 2012; Di Ruggero 2014). This has been due to controversies and public opposition that emerge from the introduction or implementation of such technologies. Unfortunately, to many decision-makers and private investors, public opposition is simply considered an obstacle to technological development – and hence as something that should be overcome. There have even been proposals to "use marketing methods [in order to] maximize the likelihood of a successful introduction" of technologies, by investigating people's attitudes (Schulte, Hart, and Van der Vorst 2004: 667). This is disconcerting, because it shifts the focus from asking why a technology is not accepted to asking how to ensure its acceptance.

Lack of social acceptance can sometimes be attributed to the fact that important ethical issues that new technologies engender are overlooked in the decision-making. For instance, public opposition to siting issues may stem from an unfair distribution of risk and benefit between a local community (that will be exposed to additional risks) and a larger region or even nation (that will enjoy the benefits). Fittingly, many humanities researchers are now considering methods for assessing the *ethics of technological risk*, and consequently the *ethical acceptability* of risky technology (e.g. Hansson 2003; Asveld and Roeser 2009). These assessments often involve conceptual philosophical contemplations.

In this chapter, I argue that only in conjunction are the concepts of social acceptance and ethical acceptability relevant to the governance of risky technology. Conceptually, it makes sense to marry these two notions because they are mostly complementary. Social acceptance studies are often incapable of capturing all the morally relevant features of risky technologies; ethical analyses do not typically include stakeholders' opinions, and they therefore lack the relevant empirical input for a thorough ethical evaluation.[3]

The chapter is organized as follows. In the next section, I will discuss a number of ethical issues that social acceptance studies cannot sufficiently cover. Section 3 will present the case of multinational nuclear waste repositories, in order to illustrate the insufficiency of social acceptance studies when assessing the broader ethical impacts of new technologies or technological projects. In section 4, I will consider the existing philosophical discussions of ethical acceptability, arguing that most of these studies are conceptual and lack empirical input. In section 5, I will present the Rawlsian Wide Reflective Equilibrium as one possible method for merging empirical social science studies on acceptance with conceptual ethical acceptability analyses. Section 6 will propose ways in which the WRE might be used to bridge the acceptance-acceptability gap for multinational repositories. Section 7 discusses an important assumption yet to be discussed in the earlier sections, namely that of national sovereignty. In section 7, I will offer my conclusions.

2 Social acceptance and neglected ethical issues

The terms *acceptance* and *acceptability* have been used in different senses throughout the literature in the social sciences and humanities. In this chapter, I make the following distinction between social acceptance and ethical acceptability:

Social acceptance refers to the fact that a new technology is accepted – or merely tolerated – by a community.

Ethical acceptability refers to a reflection on a new technology that takes into account the moral issues that emerge from its introduction.

The former concept largely aligns with studies in social psychology that assess the level of acceptance of a new technology and identify potential hurdles, while the latter concept best aligns with the literature on the ethics of technology. In the discussion of risky technologies, a distinction is often made between the actual acceptance of technology and the normative questions concerning which levels of risk *should* be acceptable to the public; I make the same distinction in this chapter (Grunwald 2000; Hansson 2003; Asveld and Roeser 2009;

Batel, Devine-Wright, and Tangeland 2013). Many authors have emphasized the interrelatedness of these two concepts where various technologies are concerned. Cowell et al., for instance, argue that acceptance is affected by perceptions of ethical concepts such as distributive and procedural justice (Cowell, Bristow, and Munday 2011). Huijts, Molin, and Steg (2012) reiterate the latter conclusion by empirically showing that in the case of sustainable energy technologies, the acceptance of individual members of the community is affected by those members' social norms, as well as by their feelings about distributive and procedural justice. Oosterlaken (2015: 364) argues that for major wind energy projects, what matters is "not only mere acceptance, but the ethical question of acceptability." Van de Poel (2016: 191) points to "the danger of equating acceptance with acceptability" and argues that we need to account for how both notions may be related. Here I build on the same line of reasoning, arguing that good governance of risky technology requires the two concepts of acceptance and acceptability to be addressed in conjunction; I present a method for bridging this gap in section 5.

The remainder of this section identifies several issues that current studies on social acceptance do not usually take into account, as well as cases that remain problematic even in light of the social acceptance that supposedly already pertains to them. Generally speaking, one could distinguish between two categories of problem, namely *principal problems* and *instrumental problems* of acceptance through the participatory process. The former relates to the fundamental ethical issues that a participatory process cannot address such as intergenerational justice. The latter is about instrumental problems associated with the participatory process, such as recognition and fair representation of stakeholders, full transparency, access to information, acknowledging the differences in power, etc. In the following paragraphs, both categories of problems are discussed in more detail. I distinguish between six main issues.

First, acceptance is sometimes based on incomplete or even faulty information. Wigley and Shrader-Frechette (1996: 72) present a case study of a uranium enrichment facility in Louisiana that asked local communities to "nominate potential sites for a proposed chemical facility."[4] While the communities did apparently nominate host sites, there were several inherent ethical problems with this situation. For one, the company never informed the local communities about the exact nature of these "chemical plants"; enrichment facilities are indeed chemical plants, but they are very specific types with radiological risks. In addition, the company never presented a Probabilistic Risk Assessment or a quantitative determination of the impacts. Thus "it [was] impossible to know, reliably, the actual risks associated with the plant" when accepting those risks (Wigley and Shrader-Frechette 1996: 72).

Second, there is the question of *which public(s)* should accept a new technology. In the last case study, concerning the site-application process, Wigley and Shrader-Frechette (1996) argue that the opinions of host communities located very close to the proposed facilities were not considered; instead, communities located farther away from the facilities were consulted. Walker (1995) presents examples of local communities opposing wind parks while the broader public endorsed this same energy technology.

Third, distributional issues underlie new technologies, both spatially and temporally. When siting risky facilities, there are several fundamental ethical issues that need to be addressed in the realm of the spatial, including questions about how the environmental burdens and benefits should be distributed. In addition, there are also more practical questions with ethical relevance, such as the matter of how to establish an acceptable distance between potential major accidents with risky technology and exposed residents (Watson and Bulkeley 2005; Gordon Walker 2010; Basta 2011).

Additionally, there are the more ethically complex issues surrounding temporal distributions, alternatively known as *intergenerational* issues.[5] For instance: at what pace we should consume non-renewable resources, and what level of change in the climatic system will be acceptable to future generations? These questions become especially intricate when new technology that could help us safeguard future interests would compromise the interests of people alive today. Such a situation gives rise to moral questions that are not easy to address in public acceptance studies. For example: do we have a moral obligation to provide benefits for or prevent losses to future generations, if that comes at a cost to ourselves? (Barry 1999; Shrader-Frechette 2000; Hillerbrand and Ghil 2008; Taebi 2011; Kermisch 2016; Kermisch and Taebi 2017).[6]

Fourth, a risky technology might be accepted for reasons that are morally wrong. This issue regularly arises in discussions of siting, and in connection with the issue of compensating local communities. Compensation is legitimate and uncontroversial when a host community is exposed to additional risks and burdens, while the benefits of new technologies (or facilities) are more widely dispersed; in such cases compensation, also referred to as community benefit, is meant to address the unequal distribution of burdens and benefits. (Himmelberger, Ratick, and White 1991; Ter Mors, Terwel, and Daamen 2012) But Hannis and Rawles (2013: 348) correctly argue that, without sound ethical guidelines regarding "who decides [or should decide] whether, or at what point, it is reasonable to expect a host community to accept [it]," compensation might well become an "exploitative, misleading or manipulative" instrument. These authors warn of situations in which compensation could be abused to "bribe" local communities (Hannis and Rawles 2013: 348).

Fifth, a technological project could be *accepted* on the basis of a faulty or unfair procedure. It has been widely acknowledged and empirically shown that, in addition to having a fair outcome (as for example in the distribution of burdens and benefits), what very much matters is having a fair procedure in decision-making (Vermunt and Törnblom 1996; Sjöberg and Drottz-Sjöberg 2001; Krütli et al. 2012). In social acceptance studies, the relevance of "procedural justice" issues has also been acknowledged, leading to a growing body of work on the participatory approach to decision-making in regard to new technologies. (Fiorino 1990; Renn, Webler, and Wiedemann 1995; Cuppen et al. 2010; Ciupuliga and Cuppen 2013; Cotton 2014) Indeed, it is now common practice to recognize a normative rationale for participation as a political right for citizens; (e.g., Ciupuliga and Cuppen 2013) "the case for participation should begin with a normative argument that a purely technocratic orientation is incompatible with democratic ideals" (Fiorino 1990: 239). However, the normativity of new technology is not to be approached only via participation. As discussed in this section, there are various other important ethical issues that a fair procedure for participation does not necessarily solve. It is crucial, however, to explicitly acknowledge procedural justice as a relevant moral issue that needs to be addressed. In addition to participation, at the very least the two other key issues of recognition and power must be considered (Sovacool and Dworkin 2014). Those who will potentially be affected by a decision must be identified and recognized; they must be able to fully and freely participate in the decision-making process, which means we need to acknowledge that some stakeholders may have fewer available opportunities to take part in such a process (Paavola and Adger 2006). Achieving procedural justice is more problematic when it comes to projects with transnational consequences, which brings me to the last issue.

Sixth, some technological projects engender international risks. For instance, some of the technological solutions presented for dealing with climate change, such as *geoengineering* (i.e., intentional climate change designed to reverse undesired change), raise serious international procedural and distributive justice issues as well as questions regarding international governance and responsibility (e.g., Pidgeon et al. 2013). The multinational character of such proposals makes it virtually impossible to address their desirability only in social acceptance studies.

This list is naturally not exhaustive. More importantly, the issues mentioned should not be viewed in isolation, because at times it is the convergence of different issues that makes a case particularly relevant from an ethical perspective. In the next section, I will present an example that shows how crucial moral aspects of a situation can easily be overlooked if we focus exclusively on "social acceptance."

3 When public acceptance alone might fail: multinational nuclear waste repositories

Despite international consensus that any country producing nuclear waste is responsible for its disposal, policymakers are increasingly considering the possibility of multinational repositories for the joint disposal of nuclear waste. This is especially true in Europe, where the European Parliament and the European Commission have already expressed interest in multinational repositories (Risoluti et al. 2008). A group of waste management organizations in several EU member states is currently exploring the feasibility of creating such repositories in Europe.[7]

Multinational repositories have serious advantages where safety, security and economics are concerned (McCombie and Chapman 2002), but they also give rise to a range of institutional, legal, financial and political issues. Furthermore, it has been widely acknowledged that they raise several ethical issues that need to be addressed (IAEA 2004; Boutellier, McCombie, and Mele 2006). In tackling these ethical issues, scholars have argued that it will be absolutely essential to establish national and local acceptance (Boutellier, McCombie, and Mele 2006; Salzer, McCombie, and Chapman 2008). That is undoubtedly a necessary requirement, but it is not a sufficient criterion, as I argue in Section 2. The associated ethical issues revolve around intergenerational and international justice. Let me elaborate on these two issues.

As regards intergenerational justice, multinational repositories could well be beneficial from the point of view of justice to posterity; they would give us access to a larger variety of geologic host sites, allowing us to choose the geological formations that best guarantee long-term protection. Moreover, the number of risky facilities would thus be reduced. This would decrease the risk of human intrusion in the far future, if knowledge about the location of the repositories were to be lost.[8]

Multinational repositories are therefore to be preferred from the perspective of compliance with intergenerational justice. However, they inevitably give rise to international *injustice* because one nation is always expected to accept another nation's waste. This injustice might not be evident at first glance, especially when the host country willingly takes the waste (or, in other words, when the criterion of *social acceptance* has been met). While this acceptance among communities and nations is necessary, it might turn out to be morally problematic. The consent of the host country could, for instance, stem from an imbalance in the economic or political power of the two countries (Bunn et al. 2001). If social acceptance is taken as the sole criterion for choosing host sites, then we could easily end up with situations in which waste is regularly transferred from richer to poorer countries, as the latter are likely to be more receptive to economic incentives.

The issue of international justice can be divided into procedural and distributive subtopics. As regards procedural justice, the issues of recognition, participation and power need to be carefully considered in the international setting. The distributive justice issue will raise questions about how to compensate and whom to compensate when we are dealing with different communities and regions in different countries.

These are just a few ethical issues that multinational nuclear waste repositories could engender, and they are not typically addressed in social acceptance studies. Similar issues are also associated with other technologies that have international and intergenerational significance, such as geoengineering.

4 Ethical acceptability and the lack of stakeholders' opinions

In the preceding sections, I argued that social acceptance studies do not typically address all the morally relevant features of risky technologies. Therefore, a single-minded focus on social acceptance can easily obscure more fundamental ethical issues. In this section, I will consider the notion of ethical acceptability as it has been used in ethics of technology.

There is a growing body of literature in applied ethics that takes up the issue of the ethical acceptability of risky technologies (e.g., Hansson 2003; Asveld and Roeser 2009; Taebi 2011). Inspired by biomedical ethics, philosophers have proposed several criteria for evaluating the ethical acceptability of technological risk, such as voluntariness, informed consent and fair compensation. The existing ethical analyses of technological risk are predominantly conceptual, and do not usually include stakeholders' opinions. I argue that a sound ethical evaluation needs empirical input; it should therefore take the opinions of stakeholders into account, for the following three reasons.

First and foremost, whenever risk is being imposed on an individual, that individual has the (moral) right to be informed about and to consent to the risk. The moral right to be informed has been formalized in environmental law with the Aarhus Convention, which grants a number of rights to the public; it mentions (i) "access to environmental information" and (ii) "public participation in environmental decision-making."[9] Consenting to this risk is an addition criterion from the *informed consent* principle. While this principle is straightforwardly applicable in biomedical ethics, where the interest of just one individual patient is usually at stake, extending it to include collective technological risk can be rather problematic. As Hansson argues, informed consent is "associated with individual veto power, but it does not appear realistic to give veto power to all individuals who are affected for instance by an engineering project" (Hansson 2006: 149). In the same vein, while we must respect the rights of each sovereign individual who is exposed to risk, modern societies would not be able to operate if all risk imposition were prohibited (Hansson 2009). Stakeholders' differing and sometimes diverging values make such an arrangement not only practically but also morally problematic (Doorn 2012).[10] Yet it is important to acknowledge the plurality of opinions among the stakeholders and to account for those opinions in decision-making as much as possible (Cuppen et al. 2015; Dignum et al. 2016). Secondly, and at a more fundamental level, one could argue that stakeholders' opinions ought to be included for the sake of pluralism – which is "a cornerstone of democracy because it features multiple centers of power, counters authoritarianism, and provides the basic grist for political debate" (Dryzek and Niemeyer 2006: 635). In the context of the acceptability of technological risk, pluralism means acknowledging the diversity of cultural and moral values (Doorn 2010; Correljé et al. 2015; Cuppen et al. forthcoming). This issue will be discussed in the next section, where I argue that diverging moral values does not necessarily mean that people cannot agree.

Thirdly, on a more practical note, stakeholders' opinions should be included because those stakeholders have unique *local* and *contextual* knowledge (Wynne 1992a; Jasanoff 2004). Against the popular belief that laypeople's understanding of risk is emotional and hence irrational, Roeser argues that emotional responses to risk – especially the responses of those who are exposed to such risk – can be an invaluable source of insight into risk-related ethical issues (Roeser 2006, 2010) So, instead of being dismissed, those emotions should be taken seriously in the ethical contemplation.[11]

5 How to bridge the gap with the Wide Reflective Equilibrium

So far I have argued that social acceptance studies do not typically take the ethical issues surrounding risky technology into account (section 3), while ethical acceptability analyses of technological risk are predominantly conceptual and do not include stakeholders' opinions (section 4). One possible tool for marrying the two concepts is the Wide Reflective Equilibrium (WRE), as introduced by Rawls (1971, 2001) and developed by Daniels (1979, 1996, 2011). This iterative method alternates between analyzing the lower levels *considered judgments* of individuals about specific situations and analyzing the top level of theoretical moral considerations; between these two levels of judgment and theory, there is a mid-level of *principles* or *rules* that we believe govern our intuition. Ideally, the WRE iterations continue until we arrive at a coherence or an *equilibrium* among the three levels.

In principle, the WRE was developed as a model of moral thinking meant to consider "a given individual at a given time" (Daniels 1979: 281). But earlier studies also proposed that it could, for instance, be used to analyze and organize public debates surrounding a specific topic (Vorstenbosch 1998). Particularly in biomedical ethics, it has proven to be a suitable method for dealing with practical moral problems (Beauchamp and Childress 2009). For instance, it has helped to integrate the moral judgments of healthcare professionals with insights from ethical theories (Van Delden and Van Thiel 1998; Van Thiel and Van Delden 2010). In the context of technological development, the WRE has been used to account for the moral judgments of the actors involved in R&D networks (Van de Poel and Zwart 2010) and to organize moral deliberation on the topic of responsibility distribution in the research setting (Doorn 2012); see also (Doorn and Taebi 2017).

I argue that the process of reaching an equilibrium via the WRE can be understood as a way of bridging the proverbial gap between acceptance and acceptability. Building on Van de Poel (2016), I argue that public acceptance studies most resemble the lower level of considered moral judgments, while ethical acceptability analysis occurs mostly at the top level of moral theory.[12] For this process to be feasible, we need to assume that people who have different interests and value systems can in principle agree about what is best for everybody. Acknowledging the plurality of moral frameworks in a democratic society (Rawls 1993), Rawls claims that people with different worldviews do at least share some common elements of their individual Wide Reflective Equilibria that pertain to an overlapping consensus. Reasonableness has an important place in this argument, because only *reasonable citizens* will weigh their own and others' considered convictions, as a result of which a *reasonable overlapping consensus* can emerge.[13]

As stressed above, the WRE approach is based on several assumptions and it is not unthinkable that a coherence between the three levels might not be achievable in a specific situation (and a consensus would be completely out of reach). Moreover, the WRE is certainly no panacea for resolving moral conflicts.

Yet, as rightfully argued by Van de Poel (2016: 191), a lack of consensus could also be a "source of debate, argumentation and reflection." In other words, one might argue that establishing a complete coherence between the three levels is the *ideal* (perhaps often unfeasible) solution while we are seeking for the best *approximation* of that ideal. More precisely, we want to investigate if an *acceptable* approximation is achievable. When there is no consensus, this endeavor could lay bare the reasons of dissensus both with regard to social acceptance and to fundamental moral questions. So, while the WRE cannot give a decisive answer to moral dilemmas, it could help us identify those dilemmas. Moreover, including stakeholders' judgment in moral dilemmas could help us formulate an informed response to such dilemmas; in the following section, I will give an example of such situations.

In summary, reflecting on the expressed judgment is an inherent part of this method; both from a technical point of view (and when it comes to the issues of technological risks and uncertainties) and from a moral point of view. In social practice, this requires that the person involved in the judgment must have both the ability and the willingness to engage in reflection and, again, this is an assumption that needs empirical substantiation,[14] but in general the purpose of this method is to facilitate a reflection and to investigate if the acceptance-acceptability gap can be sufficiently bridged.[15]

6 How to bridge the acceptance-acceptability gap for multinational repositories

Let me elaborate on how the framework of WRE could be used to bridge the acceptance-acceptability gap in the earlier discussed case of multinational repositories. In other words, how can we discover whether a *reasonable overlapping consensus* can be reached in such a case?[16] As mentioned in section 3, the ethical issues associated with multinational repositories revolve around international (procedural) and intergenerational justice. Following the WRE analogy, these justice notions must therefore be placed at the top level of abstract moral theory. The bottom level is connected to the considered opinions of stakeholders in the different countries involved. The top and bottom level should then resonate with the mid-level of principles, which should guide and govern the development of such repositories.

So the first question is whether the notions of justice that are discussed in the philosophy literature have any bearing on the mid-level principles. Such analysis does not have to start from scratch, since issues of justice surrounding nuclear energy production and waste management have been discussed for at least three decades. The very idea of disposing of nuclear waste deep underground stems from an interpretation of the notion of intergenerational justice: "[r]adioactive waste shall be managed in such a way that will not impose undue burdens on future generations"(IAEA 1995: 7). Likewise, various procedural justice principles have played a role in shaping nuclear waste management policies. One might think of the principles of transparency and openness in nuclear waste management, or the principle of early and inclusive participation (COWAM 2007). All these considerations are, however, mainly about *national* radioactive waste management policies; to what extent would they apply to multinational repositories? Considering the international risk and the requirements of international decision-making, new or modified principles may be needed to govern multinational repositories.

The aim of applying the WRE method is, therefore, to determine whether there is an overlapping consensus to be found regarding the principles for good governance of multinational repositories. The key questions here are whether the existing national principles (i) sufficiently encompass the transnational and intergenerational risk of multinational repositories, and (ii) sufficiently reflect stakeholders' opinions in the different countries involved.

As mentioned earlier, one aim of bridging the acceptance-acceptability gap is to explicitly address the ethical issues at hand. This conceptual analysis, however, can sometimes only lay bare certain ethical dilemmas. Section 3 gives an example of this phenomenon, showing that while multinational repositories are to be preferred from the perspective of justice to future generations, they can create intragenerational/international injustice. Indeed, this dilemma could be addressed in a conceptual normative analysis, but also at this level, the plurality of the opinions of those who are performing such analysis will become relevant; it is likely that there would be different ethically defensible solutions to this dilemma. In a sense, the bottom-up analysis of the considered judgments of stakeholders might *validate* different moral judgments. One could argue that, other things being equal, the ethical analysis of risky technology that counts on the support of those who are exposed to those risks is the most defensible one. This shows how the two concepts of social acceptance and ethical acceptability could be best complementary.

Finally, for facilitating the WRE process, learning among the stakeholders should be incentivized. This will allow them to reflect on the existing principles, the existing theories of justice and each other's opinions. Ideally, we want stakeholders in different countries to answer questions regarding the governance of these multinational repositories without knowing whether waste will be disposed of in their country (or even their local community) or elsewhere.[17] Establishing such an ideal situation, however, will prove very difficult if not impossible; we should therefore find the best approximation of this state of affairs. For instance, stakeholders could be asked to answer all questions as if they were in the position of hosting the waste repository. This might generate the most risk-averse answers, but in this way we could ensure that a possible consensus would be fair to all participants.

7 Should we take state sovereignty for granted?

Before moving to the conclusions, let me discuss two important yet implicit assumptions upon which my argument is founded. First, my argument about the need for good governance of risky technologies with international and intergenerational risks assumes that there is a *collective interest* to be determined beyond national and generational borders. So, when these risks have been governed well, it could serve this collective interest. Second, and in conjunction with the previous assumption, I seem to silently assume that nation states must be the guardians of this collective international and transgenerational interest. For instance, the critique regarding the lack of social acceptance when dealing with international risks implies that social acceptance can "only" be considered as social acceptance confined within one nation state. In other words, *transnational* social acceptance can only exist as the *sum* of social acceptance within multiple (perhaps neighboring) states. Furthermore, I criticize a sole focus of social acceptance for decision-making on multinational disposal in that it neglects international (distributive and procedural) justice; this seems to presuppose nationally sovereign states that need to negotiate and agree on decision-making and the distributions of burdens and benefits between these states. In short, I seem to have taken national sovereignty for granted. This could be challenged from a normative and a pragmatic perspective.

From a normative perspective, one can question the moral limits of nation states' sovereignty when it is potentially conflicting something morally more compelling, for instance *human rights*. Rawls (2002) argues that a serious violation of human rights is a sufficient ground for taking action against the violator in the international arena. Raz (2010: 328) approaches this slightly differently and argues that human rights are rights "whose violation can justify any international action against violators, provided that they are actions which normally would be impermissible being violations of state sovereignty." Similarly, we could raise the question of whether there is an international responsibility that goes beyond the sum of national responsibilities, for instance for dealing with international risks. One might argue that an institution such as the European Union (EU) is an embodiment of international or supranational responsibilities, but also in the EU, the responsibilities lie primarily with the nation states and, in addition, the need for European governance is emphasized.

This brings me to the pragmatic challenges to national sovereignty. Indeed, there is a case to be made against sole national sovereignty in governing certain risks whose consequences will be (potentially) felt beyond national borders. Nuclear risk is clearly an example that poses such a challenge, because – as the former Director General of the International Atomic Energy Agency, Hans Blix (1986) has correctly said: "a nuclear accident somewhere is a nuclear accident everywhere." Yet no one would argue for giving up national sovereignties altogether; the crucial role that national states (and regulators) play in ensuring nuclear safety in their countries is widely acknowledged. Rather, the argument is about the extent to which national sovereignty needs to be seen as an absolute notion. The existence of international agreements – also for safeguarding nuclear safety – is an evidence of countries' willingness to partially renounce their national responsibilities by subjecting themselves to these agreements.

In so far as nuclear risk is concerned, the argument has been made that we might have to think beyond nation states for their governance. Historically speaking, each nuclear accident has contributed to a further shift of national responsibilities to international bodies such as the International Atomic Energy Agency (IAEA) and, by that, accepting certain limitations to national sovereignty. The Chernobyl accident, for instance, marks the beginning of much of what is already in place in the global nuclear safety regime (Bunn and Heinonen 2011), including the most important instrument for international governance of nuclear safety, namely the IAEA's Convention on Nuclear Safety (CNS). Ironically, this prominent international convention has as a key objective "to achieve and maintain a high level of nuclear safety worldwide through the enhancement of national measures and international co-operation" (IAEA 1994; Article 1; own italics).

While no one seems to categorically disregard national responsibilities for governing risks, the current strong focus on national sovereignty might be insufficient when we need to deal with the increasingly international (and intergenerational) nuclear risk challenges. Elsewhere, Maximilian Mayer and I argued for a push towards "global governance of nuclear safety" (Taebi and Mayer 2017: 19). This argument is, of course, not an attempt to renounce national sovereignties. Instead, it is an attempt to call attention to the need for the governance of nuclear risks beyond nation states. This is very much needed considering the changing landscape of future nuclear energy, tilting towards Asian countries (with less experience with this technology), but also considering the new developments that aim at the disposal of nuclear waste multinationally. At a minimum, such a change could be established by introducing (or reinforcing) transnational governance regimes, including elements of international monitoring and verifications for ensuring better nuclear safety.[18]

A potential objection to global governance approaches is that smaller (and less influential) countries need to give up part of their sovereignties and what they get in return might not be very clear. One way of circumventing this problem is to think of such approaches globally but to enforce them more regionally, where the benefits of not being exposed to the neighbors' additional risk might be considered faster (Taebi and Mayer 2017). Indeed, this argument does not only relate to nuclear risk, but to any other risk that could go beyond geographic and generational borders; such global (or regional) approaches to their governance might be more feasible. Such approaches need to still consider limits for national sovereignty, which will probably remain a serious challenge in practice, but if successful there is a great potential to improve risk governance, for instance by emphasizing the role that other actors – most prominently non-governmental institutions – could play that are not necessarily confined by national borders.[19]

8 Conclusion

In this chapter, I have argued that concentrating solely on social acceptance threatens to obscure several important moral issues, especially when it comes to technologies with international and intergenerational risks. Good governance of risky technology must involve addressing both social acceptance and ethical acceptability, because it is only in conjunction that these two concepts gain serious relevance for policy-making. Conceptually, it is helpful to combine these notions, because they are mostly complementary; social acceptance studies are often in need of an ethical addendum, while existing ethical analysis would very much benefit from including stakeholders' opinions. One method for bridging this gap is the Wide Reflective Equilibrium, which aims to establish *coherence* among the three levels of ethical theory, guiding principles and stakeholders' considered moral judgments. While a complete coherence seems to be the ideal (perhaps unrealistic) solution, we must seek the best *approximation* of that ideal. More precisely, we want to investigate if an *acceptable* approximation of that ideal, or a *reasonable overlapping consensus* is achievable.

Reflecting on an expressed judgment is an inherent part of this method, which means that people should have the ability and the willingness to engage in reflection. Hence, according to this framework, reaching a shared opinion does not necessarily require all stakeholders to have the same moral framework or the same value system. What it does require is that all stakeholders be *reasonable* citizens – in the Rawlsian sense – who are willing to reflect on their opinions and consider the opinions of others.

Section 6 elaborates on how the WRE analysis could be applied to the case of multinational nuclear waste repositories. My aim has been to show several steps for implementing the WRE in a hypothetical situation. In so doing, there are several potential problems and difficulties, such as how to deal with different (and diverging) resolutions of moral dilemmas and how to incentivize the learning process (and thereby arriving at considered moral judgments). I have argued that, at the minimum, the WRE method could help identify the underlying reasons for dissensus both with regard to social acceptance and ethical acceptability. Moreover, while the WRE cannot give a decisive answer to moral dilemmas, including stakeholders' judgment in moral dilemmas could help us formulate an informed response to such dilemmas.

Indeed, the usability of WRE for bridging the acceptance-acceptability gap needs to be empirically tested, but if successful, the proposed approach in this chapter could enrich conceptual ethical analysis by adding stakeholders' moral judgments. At the same time, it could broaden social science studies by adding an explicit analysis of the moral aspects of technology. This endeavor is worthwhile, because it is only when they are discussed in conjunction that social acceptance and ethical acceptability analyses are relevant for good governance of risky technologies.

Finally, the arguments in this paper seem to be founded on an assumption of national sovereignty. Some challenges (both normative and from a pragmatic point of view) have been presented in this paper. While no serious risk governance approach dismisses national sovereignty altogether, there is a need to strike a fine balance between national sovereignty on the one hand and having systems of international supervision, monitoring and verification on the other. That is, there are instances in which nation states might not be the best guardians of international and intergenerational interests.

Notes

1 Sections 1–6 of this paper are drawing on an earlier published paper with *Risk Analysis* (Taebi 2017). The discussions of national sovereignty versus international responsibility have been added to this draft.
2 These methods have also been criticized for other reasons, such as their inability to assign objective probabilities due to uncertainties (Doorn and Hansson 2011).
3 It should be mentioned that some ethical theories such as different forms of preferentialism do consider people's actual preferences and wishes as necessary input for ethical decision-making. These theories are, however, not very influential in applied ethics and in the ethics of risk, which is the primary focus of this chapter.
4 This is a quotation from the draft Environmental Impact Statement of the US Nuclear Regulatory Commission (NRC). It is quoted here from the following reference: Wigley and Shrader-Frechette (1996: 71)
5 Strictly speaking, we must distinguish between temporal and intergenerational issues, because not all temporal issues are also intergenerational. The question of how to distribute tax burdens over a period of a few years does have a temporal component, but it is not intergenerational.
6 There are some studies that have explicitly addressed these future effects in the course of public deliberation. There are two examples of the deliberations of mini-publics in the areas of fishery decision-making and Canadian nuclear waste management; see MacKenzie and O'Doherty (2011); NWMO (2005). Another example involves evolutionary game theory in economics; see for instance (Young (1994). These are, however, exceptions to the rule.
7 See the website of the European Repository Development Organization for more information: http://erdo-wg.eu/.
8 Elsewhere I defend this claim in detail (Taebi 2012).
9 While this convention primarily refers to "the state of the environment," it also includes "the state of human health and safety where this can be affected by the state of the environment." This quotation is from the website of the United Nations Economic Commission for Europe; see http://ec.europa.eu/environment/aarhus/ (accessed on February 1st 2016).
10 Doorn puts forward this argument for different conceptions of responsibility among different team members in R&D networks, but the rationale of the argument applies to any situation in which "acceptance" will depend on diverging and sometimes conflicting values.
11 See also (Taebi, Roeser, and Van de Poel (2012); Roeser and Pesch (2016).
12 While I follow Van de Poel (2016) in applying the coherentist approach for relating the two concepts of acceptance and acceptability, our conceptualizations of the notions and the relation between them are slightly different. Van de Poel conceives acceptance as "an equilibrium in which moral principles and background theories are adjusted to given considered judgments" while acceptability should "also critically scrutinize considered judgments from a variety of moral theories and background principles" (191) In this conceptualization, acceptability is the more comprehensive notion that inherently encompasses acceptance. I argue that acceptance takes place at the level of considered judgment about a specific situation, while acceptability occurs at the top level of applying moral theory to that specific situation. So, I conceive of them as two distinct concepts that could be connected through the WRE and should ideally culminate in the mid-level guiding principles with *sufficient* bearing on both moral theory and stakeholders' judgments.
13 Reasonable citizens, in Rawls's understanding, are those who have the "willingness to propose and to abide by, if accepted, what they think others as equal citizens with them might reasonably accept as fair terms of social cooperation" (Rawls 1995: 149).

14 The literature on "reflective learning" provides part of this substantiation. Most notably, Van de Poel and Zwart have empirically tested this claim by applying it to the R&D Network and to achieving overlapping consensus about the moral issues associated with a sewage treatment technology (Van de Poel and Zwart 2010).

15 Let me reiterate that the WRE is only one possible method for doing this. Another method is *discourse ethics*, as most prominently defended by Jürgen Habermas. Discourse ethics rests on the assumption that it is the engagement in communicative action that helps us to recognize the normative rightness of an argument and it was presented by Habermas for structuring the deliberation between different stakeholders that do not necessarily subscribe to the same values. In this way, Habermas's discourse ethics claims to be able to assess the moral rightness of a judgment by ensuring the impartiality of the process of making judgments, unlike Rawls who focuses on the impartiality of the individuals involved in making a moral judgment. It is not my intention to compare the Rawlsian and Habermasian approaches here. My aim in this chapter is only to show the potential and difficulties of the WRE method, as a method that has been used in other areas of applied ethics too. Indeed, these very short accounts do not do justice to Rawls's and Habermas's sophisticated and extensive discussions. Interested readers should consider original sources by Rawls (1993, 2001) and Habermas (1990, 1996) and their exchange on the WRE and other related issue (Habermas 1995; Rawls 1995).

16 It goes without saying that this endeavor does not imply that such a reasonable overlapping consensus exists. The outcome of the analysis could very well be that consensus is impossible.

17 Rawls refers to decisions made behind a *veil of ignorance* when participants "do not know how the various alternatives will affect their own particular case and they are obliged to evaluate cases solely on the basis of general considerations" (Rawls 1971: 118).

18 See Taebi and Mayer (2017) for an elaborate defense of this argument.

19 See Crawford and Watkins (2010) and Murphy (2010) for an elaborate discussion of international responsibilities.

References

Asveld L., Roeser S. (eds.) (2009) *The Ethics of Technological Risk*. London: Earthscan.

Barry B. (1999) 'Sustainability and Intergenerational Justice', in: *Fairness and Futurity: Essays on Environmental Sustainability and Social Justice*, edited by Dobson A., 93–117. New York, NY: Oxford University Press.

Basta C. (2011) 'Siting Technological Risks: Cultural Approaches and Cross-Cultural Ethics', *Journal of Risk Research*, 14(7), 799–817.

Batel S., Devine-Wright P., Tangeland T. (2013) 'Social Acceptance of Low Carbon Energy and Associated Infrastructures: A Critical Discussion', *Energy Policy*, 58, 1–5.

Beauchamp T. L., Childress J. F. (2009) *Principles of Biomedical Ethics*. 6th ed. New York, NY and Oxford: Oxford University Press.

Blix H. (1986) 'The Influence of the Accident at Chernobyl', *Lecture Delivered at Round Table No. 7, on 'The Future for Nuclear Power' at the 13th Congress of the World Energy Conference*. Cannes, France: International Atomic Energy Agency, Division of Public Information.

Boutellier C., McCombie C., Mele I. (2006) 'Multinational Repositories: Ethical, Legal and Political/Public Aspects', *International Journal of Nuclear Law*, 1(1), 36–48.

Bunn M., Heinonen O. (2011) 'Preventing the Next Fukushima', *Science*, 333(6049), 1580–1. doi:10.1126/science.1209668.

Bunn M., Holdren J. P., Macfarlane A., Pickett S. E., Suzuki A., Suzuki T., Weeks J. (2001) 'Interim Storage of Spent Nuclear Fuel: A Safe, Flexible, and Cost-Effective Near-Term Approach to Spent Fuel Management', Managing the Atom Project, Harvard University, Cambridge, MA, and Project on Sociotechnics of Nuclear Energy, University of Tokyo.

Chung K. (1990) 'Nuclear Power and Public Acceptance', *IAEA Bulletin*, 32(2), 13–15.

Ciupuliga A. R., Cuppen E. (2013, September) 'The Role of Dialogue in Fostering Acceptance of Transmission Lines: The Case of a France – Spain Interconnection Project', *Energy Policy*, 60, 224–33. doi:10.1016/j.enpol.2013.05.028.

Correljé A., Cuppen E., Dignum M., Pesch U., Taebi B. (2015) 'Responsible Innovation in Energy Projects: Values in the Design of Technologies, Institutions and Stakeholder Interactions', in: *Responsible Innovation*. Vol. II, edited by Van den Hoven J., Koops E. J., Romijn H. A., Swierstra T. E., Oosterlaken I. Heidelberg: Springer.

Cotton M. (2014) *Ethics and Technology Assessment: A Participatory Approach*. Heidelberg: Springer. Available at http://link.springer.com/content/pdf/10.1007/978-3-642-45088-4.pdf.

Covello V. T., Merkhofer M. W. (1993) *Risk Assessment Methods: Approaches for Assessing Health and Environmental Risks*. New York, NY: Plenum Press.

COWAM (2007) *Quality of Decision-Making Processes: Decision-Making Processes in Radioactive Waste Governance – Insights and Recommendations*. *Work Package 3*. Paris: COWAM II. Available at www.cowam.com/IMG/pdf_cowam2_WP3_v2.pdf.

Cowell R., Bristow G., Munday M. (2011) 'Acceptance, Acceptability and Environmental Justice: The Role of Community Benefits in Wind Energy Development', *Journal of Environmental Planning and Management*, 54(4), 539–57.

Crawford J., Watkins J. (2010) 'International Responsibilities', in: *The Philosophy of International Law*, edited by Besson S., Tasioulas J., 283–98. Oxford and New York, NY: Oxford University Press.

Cuppen E., Breukers S., Hisschemöller M., Bergsma E. (2010) 'Q Methodology to Select Participants for a Stakeholder Dialogue on Energy Options From Biomass in the Netherlands', *Ecological Economics*, 69(3), 579–91.

Cuppen E., Brunsting S., Pesch U., Feenstra Y. (2015) 'How Stakeholder Interactions Can Reduce Space for Moral Considerations in Decision Making: A Contested CCS Project in the Netherlands', *Environment and Planning A*, 47(9), 1963–78.

Cuppen, E., Pesch, U., Remmerswaal, S., Taanman, M. (2016) "Normative Diversity, Conflict and Transition: Shale Gas in the Netherlands." *Technological Forecasting and Social Change*, November. https://doi.org/10.1016/j.techfore.2016.11.004.

Daniels N. (1979) 'Wide Reflective Equilibrium and Theory Acceptance in Ethics', *Journal of Philosophy*, 76(5), 256–82.

Daniels N. (ed.) (1996) *Justice and Justification: Reflective Equilibrium in Theory and Practice*. Cambridge: Cambridge University Press.

Daniels N. (2011) 'Reflective Equilibrium', in: *The Stanford Encyclopedia of Philosophy*, edited by Edward N. Zalta. Available at http://plato.stanford.edu/archives/win2013/entries/reflective-equilibrium/.

Dignum M., Correljé A., Cuppen E., Pesch U., Taebi B. (2016) 'Contested Technologies and Design for Values: The Case of Shale Gas', *Science and Engineering Ethics*, 22(4), 1171–91.

Di Ruggero O. (2014) *Anticipating Public Acceptance: The Hydrogen Case*. PhD Thesis, Delft University of Technology.

Doorn N. (2010) 'Applying Rawlsian Approaches to Resolve Ethical Issues: Inventory and Setting of a Research Agenda', *Journal of Business Ethics*, 91(1), 127–43.

Doorn N. (2012) 'Exploring Responsibility Rationales in Research and Development (R&D)', *Science, Technology & Human Values*, 37(3), 180–209.
Doorn N., Hansson S. O. (2011) 'Should Probabilistic Design Replace Safety Factors?', *Philosophy & Technology*, 24(2), 151–68.
Doorn, N., Taebi, B. (2018) "Rawls' Wide Reflective Equilibrium as a Method for Engaged Interdisciplinary Collaboration: Potentials and Limitations for the Context of Technological Risks." *Science, Technology and Human Values*, 43(3): 487–517.
Dryzek J. S., Niemeyer S. (2006) 'Reconciling Pluralism and Consensus as Political Ideals', *American Journal of Political Science*, 50(3), 634–49.
Fiorino D. J. (1990) 'Citizen Participation and Environmental Risk: A Survey of Institutional Mechanisms', *Science, Technology & Human Values*, 15(2), 226–43.
Flynn R., Bellaby P. (eds.) (2007) *Risk and the Public Acceptance of New Technologies*. New York, NY: Palgrave Macmillan.
Grunwald A. (2000) 'Technology Policy Between Long-Term Planning Requirements and Short-Ranged Acceptance Problems. New Challenges for Technology Assessment', in: *Vision Assessment: Shaping Technology in 21st Century Society*, edited by Grin J. J., 99–147. Berlin: Springer.
Habermas J. (1990) *Moral Consciousness and Communicative Action*, translated by Lenhardt C., Nicholsen S. W. Cambridge, MA: MIT Press.
Habermas J. (1995) 'Reconciliation Through the Public Use of Reason: Remarks on John Rawls's Political Liberalism', *The Journal of Philosophy*, 92(3), 109–31. doi:10.2307/2940842.
Habermas J. (1996) *Between Facts and Norms: Contributions to a Discourse Theory of Law and Democracy*, translated by Rehg W. Cambridge, MA: MIT Press.
Hannis M., Rawles K. (2013) 'Compensation or Bribery? Ethical Issues in Relation to Radwaste Host Communities', in: *Social and Ethical Aspects of Radiation Risk Management*, edited by Oughton D., Hansson S. O. Amsterdam: Elsevier.
Hansson S. O. (2003) 'Ethical Criteria of Risk Acceptance', *Erkenntnis*, 59(3), 291–309.
Hansson S. O. (2006) 'Informed Consent Out of Context', *Journal of Business Ethics*, 63(2), 149–54.
Hansson S. O. (2009) 'An Agenda for the Ethics of Risk', in: *The Ethics of Technological Risk*, edited by Asveld L., Roeser S., 11–23. London: Earthscan.
Hillerbrand R., Ghil M. (2008) 'Anthropogenic Climate Change: Scientific Uncertainties and Moral Dilemmas', *Physica D: Nonlinear Phenomena*, 237(14–17), 2132–8.
Himmelberger J. J., Ratick S. J., White A. L. (1991) 'Compensation for Risks: Host Community Benefits in Siting Locally Unwanted Facilities', *Environmental Management*, 15(5), 647–58.
Huijts N. M. A., Molin E. J. E., Steg L. (2012) 'Psychological Factors Influencing Sustainable Energy Technology Acceptance: A Review-Based Comprehensive Framework', *Renewable and Sustainable Energy Reviews*, 16(1), 525–31.
IAEA (1994) *Convention on Nuclear Safety: Final Act. IAEA Document INFCIRC/449/ Add.1*. Vienna: International Atomic Energy Agency. Available at https://www.iaea.org/publications/documents/treaties/convention-nuclear-safety.
IAEA (1995) *The Principles of Radioactive Waste Management*. Radioactive Waste Safety Standards Programme. Vienna: IAEA.
IAEA (2004) *Developing Multinational Radioactive Waste Repositories: Infrastructural Framework and Scenarios of Cooperation*. Vienna: IAEA.
Jasanoff S. (2004) 'Science and Citizenship: A New Synergy', *Science and Public Policy*, 31(2), 90–4.

Kermisch C. (2016) 'Specifying the Concept of Future Generations for Addressing Issues Related to High-Level Radioactive Waste', *Science and Engineering Ethics* 22(6): 1797–1811.

Kermisch, C., Taebi, B. (2017) "Sustainability, Ethics and Nuclear Energy: Escaping the Dichotomy," *Sustainability* 9(3): 446.

Krütli P., Stauffacher M., Pedolin D., Moser C., Scholz R. W. (2012) 'The Process Matters: Fairness in Repository Siting for Nuclear Waste', *Social Justice Research*, 25(1), 79–101.

MacKenzie M. K., O'Doherty K. (2011) 'Deliberating Future Issues: Minipublics and Salmon Genomics', *Journal of Public Deliberation*, 7(1 – Article 5).

McCombie C., Chapman N. (2002) 'Sharing the Waste Burden', *Nuclear Engineering International*, 47(580), 27–30.

Murphy L. (2010) 'International Responsibilities', in: *The Philosophy of International Law*, edited by Besson S., Tasioulas J., 299–315. Oxford and New York, NY: Oxford University Press.

NRC (1975) *Reactor Safety Study: An Assessment of Accident Risks in U.S. Commercial Nuclear Power Plants. WASH-1400-MR; NUREG-75/014-MR.* Washington, DC: Nuclear Regulatory Commission.

NWMO (2005) *Choosing a Way Forward: The Future Management of Canada's Used Nuclear Fuel (Final Study)*. Ottawa (Ontario), Canada: Nuclear Waste Management Organization. Available at www.nwmo.ca/studyreport.

Oosterlaken I. (2015) 'Applying Value Sensitive Design (VSD) to Wind Turbines and Wind Parks: An Exploration', *Science and Engineering Ethics*, 21(2), 359–379.

Paavola J., Adger W. N. (2006) 'Fair Adaptation to Climate Change', *Ecological Economics*, 56(4), 594–609.

Pidgeon N., Parkhill K., Corner A., Vaughan N. (2013, May) 'Deliberating Stratospheric Aerosols for Climate Geoengineering and the SPICE Project', *Nature Climate Change*, 3, 451–7.

Rawls J. (1971) *A Theory of Justice, Revised Edition*. 1999th ed. Cambridge, MA: The Belknap Press of Harvard University Press.

Rawls J. (1993) *Political Liberalism: Expanded Edition*. 2005th ed. New York, NY: Columbia University Press.

Rawls J. (1995) 'Political Liberalism: Reply to Habermas', *The Journal of Philosophy*, 132–80.

Rawls J. (2001) *Justice as Fairness: A Restatement*. Cambridge, MA: Belknap Press.

Rawls J. (2002) *The Law of Peoples*. 4th ed. Cambridge, MA and London: Harvard University Press.

Raz J. (2010) 'Human Rights Without Foundations', in: *The Philosophy of International Law*, edited by Besson S., Tasioulas J., 321–38. Oxford and New York, NY: Oxford University Press.

Renn O., Webler T., Wiedemann P. (eds.) (1995) *Fairness and Competence in Citizen Participation: Evaluating Models for Environmental Discourse*. Vol. 10. Dordrecht: Kluwer Academic Publishers.

Risoluti P., McCombie C., Chapman N., Boutellier C. (2008) 'Legal & Business Options for Developing a Multinational/Regional Repository (Work Package 1)', *SAPIERR II, Strategic Action Plan for Implementation of European Regional Repositories: Stage 2*. Brussels: European Commission Community Research.

Roeser S. (2006) 'The Role of Emotions in Judging the Moral Acceptability of Risks', *Safety Science*, 44(8), 689–700. doi:10.1016/j.ssci.2006.02.001.

Roeser S. (ed.) (2010) *Emotions and Risky Technologies*. Dordrecht: Springer.

Roeser S., Pesch U. (2016) 'An Emotional Deliberation Approach to Risk', *Science, Technology & Human Values*, 41, 274–97.

Salzer P., McCombie C., Chapman C. (2008) 'Responsibilities and Financial Liabilities (Work Package 2)', *SAPIERR II, Strategic Action Plan for Implementation of European Regional Repositories: Stage 2*. Brussels: European Commission Community Research.

Schulte I., Hart D., Van der Vorst R. (2004) 'Issues Affecting the Acceptance of Hydrogen Fuel', *International Journal of Hydrogen Energy*, 29(7), 677–85.

Shrader-Frechette K. (2000) 'Duties to Future Generations, Proxy Consent, Intra- and Intergenerational Equity: The Case of Nuclear Waste', *Risk Analysis*, 20(6), 771–8.

Sjöberg L. (2004) 'Local Acceptance of a High Level Nuclear Waste Repository', *Risk Analysis*, 24(3), 737–49.

Sjöberg L., Drottz-Sjöberg B. M. (2001) 'Fairness, Risk and Risk Tolerance in the Siting of a Nuclear Waste Repository', *Journal of Risk Research*, 4(1), 75–101.

Sovacool B. K., Dworkin M. H. (2014) *Global Energy Justice: Problems, Principles, and Practices*. Cambridge: Cambridge University Press.

Taebi B. (2011) 'The Morally Desirable Option for Nuclear Power Production', *Philosophy & Technology*, 24(2), 169–92.

Taebi B. (2012) 'Multinational Nuclear Waste Repositories and Their Complex Issues of Justice', *Ethics, Policy & Environment*, 15(1), 57–62.

Taebi B. (2017) 'Bridging the Gap Between Social Acceptance and Ethical Acceptability', *Risk Analysis*, 37(10), 1817–27.

Taebi B., Mayer M. (2017) 'By Accident or by Design? Pushing Global Governance of Nuclear Safety', *Progress in Nuclear Energy*, 99, 19–25.

Taebi B., Roeser S., Van de Poel I. (2012) 'The Ethics of Nuclear Power: Social Experiments, Intergenerational Justice, and Emotions', *Energy Policy*, 51, 202–6.

Ter Mors E., Terwel B. W., Daamen D. D. L. (2012) 'The Potential of Host Community Compensation in Facility Siting', *International Journal of Greenhouse Gas Control*, 11(Suppl), S130–S138.

Van Delden J. M., Van Thiel G. J. M. W. (1998) 'Reflective Equilibrium as a Normative-Empirical Model in Bioethics', in: *Reflective Equilibrium*, edited by van der Burg W., van Willigenburg T., 251–9. Dordrecht: Kluwer Academic Publishers.

Van de Poel I. R. (2016) 'A Coherentist View on the Relation Between Social Acceptance and Moral Acceptability of Technology', in: *Philosophy of Technology After the Empirical Turn*, edited by Franssen M., Vermaas P. E., Kroes P., Meijers A. W. M., 177–93. Philosophy of Engineering and Technology 23. Switzerland: Springer. doi:10.1007/978-3-319-33717-3_11.

Van de Poel I. R., Zwart S. D. (2010) 'Reflective Equilibrium in R & D Networks', *Science, Technology & Human Values*, 35(2), 174–99.

Van Thiel G. J. M. W., Van Delden J. (2010) 'Reflective Equilibrium as a Normative Empirical Model', *Ethical Perspectives*, 17(2), 183–202.

Vermunt R., Törnblom K. Y. (1996) 'Introduction: Distributive and Procedural Justice', *Social Justice Research*, 9(4), 305–10.

Vorstenbosch J. (1998) 'Reflective Equilibrium and Public Debate: How to Cast the Public's Web of Beliefs Broadly Enough', in: *Reflective Equilibrium: Essays in Honour of Robert Heeger*, edited by Van der Burg W., van Willigenburg T., 177–90. Dordrecht: Kluwer Academic Publishers.

Walker G. (1995) 'Renewable Energy and the Public', *Land Use Policy*, 12(1), 49–59.

Walker G. (2010) 'Environmental Justice, Impact Assessment and the Politics of Knowledge: The Implications of Assessing the Social Distribution of Environmental Outcomes', *Environmental Impact Assessment Review*, 30(5), 312–18.
Watson M., Bulkeley H. (2005) 'Just Waste? Municipal Waste Management and the Politics of Environmental Justice', *Local Environment*, 10(4), 411–26.
Wigley D. C., Shrader-Frechette K. (1996) 'Environmental Justice: A Louisiana Case Study', *Journal of Agricultural and Environmental Ethics*, 9(1), 61–82.
Wüstenhagen R., Wolsink M., Bürer M. J. (2007) 'Social Acceptance of Renewable Energy Innovation: An Introduction to the Concept', *Energy Policy*, 35(5), 2683–91.
Wynne B. (1992a) 'Misunderstood Misunderstanding: Social Identities and Public Uptake of Science', *Public Understanding of Science*, 1(3), 281–304.
Wynne B. (1992b) 'Risk and Social Learning: Reification to Engagement', in: *Social Theories of Risk*, edited by Krimsky S., Golding D., 275–97. Westport, CT: Praeger.
Young H. P. (1994) *Equity: In Theory and Practice*. Princeton, NJ: Princeton University Press. Available at https://books.google.nl/books?hl=nl&lr=&id=H0IQ0PKZ4WYC&oi=fnd&pg=PR11&dq=peyton+young+&ots=CFHeQBTgwi&sig=musCPy2MAYuDKh7FwCG_cGUJ6iI.

5 The right to enjoy the benefits of scientific progress for small farmers facing pesticides hazards

Leslie London

1 Introduction

The use of pesticides continues to pose significant health and environmental hazards, despite scientific and technological advances in agricultural and industrial processes. These risks are borne disproportionately by resource-poor countries, communities and individuals across the world. Whereas less than 25% of global pesticide use occurs in developing countries, over 90% of pesticide poisonings and 99% of fatalities continue to occur in Low and Middle-Income Countries (LMICs) (Lekei, Ngowi, and London 2016; United Nations General Assembly 2017a). This disparity arises precisely because these countries lack the institutional capacity to control pesticide hazards as a result of weak regulatory systems, porous borders permitting the import of highly hazardous pesticides, inadequate or absent inspection capacity, lack of skilled human resources, weak or absent surveillance systems, extension services preoccupied with boosting production rather than reducing human and environmental risks, lack of farmer support and training, and the powerful influence exercised by the pesticide industry over LMIC governments and their agricultural officials (London and Rother 2000; Kishi and Ladou 2001; Murray et al. 2002; Rosenthal 2003; Konradsen 2007; Rother, Ngowi, and London 2009; London 2011; Lekei, Ngowi, and London 2014a; Lekei, Ngowi, and London 2016).

The reasons for the ongoing use of potentially hazardous pesticides in countries with the least capacity to manage such pesticide use safely or to prevent poisoning, both acute and chronic, relate to pressures on farmers to increase food productivity, and on governments to put agricultural production ahead of considerations of human health and environmental protection. This situation pertains, notwithstanding many states committing to a range of international and regional declarations and conventions designed to prevent (or at least ameliorate) the worst consequence of uncontrolled and unsafe pesticide use in poor countries. For example, of the 161 countries having ratified the Rotterdam Convention on Prior Informed Consent,[1] 111 (69%) are LMICs (Table 5.1). In fact, the density of ratifications amongst LMICs for the four pesticide-linked conventions is about 20% higher for LMICs than for HICs (89% versus 69% respectively), confirming that there is no shortage of international legal benchmarks for some key aspects of pesticide management in most developing countries.

Table 5.1 Country ratifications of conventions applicable to pesticides

Convention	*Year adopted*	*Main aim*	*Number of ratifications (%)*	
			*HIC*s (n=78)*	*LMIC*s (n=140)*
Stockholm Convention on Persistent Organic Pollutants	2001	Mindful of the precautionary approach, to protect human health and the environment from persistent organic pollutants (POPs)	55 (71%)	125 (89%)
Rotterdam Convention on Prior Informed Consent	1998	To promote shared responsibility and cooperative efforts in the international trade of certain hazardous chemicals so as to protect human health and the environment from potential harm and to contribute to their environmentally sound use	51 (65%)	111 (79%)
The Basel Convention on the Control of Trans-boundary Movements of Hazardous Wastes and Their Disposal	1989	To reduce transboundary movements of wastes to a minimum consistent with the environmentally sound and efficient management; to minimise amount and toxicity of hazardous wastes generated; ensure their environmentally sound management; assist developing countries	54 (69%)	128 (91%)
Montreal Protocol on Substances that Deplete the Ozone Layer under the Convention	1989	To reduce the production and consumption of ozone depleting substances in order to reduce their abundance in the atmosphere, and thereby protect the earth's fragile ozone layer.	56 (72%)	132 (94%)

Source for Ratifications: https://treaties.un.org/;

*Country classifications derived from World Bank list of economies on the World Databank (databank.worldbank.org/data/download/site-content/CLASS.xls)

Unsurprisingly, it has been argued that the ongoing burden of pesticide-related morbidity and mortality is a human rights concern (Dinham and Malik 2003; Rosenthal 2003; London 2003, 2009, 2011) which reflects global inequalities in power, resources and capacity. Far from securing food security, the way in which pesticide use is manifest globally and the dependence on hazardous chemicals for food production is said to undermine the right to food and health for present and future generations (United Nations General Assembly 2017a).

The human rights framework for health in relation to pesticides

Adopting a rights-based approach to environmental toxicants has led the UN to establish a Special Rapporteur on Toxic Wastes,[2] whose mandate is to prevent the dumping of hazardous substances and waste, address the whole life-cycle of hazardous products (cradle-to-grave approach) through monitoring and information dissemination, promote best practices in the management of hazardous chemicals and protect environmental human rights defenders from victimisation (United Nations General Assembly 2017b). Similarly, the mandate of the UN Special Rapporteur on the Right to Food includes the right of people to food of adequate quality (United Nations General Assembly 2017a) which has been interpreted as implying food that is free of hazardous contaminants such as pesticides (CESCR 1999).

Furthermore, the Right to Health contained in paragraph 12 of the International Covenant on Economic, Cultural and Social Rights (ICECSR), a covenant ratified by 164 countries across the globe, recognises the "right of everyone to the enjoyment of the highest attainable standard of physical and mental health" as including "improvement of all aspects of environmental and industrial hygiene" and the "prevention, treatment and control of epidemic, endemic, occupational and other diseases" (UN General Assembly 1966). This has been reinforced in the UN Expert Committee interpretation of the Right to Health in General Comment 14, which describes the right to health as "not only . . . timely and appropriate health care but also . . . the underlying determinants of health" which include "healthy occupational and environmental conditions" and "improvement of all aspects of environmental and industrial hygiene" (ICECSR Article 12.2 (b)) as well as measures to prevent occupational accidents and diseases, to reduce or prevent population exposure to harmful chemicals and minimise, to the extent reasonably practicable, health hazards in the working environment (CESCR 2000). Coupled with Article 7 of the ICESCR, which recognises "the right of everyone to the enjoyment of just and favourable conditions of work which ensure . . . safe and healthy working conditions," global human rights standards reflect a high level of attention to ensuring safety in relation to pesticides, both for working populations and for populations exposed through other environmental pathways, particularly food consumption. Additionally, the Strategic Approach to International Chemicals Management (SAICM), adopted by the International Conference on Chemicals Management in 2006, includes a founding declaration that explicitly commits to respect human rights under the framework, and a later resolution in 2015 which encourages, on a non-binding basis, the use of alternatives to highly hazardous pesticides (United Nations Environment Programme, undated).

However, framing a protection as a human right does not, of itself, mean that people will benefit. For a rights-holder to be able to claim an entitlement, there must be a duty-bearer, and under international human rights law, the state is usually that duty-bearer. The enjoyment of any human right therefore creates state obligations to respect, protect and fulfil rights through domestication of those international agreements which the state has ratified.

The obligation to respect imposes on states a negative duty to desist from passing laws that conflict with treaty provisions and/or which violate people's rights. Thus, for example, a state which mandates the use of hazardous pesticides as a condition for the receipt of agricultural outreach services, or as part of land restitution, would be breaching its obligation to respect people's human rights. The obligation to protect requires states to take action to protect people from violations perpetrated by third parties. A functioning registration system for pesticide that prevents companies from registering highly hazardous chemicals which expose populations to toxic pesticide hazards is an example of a state meeting its obligation to protect from a third party – the company manufacturing and/or distributing the chemical. Lastly, state obligations to fulfil rights implies active and positive steps by the state – such as budgeting, providing services and building infrastructure – to enable the substantive elements of that right to be met. In relation to ensuring safety and health related to pesticides, state fulfilment of human rights would, for example, imply state provision of extension services geared to reducing pesticide exposure (through, for example, the promotion of Integrated Pest Management or of organic production) and support for small farmers accessing markets for their products produced through safer production systems.

While the international human rights framework provides an extensive institutional system for protection of the most vulnerable, there are some caveats to be noted (London 2008). Firstly, while state obligations are key to realising rights, it is also increasingly being recognised that the agency of people affected by rights violations, particularly vulnerable and marginal groups, is key to ensuring state accountability in meeting rights obligations. By strengthening their agency, human rights systems enable those affected to change the conditions which render them vulnerable to human rights violations (London 2007). Social movements of rural agricultural populations are thus key to protecting rural populations, including farm workers, violations of their rights regarding toxic pesticide exposure (Barraza et al. 2013; Sineiro and Berger 2012). Secondly, rights are sometimes reduced to individual claims for particular resources or freedoms. This is an excessively narrow view that preferences civil and political rights over socio-economic rights, which are typically realisable only in a collective context – usually for populations or a community rather than for individuals. Lastly, while the state is considered the primary duty-bearer under human rights systems, there is increasing attention to the questions of non-state actors, particularly transnational corporations, having human rights responsibilities (Weissbrodt and Kruger 2003; Arnold 2010). These responsibilities, though of a lesser order than state obligations, provide an important vehicle to avoid violations of rights of the most vulnerable populations across the globe by private corporations, many of whom are larger economic entities that are some of the poorest nation states in the developing world.

2 The right to enjoy the benefits of scientific progress

One of the rights contained in the ICESCR that has received relatively little attention to date is the right to enjoy the benefits of scientific progress (REBSP). Article 15 directs states to "recognize the right of everyone to enjoy the benefits of scientific progress and its applications," and links this right to a set of mandates on states to respect the autonomy of scientific research, take steps to ensure the development and diffusion of science, and to encourage the development of international contacts and cooperation in science (Chapman 2009). Two elements of this right should be evident.

Firstly, the idea of "progress" implies a recognition that scientific advances are made over time, even if this progress does not follow in a linear fashion. For science to progress, it has to build on preceding knowledge and generate new understandings and applications.

Secondly, the right makes the entitlement to "benefit" a right enjoyed by everyone. This, in turn, implies that the mere progress in scientific knowledge in itself is insufficient for meeting the intention of the right, which is to ensure humans benefit from science, but must be accompanied by a process whereby people are able to benefit in an equitable way. Importantly, while the ICESCR also recognises the intellectual property of the inventors and creators of scientific knowledge who themselves enjoy the right "to benefit from the protection of the moral and material interests resulting from any scientific . . . production of which he [sic] is the author," the covenant is also clear in placing public benefits at the forefront of this right. This means that, if science is to benefit people, the state is obliged to ensure two conditions.

Firstly, where science has generated new knowledge with applications, states must ensure that such knowledge and its applications are distributed and made available to everyone because there is a universal right to share in the benefits of scientific advancement. Moreover, because of the imperative of human rights to preference the most vulnerable and marginalised, the state's obligation extends to ensuring that such knowledge and its applications is made available particularly to those most in need (Chapman 2009) – whether through active dissemination by the state or through science systems that receive state support to disseminate scientific outcomes.

Secondly, basic scientific research is directed toward the generation of new knowledge and not specifically to advance human betterment. Moreover, changes in the scientific landscape over the past five decades have seen the privatisation of scientific research on a huge scale such that much research is profit-driven with private interests driving the choice of research (Greenberg 2007; Chapman 2009; Donders 2011). Sharing the concrete benefits of such research targeting lucrative applications will be unlikely to benefit everyone and particularly unlikely to benefit poor and marginalised populations. Indeed, the great neglect of the REBSP over many years, with the resultant denial of access to the benefits of scientific advancement for the poor and marginalised, has been attributed to poor state policy, government inaction, lack of private sector accountability, poverty and poor education (UNGA 2014). This implies that if states are to ensure benefits from science accrue to everyone (rather than those who can pay), states are obliged to intervene to support the development of a science system in which research is able to generate outcomes that serve public benefit (Chapman 2009). Moreover, consistent with the specific legal regime of the ICESCR, the REBSP would be subject to the concept of progressive realisation, in that states must take both immediate steps and, over time, progressively expand their legislative, administrative, financial, educational, social and other measures (including judicial remedies) to achieve the full realisation of the right (Donders 2011).

Thus, the REBSP presents two key levers to benefit marginal populations such as small farmers facing pesticide hazards. Firstly, it places an onus on states to create an infrastructure for science that is not captured for private benefit (Resnick 2007), but that is able to create public benefits, for example, by investing in research to support farming systems that reduce reliance on and exposure to hazardous pesticides. Secondly, the state is then obliged, whether through non-state intermediaries such as universities, non-profits or private sector entities, to ensure the dissemination of such benefits to those who need its applications.

In taking this agenda forward, it could be argued that states should therefore (i) develop an intellectual property system that enables the REBSP and balances IP rights with public benefit); (ii) adopt an overarching science policy reflecting the REBSP; (iii) mobilize state funding for research in neglected areas and incentives for private sector funding of such areas; (iv) adhere to stated commitment to funding R&D; (v) support human resource capacity development – both to do the research and to support implementation of its applications; (vi) implement regulatory systems that encourage innovation for public benefit (e.g. expedited registration for products meeting certain criteria); (vii) invest in operational research to test implementation; (viii) negotiate costs for new safer and effective technology using state tenders; (ix) undertake public education; (x) implement appropriate regulatory action to ringfence public sources (such as tax); and (xi) design appropriate public private partnerships (London, Cox, and Coomans 2016).

3 Applying the REBSP to small farmers facing pesticide exposures

In South Africa, post-apartheid land restitution policies have sought to return black farmers evicted under apartheid to ancestral lands and to support their development as profitable farmers. This category of farmer, called "emergent farmer" in policy language, includes a range of rural residents with varying degrees of experience and expertise in farming who enter or re-enter agricultural production with variable levels of capital investment (Hart 2007). State policy links redress and equity to the prospect of helping such farmers on the trajectory to becoming commercially competitive with existing large-scale agriculture. However, research has shown that the laudable policy intent has not been realised in practice: emergent farmers often have little extension support, poor access to markets and lack the capital to transition to commercial farming. It is unclear what they are emerging from, nor what the final endpoint is of their trajectory. However, one aspect is clear in the lives of most emergent farmers – the pressures on emergent farmers to boost production in order to meet policy objectives and thereby access further state support are substantial (Xaba 2015), and that drives a turn toward the use of chemicals for pest control (Rother, Hall, and London 2008). For that reason, emergent farmers may be particularly vulnerable to the adverse impacts of pesticides.

The chapter now outlines a case study of a farmer in northern KwaZulu-Natal to illustrate the challenges posed to human health and the environment, and what a programme to realise the Right to Enjoy the Benefits of Scientific Progress might mean for reducing farmer vulnerability.

The setting of the Makhatini Flats is an agriculturally intense area of the northern KwaZulu-Natal province of South Africa, consisting of approximately 1500 small-scale farms of which about 20% are part of a state irrigation scheme with the balance in a "dry-land" area reliant on rain for water for their crops. As would be expected, farms in the irrigation area tend to be larger. Because of the temperate climate, mixed cropping is practised throughout the year (Naidoo et al. 2010). It is one of the major areas for emergent farmers and has seen a sizeable investment by the South African National Department of Agriculture in infrastructure, principally because of an explosive growth in GM crop trials and GM cotton cultivation in the area (Thirtle et al. 2003; Gouse et al. 2005). The area is also close to the Mozambique and Swaziland borders and is subject to a vector control programme for malaria which involved household residual spraying to interrupt mosquito-borne transmission. The pesticides used in the programme have switched between DDT and pyrethroids to cope with insect resistance over many years.

Although agricultural outreach services are provided in the area, the reach of technical support to small farmers is limited in South Africa in general (Stull, Bell, and Ncwadi 2016; Okunlola et al. 2016) and in the Makhatini area in particular (Fok 2003; Pringle et al. 2010). In fact, small farmers are most likely to get advice on pest control methods from their fellow farmers, representatives of pesticide companies operating in the area, small vendors retailing pesticides, or from trainings organised by the pesticide industry (Rother, Hall, and London 2008), a situation not dissimilar to other developing countries, such as Tanzania (Lekei, Ngowi, and London 2014a) where pesticide retailers dominate the information sources for small farmers, but are themselves poorly informed about health and safety related to pesticides (Lekei, Ngowi, and London 2014b).

4 A case study

Mrs Mkhize (pseudonym used) is an emergent farmer and a grandmother of four who farms in the dry-land area. She grows maize, vegetables and a limited amount of sorghum. Her plot is located about 4 km from her homestead so in peak season, she sleeps overnight in a lean-to structure on her fields so that she can start working early (before it gets too hot to work in the fields). She is dependent on farming to support her family of 12 persons given high rural unemployment and the fact that her two daughters, living in the city, have sent their youngest children to Mrs Mkhize to look after. She received a start-up farming pack from an extension officer three years ago, but gets little information or visits from any government officials.

Confronted with evidence of a pest infiltration of her crop, she consults with a fellow farmer who advises her to purchase a particular pesticide he had used with good effect for a similar problem. Mrs Mkhize undertakes the arduous trip to the nearest town more than 150 km away to find an agricultural coop able to sell her the pesticide, which turns out to be metasystox, a class I organophosphate insecticide – according to the WHO classification, a highly hazardous pesticide. She returns from the town with a large container (5 litres) of the concentrate and verbal instructions from the co-op assistant in how to apply it since the pesticide insert is not in a language she understands, nor is she sufficiently literate to be able to read and understand small print technical information contained on a pesticide insert. She is also not aware of the significance of the red band on the label which indicates the pesticide is highly hazardous in terms of WHO criteria.

Mrs Mkhize borrows a backpack from a fellow farmer to apply the pesticide as she lacks the capital to purchase her own. The backpack is old and leaks as a result of years of overuse. Mrs Mkhize has no respirator, gloves or overall to wear whilst applying the pesticide for protection. Even if she could afford protective clothing, it is too hot to wear gloves and a mask whilst working in the fields. State agricultural extension officers are not able to advise her on its use since they are themselves uninformed and, in any event, do not visit Mrs Mkhize's farm more than twice or thrice a year so she hardly sees them.

The pesticide is evidently effective in controlling the pests, and within two weeks, the infestation appears to have been cleared. Mrs Mkhize still has about 4 litres of the concentrate left, since the 5-litre container of metasystox was all they had in stock at the time of purchase.

During the period of application, Mrs Mkhize sleeps in her lean-to. At night, when she goes to sleep, the pesticide container is stored in the same room where she sleeps. Mrs Mkhize uses the container, still full of its content, as a stand in her room for her candle before she goes to sleep. As a result, melted candle wax adorns the container lid (Figure 5.1). When asked about the pesticide, Mrs Mkhize has no knowledge of its toxicity or why it has a label marked in red.

Mrs Mkhize is therefore exposed to a highly toxic pesticide that has been phased out in most northern countries for health and environmental reasons (United Nations 2009). Because of her working conditions (including lack of protective clothing, damaged backpack sprayer and hazardous hygiene practices such as mounting a candle on the lid) and lack of awareness, she is at risk for high exposure. Farmers facing the same challenges as Mrs Mkhize are not uncommon in South Africa, nor indeed, in other parts of the developing world. There are multiple violations of Mrs Mkhize's human rights and probably of the human rights of family members and other rural residents living nearby who may be put at risk by the unsafe use of a hazardous pesticide. Her right to a safe environment

Figure 5.1 Small farmer and her pesticide container, Northern Kwazulu Natal, South Africa

and her right to health are both compromised by the circumstances under which she is forced to secure her livelihood, and might be affecting the health of others in her family and living nearby.

The case illustrates how human rights are indivisible and often one right may be instrumental for the realisation of another right. Thus, for example, Mrs Mkhize's right to a safe environment, to health, to safe working conditions and to dignity are all compromised by the circumstances under which she procures and uses the metasystox. Importantly, her inability to access information in a meaningful way so as to make decisions to protect her health and that of people around her means that she is not empowered to exercise agency in defending her rights. This reflects a failure of the state to ensure her right to education as well as access to information. At multiple levels, the system has let her down. By creating a system of land redress linked to cultivating a class of emergent farmers, the state has violated her rights by setting her onto the pesticide treadmill (Nicholls et al. 1997) which she needs in order to keep state support. By failing to control the availability of class I pesticides unsuited for emergent farmers, the state has failed to protect her; and by failing to provide adequately resourced and trained extension officers able to link her produce to markets to encourage safer methods of pest control, the state has failed to fulfil its rights obligations.

However, it is also the case that the lack of research and development into solutions for small farmers is an underlying reason as to why Mrs Mkhize needs to secure a highly toxic method for pest control. For small farmers facing persistent pest problems, scientific solutions more suited to small farmers' needs might focus on novel non-toxic methods of pest control that do not rely on toxic chemicals. For example, Integrated Pest Management is an approach which emphasises a comprehensive toolkit of pest control methods, including scouting, mechanical barriers, and the use of less toxic agents. If state agencies charged with a research mandate, such as South Africa's Agricultural Research Council, were to invest greater resources into researching safer and less hazardous methods of pest control that are suited to small farmers, it would be farmers like Mrs Mkhize who benefit, rather than the large commercial farmers who already run well-resourced operations, who benefit from state-supported trials of GM crops, for example. Similarly, shaping research calls emanating from state funders could be used to encourage universities to pursue research into methods suited for pest control amongst small farmers – both to promote less use of toxic chemicals (reliant on the hierarchy of controls to avoid, substitute or achieve safer design) and, where there are no feasible alternative methods, to develop newer and less toxic agents to control pests. For example, a recent trial of safe storage of pesticides amongst rural Sri Lankan farmers tested a novel semi-buried barrel as a low-cost method for preventing suicide with pesticides in a country known for use of pesticides as an agent for suicide (Pearson et al. 2011). Mrs Mkhize's problem might have been eminently preventable using different agronomic approaches and/or non-chemical methods.

Labelling has long been recognised as a key requirement for preventing poisoning. However, poor comprehensibility of labelling by low education populations is a common and long-known problem (Rother 2008). Scientific research into hazard communication with low education populations has generated novel and tested methods more suitable for communicating risk than detailed paper inserts filled with scientific jargon that is unintelligible to most individuals, let alone rural farmers (Dalvie, Rother, and London 2014; Rother 2005; Rother 2014). If Mrs Mkhize was able to access information in a language she understood and that was presented in a simple, jargon-free manner, or if the visual communication tools were explicit in conveying risk messages, she might have realised how dangerous the metasystox was, and have been able to exercise choice of an alternative and safer method of pest control, at a reasonable cost she could afford.

Yet, the state continues to use an outdated regulatory system that relies on the label and package insert as the only statutory measure to communicate hazards to end-users of pesticides. In fact, it has been argued that such measures serve only to protect the pesticide company from possible litigation arising from a poisoning, rather than providing any meaningful preventive information usable to at-risk populations (London and Rother 2000; Dalvie, Rother, and London 2014). This is a system that is failing small farmers because registration takes no account of the use circumstances under which a chemical submitted for registration or re-registration occurs. Under South Africa's regulatory system, it would be Mrs Mkhize who was at fault for purchasing and using a pesticide in a way that was inconsistent with the label – a label she could not read – when the state has not addressed the multiple obstacles facing Mrs Mkhize if she were to try pest control methods that were less toxic.

At the very least, mandating training as a condition for the purchase and use of pesticides should be the norm, as should be registration of staff who sell pesticides so that some quality could be established in the information provided to end-users. Training of extension staff should provide sound, science-based advice aimed at reducing pesticide hazard rather than replicating the current status quo dominated by pesticide use – which is highly influenced by the pesticide industry (Rother, Hall, and London 2008). The REBSP would extend not only to ensuring the extension staff are properly trained so as to disseminate scientific advances appropriately, but also to develop the capacity of researchers to pursue methods more suited to answer the research questions relevant to small farmers. As Hart (2007) points out, social sciences have much to offer in better understanding how to advance the well-being of small farmers like Mrs Mkhize.

The REBSP would also demand that states implement regulatory systems that encourage innovation for public benefit. Thus, for example, an application for a new product suited to small farmers like Mrs Mkhize that reduces risk to humans and the environment should enjoy expedited registration. Where basic scientific research identifies an opportunity to reduce risk in managing pesticide, state obligations would expect the state to invest in operational research to test implementation so that Mrs Mkhize might reap the practical benefit of the new findings. Moreover, if the new technology to benefit Mrs Mkhize was to be patented by the inventor, the state should ensure a system that does not allow intellectual property (IP) to become a barrier to public dissemination of science to those who need it most. While the REBSP recognises that inventors need to enjoy fair reward for their role in creating intellectual property, a new pest control method with lower risk could be made available to Mrs Mkhize through utilisation of any the TRIPS flexibilities that apply to public health, thereby balancing IP protection with ensuring public benefit from science (Donders 2011; UNGA 2014).

There is also an important gender dimension to be considered; in that women are particularly vulnerable, and Mrs Mkhize's status as a poor black rural farmer brings in multiple axes of vulnerability. The REBSP is particularly important for redressing discrimination and ensuring that the most vulnerable members of society are able to benefit from scientific findings (UNGA 2014). Ensuring non-discrimination in access to the REBSP would be an immediate obligation on the state (Donders 2011).

Lastly, Mrs Mkhize bought a pesticide manufactured by a company with its headquarters in a developed country. Many of these companies are large multinationals that claim to have stellar corporate social responsibility records. However, as argued by the UN Special Rapporteur on Toxics, "The issues presented by hazardous substances are far too international – involving global supply chains, transnational corporations, foreign investment and transboundary movement of pollution and waste – to be effectively addressed through a nationalistic approach" (UN General Assembly 2017c: 11–12). Practising cradle to grave product stewardship would mean that the company manufacturing metasystox has responsibilities to ensure as far as possible that its product does not end up as a candle holder in a rural farm shelter in South Africa. Developed country governments have obligations outside their territories to ensure their country's corporations do not disseminate products in ways that violate the rights of vulnerable populations in poor countries (ETO 2013; UN General Assembly 2017c).

5 Conclusion

The state needs to locate pesticide safety within an overarching science policy reflecting the REBSP, rather than leaving pesticide safety to market forces. Framing scientific research within a human rights paradigm consistent with the REBSP generates an obligation on governments and responsibilities on private sector stakeholders, to create an enabling environment for scientific research that both generates new knowledge for the benefit of the most vulnerable and mandates the diffusion of that knowledge to those who might benefit. For small farmers like Mrs Mkhize, there is no entitlement to claim a newer and safer pesticide or application system; rather she can expect that the states ensures there is a scientific research system that tries to address the main problems she faces, and disseminates that knowledge to her and other small famers, making sure she can access its benefits as a member of a highly vulnerable group. The REBSP offers researchers, activists, policy-makers and civil society, novel opportunities to protect the health of small farmers exposed to pesticides in developing countries.

Acknowledgements

The author wishes to thank his colleague, Fons Coomans, coordinator of the Maastricht Centre for Human Rights, for inspiring him to think about exploring these rights issues in relation to environmental justice and pesticide safety for small farmers and Tshepo Phakisi for assistance with the literature review for this chapter.

Notes

1 The Rotterdam Convention is aimed at addressing the uncontrolled export of highly hazardous chemicals to developing countries unable to manage such chemicals safely. The Convention provides for the formal dissemination of information, particularly whether the chemical is banned or restricted in the exporting country, so that receiving countries can decide if they wish to import the chemical. The Convention is thus intended to promote a shared responsibility between exporting and importing countries in protecting human health and the environment from the harmful effects of such chemicals, and it relies on the exchange of information about potentially hazardous chemicals that may be exported and imported. See www.pic.int.

2 The full title of the post is: Special rapporteur on the implications for human rights of the environmentally sound management and disposal of hazardous substances and wastes; abbreviated to: Special rapporteur on toxic wastes – see www.ohchr.org/EN/Issues/Environment/ToxicWastes/Pages/SRToxicWastesIndex.aspx.

References

Arnold D. G. (2010) 'Transnational Corporations and the Duty to Respect Basic Human Rights', *Business Ethics Quarterly*, 20(3), 371–99.

Barraza D., Jansen K., van Wendel de Joode B., Wesseling C. (2013, January–March) 'Social Movements and Risk Perception: Unions, Churches, Pesticides and Bananas in Costa Rica', *International Journal of Occupational and Environmental Health*, 19(1), 11–21.

Chapman A. (2009) 'Towards an Understanding of the Right to Enjoy the Benefits of Scientific Progress and Its Applications', *Journal of Human Rights*, 8, 1–36.

Dalvie M. A., Rother H. A., London L. (2014) 'Chemical Hazard Communication Comprehensibility in South Africa: Safety Implications for the Adoption of the Globally Harmonized System of Classification and Labeling of Chemicals', *Safety Science*, 61, 51–8.

Dinham B., Malik S. (2003, January–March) 'Pesticides and Human Rights', *International Journal of Occupational and Environmental Health*, 9(1), 40–52.

Donders Y. (2011) 'The Right to Enjoy the Benefits of Scientific Progress: In Search of State Obligations in Relation to Health', *Med Health Care and Philos*, 14, 371–81.

ETO (2013) *Maastricht Principles on Extraterritorial Obligations of States in the Area of Economic, Social and Cultural Rights*. Heidelberg: FIAN International. Available at www.etoconsortium.org/nc/en/main-navigation/library/maastricht-principles/?tx_drblob_pi1%5BdownloadUid%5D=23. Date Accessed: 13 January 2017.

Fok M. (2003) *Report of a Mission in South Africa. Technical Assistance to the Implementation of a Socio-Economic Survey in the Makhatini Flats, March 14–25, 2003*. Montpellier: CIRAD. Available at https://agritrop.cirad.fr/513795/1/ID513795.pdf. Date Accessed: 13 January 2018.

Gouse M., Kirsten J., Shankar B., Thirtle C. (2005) 'Bt Cotton in KwaZulu-Natal: Technological Triumph But Institutional Failure', *AgBiotechNet*, 7(134), 1–7.

Greenberg D. S. (2007) *Science for Sale: The Perils, Rewards, and Delusions of Campus Capitalism*. Chicago, IL and London: University of Chicago Press.

Hart T. (2007) 'The Socioeconomics of Subsistence Farmers and the Contribution of the Social Sciences to Agricultural Development', in: *Science-Based Improvements of Rural/Subsistence Agriculture: Forum Proceedings*, edited by Ntutela S., Gevers W., Ramaite R., 69–82. Pretoria: The Academy of Science of South Africa.

Kishi M., Ladou J. (2001) 'International Pesticide Use', *International Journal of Occupational and Environmental Health*, 7, 259–65.

Konradsen F. (2007) 'Acute Pesticide Poisoning – A Global Public Health Problem', *Danish Medical Bulletin*, 54(1), 58–9.

Lekei E. E., Ngowi A. V., London L. (2014a) 'Farmers' Knowledge, Practices and Injuries Associated With Pesticide Exposure in Rural Farming Villages in Tanzania', *BMC Public Health*, 14, 389. Available at https://bmcpublichealth.biomedcentral.com/articles/10.1186/1471-2458-14-389.

Lekei E. E., Ngowi A. V., London L. (2014b) 'Pesticide Retailers' Knowledge and Handling Practices in Selected Towns of Tanzania', *Environ Health*, 13, 79. doi:10.1186/1476-069X-13-79.

Lekei E. E., Ngowi A. V., London L. (2016) 'Under-reporting of acute pesticide poisoning in Tanzania: Modelling results from two cross-sectional studies', *Environ Health*, 15(1), 118.

London L. (2003) 'Human Rights, Environmental Justice, and the Health of Farm Workers in South Africa', *International Journal of Occupational and Environmental Health*, 9, 59–68.

London L. (2007) '"Issues of Equity Are Also Issues of Rights": Lessons From Experiences in Southern Africa', *BMC Public Health*, 7, 14. Available at www.biomedcentral.com/content/pdf/1471-2458-7-14.pdf.

London L. (2008) 'What Is a Human-rights Based Approach to Health and Does It Matter?', *Health and Human Rights*, 10(1), 65–80. Available at www.hhrjournal.org/2013/09/13/what-is-a-human-rights-based-approach-to-health-and-does-it-matter/.

London L. (2009) 'Neurobehavioural Methods, Effects and Prevention: Workers Human Rights Are Why the Field Matters for Developing Countries', *Neurotoxicology*, 30, 1135–43.

London L. (2011) 'Human Rights and Health: Opportunities to Advance Rural Occupational Health', *International Journal of Occupational and Environmental Health*, 17, 80–92.

London L., Cox H., Coomans F. (2016) 'Drug-Resistant TB: Implementing the Right to Health Through the Right to Enjoy the Benefits of Scientific Progress', *Health and Human Rights*, 18(1), 25–41. Available at https://cdn2.sph.harvard.edu/wp-content/uploads/sites/13/2016/06/London1.pdf.

London L., Rother H. A. (2000) 'People, Pesticides and the Environment: Who Bears the Brunt of Backward Policy in South Africa?', *New Solutions*, 10(4), 339–50.

Murray D., Wesseling C., Keifer M., Corriols M., Henao S. (2002) 'Surveillance of Pesticide Related Illness in the Developing World', *International Journal of Occupational and Environmental Health*, 8, 243–8.

Naidoo S., London L., Rother H.-A., Burdorf A., Naidoo R. N., Kromhout H. (2010) 'Pesticide Safety Training and Practices in Women Working in Small-scale Agriculture in South Africa', *Occupational and Environmental Medicine*, 67, 823–8.

Nicholls C. I., Altieri M. A. (1997) 'Conventional Agricultural Development Models and the Persistence of the Pesticide Treadmill in Latin America', *International Journal of Sustainable Development & World Ecology*, 4(2), 93–111.

Okunlola A., Ngubane M., Cousins B., du Toit A. (2016) *Challenging the Stereotypes: Small-Scale Black Farmers and Private Sector Support Programmes in South Africa. A National Scan Research Report*. Bellville: PLAAS: Institute for Poverty, Land and Agrarian Studies, University of the Western Cape.

Pearson M., Konradsen F., Gunnell D., Dawson A. H., Pieris R., Weerasinghe M., Knipe D. W., Jayamanne S., Metcalfe C., Hawton K., Wickramasinghe A. R., Atapattu W., Bandara P., de Silva D., Ranasinghe A., Mohamed F., Buckley N. A., Gawarammana I., Eddleston M. (2011) 'A Community-based Cluster Randomised Trial of Safe Storage to Reduce Pesticide Self-poisoning in Rural Sri Lanka: Study Protocol', *BMC Public Health*, 11, 879.

Pringle D., Williams M., Mtshali S., Ashton D. (2010) *Scoping Report Relating to Makathini Sugar Cane Project Environmental Impact Assessment (EIA)*. Hillcrest: Phatisa Equity (Phatisa). Available at www.andisaagri.com/images/files/Scoping%20Report%20-%20Makathini%20Sugar%20Cane%20Project%20EIA%20PDF%20(SMALL%20FILE).pdf. Date Accessed: 13 January 2018.

Resnick D. B. (2007) *The Price of Truth: How Money Affects the Norms of Science*. Oxford and New York, NY: Oxford University Press.

Rosenthal E. (2003, January–March) 'The Tragedy of Tauccamarca: A Human Rights Perspective on the Pesticide Poisoning Deaths of 4 Children in the Peruvian Andes', *International Journal of Occupational and Environmental Health*, 9(1), 53–8.

Rother H. A. (2005) 'Researching Pesticide Risk Communication Efficacy for South African Farm Workers', *Occupational Health Southern Africa*, 11(3), 20–6.

Rother H. A. (2008) 'South African Farm Workers' Interpretation of Risk Assessment Data Expressed as Pictograms on Pesticide Labels', *Environmental Research*, 108(3), 419–27.

Rother H. A. (2014) 'Communicating Pesticide Neurotoxicity Research Findings and Risks to Decision-makers and the Public', *NeuroToxicology*, 45, 327–37.

Rother H. A., Hall R., London L. (2008) 'Pesticide Use Among Emerging Farmers in South Africa: Contributing Factors and Stakeholder Perceptions', *Development Southern Africa*, 25(4), 399–424.

Rother H. A., Ngowi A. V. F., London L. (2009) 'WAHSA Action on Pesticides – Building Capacity to Reduce Hazardous Pesticide Exposures in the SADC', *Occupational Health Southern Africa*, 15(Special WAHSA Issue), 36–45.

Sineiro C., Berger M. (2012) 'The International Peasant Movement and the Struggle for Environmental Justice in Brazil: An Interview With Cleber Folgado From Movimiento de Pequeños Agricultores (MPA), Vía Campesina', *Brazil. Environmental Justice*, 5(2), 111–14. doi:10.1089/env.2011.0026.

Stull V., Bell M. M., Ncwadi M. (2016) 'Environmental Apartheid: Eco-health and Rural Marginalization in South Africa', *Journal of Rural Studies*, 47, 369–80.

Thirtle C., Beyers L., Ismael Y., Piesse J. (2003) 'Can GM-Technologies Help the Poor? The Impact of Bt Cotton in Makhathini Flats, KwaZulu-Natal', *World Development*, 31(4), 717–32.

UN Committee on Economic, Social and Cultural Rights (CESCR) (1999, May 12) *General Comment No. 12: The Right to Adequate Food (Art. 11 of the Covenant)*. Available at www.refworld.org/docid/4538838c11.html. Date Accessed: 9 January 2018.

UN Committee on Economic, Social and Cultural Rights (CESCR) (2000, August 11) *General Comment No. 14: The Right to the Highest Attainable Standard of Health (Art. 12 of the Covenant)*. E/C.12/2000/4. Available at www.refworld.org/docid/4538838d0.html. Date Accessed: 9 January 2018.

UN General Assembly 'International Covenant on Economic, Social and Cultural Rights' (1966, December 16) *United Nations, Treaty Series*. Vol. 993, p. 3. Available at www.refworld.org/docid/3ae6b36c0.html. Date Accessed: 9 January 2018.

United Nations (2009) *Consolidated List of Products Whose Consumption and/or Sale Have Been Banned, Withdrawn, Severely Restricted or not Approved by Governments*. Thirteenth Issue (December 2004–December 2006). Geneva: UN Department of Economic and Social Affairs ST/ESA/321.

United Nations Environment Programme (undated) *Strategic Approach to International Chemicals Management. SAICM Texts and Resolutions of the International Conference on Chemicals Management*. Geneva: UNEP. Available at www.saicm.org/Portals/12/Documents/saicmtexts/New%20SAICM%20Text%20with%20ICCM%20resolutions_E.pdf. Date Accessed: 13 January 2017.

United Nations General Assembly 'Report of the United Nations High Commissioner for Human Rights' (2014, April 1) *Report on the Seminar on the Right to Enjoy the Benefits of Scientific Progress and Its Applications*. UN Doc A/HRC/26/19.

United Nations General Assembly 'Report of the Special Rapporteur on the Right to Food' (2017a, January 24) UN Doc A/HRC/34/48.

United Nations General Assembly 'Report of the Special Rapporteur on the Implications for Human Rights of the Environmentally Sound Management and Disposal of Hazardous Substances and Wastes' (2017b, January 24) UN Doc A/HRC/34/41.

United Nations General Assembly 'Report of the Special Rapporteur on the Implications for Human Rights of the Environmentally Sound Management and Disposal of Hazardous Substances and Wastes' (2017c, July 20) UN Doc A/HRC/36/41.

Weissbrodt D., Kruger M. (2003) 'Norms on the Responsibilities of Transnational Corporations and Other Business Enterprises With Regard to Human Rights', *The American Journal of International Law*, 97(4), 901–22.

Xaba V. (2015) *Budget Policy Speech 2015/2016, Department of Agriculture and Rural Development*. Pietermaritzburg: KwaZulu-Natal Province. Available at www.kzndard.gov.za/images/Documents/PolicyDocuments/Budget-Policy-Speech-2015-2016.pdf. Date Accessed: 13 January 2018.

6 The politics of hypothesis

An inquiry into the ethics of scientific assessment

Gaston Meskens

1 Introduction: scientific challenges in Fukushima

On 11 March 2011, an earthquake with a magnitude of 9.0 hit Japan, followed by a tsunami which struck coastal Japan, including the northeastern coast. In addition to the great loss of life and devastation caused by the earthquake and the tsunami, the tsunami also led to the nuclear accident at the Fukushima Daiichi nuclear power plant, located at that northeastern coast. As a consequence of the accident, radionuclides were released from the plant into the atmosphere, and were deposited on land and into the ocean. There were also direct releases into the sea. Citizens within a radius of 20 km around the site and from other specific contaminated areas were evacuated, and those within a radius of 20–30 km were instructed to shelter before later being advised to voluntarily evacuate. Restrictions were placed on the distribution and consumption of food and the consumption of drinking water (IAEA 2015). As it is known, radioactive iodine (I-131) isotopes are part of a radioactive release from a damaged nuclear reactor, and it can be incorporated into the human body through inhalation or ingestion of contaminated food and milk (Dreger et al. 2015). Uptake of radioactive iodine may increase the risk of thyroid cancer, particularly in children. The younger the age at exposure, the higher the risk is for developing thyroid cancer (World Health Organisation 2011).

In May 2016, a paper was published in the journal 'Epidemiology' entitled 'Thyroid Cancer Detection by Ultrasound Among Residents Ages 18 Years and Younger in Fukushima, Japan: 2011 to 2014'. In the paper, the claim is developed (and empirically underpinned) that 'An excess of thyroid cancer has been detected by ultrasound among children and adolescents in Fukushima Prefecture within 4 years of the release, and is unlikely to be explained by a screening surge' (Tsuda et al. 2016: 316). That claim has been contested since its publication, not only by the Japanese authorities and by TEPCO (the owner of the Fukushima nuclear power plant), but also by scientists in various publications (see, among others, Takamura et al. 2016; Vaccarella et al. 2016; Williams 2015b), and in a letter to the editor of Epidemiology by a group of scientists who served as members of an International Expert Working Group established by the World Health Organization to perform an initial assessment of the health consequences of the accident

(Wakeford et al. 2016). One reaction to the original claim may summarise the critique best:

> The evidence suggests that the current prevalence of thyroid cancer found by ultrasound screening in Fukushima Prefecture represents a normal finding. This does not exclude the possibility that a very small number of cancers may be radiation induced. An increase due to radiation will probably be detectable in the future among the youngest-at-exposure group from the most exposed areas, but it will be much smaller than the increase seen after Chernobyl.
>
> (Williams 2015a)

Overall, the scientific critiques on the original paper can be summarised as follows (see, among others, Yamashita et al. 2018):

1. It is too early to draw conclusions. In the case of the Chernobyl accident, one has observed a rise of thyroid cancer in children (0–14y) and adolescents (15–19y), but only after 5 and 7 years after the accident respectively, with a peak in incidence after 10 and 15 years respectively;
2. The radiological impact on humans and the environment in Fukushima is lower when compared to Chernobyl, because the radioactivity released from the damaged nuclear reactor was lower;
3. However, while critiques 1 and 2 refer to facts related to the accident itself (of which the consequences could be taken into account in the interest of a proper understanding of the issue), the third critique is the most interesting. In Fukushima, after the accident, the authorities conducted a screening of all children of age 18 years and younger, applying an ultrasound detection technique to look for eventual anomalies of the thyroid. However, evidence from research shows that the number of thyroid cancers one would detect with an ultrasound screening among a normal population could be up to 150 times higher compared to the number of thyroid cancers observed among people who would go to the doctor with health complaints and who would consequently be diagnosed as having thyroid cancer. In other words, in a normal population, unaffected by a nuclear accident, most of the thyroid cancers remain largely undetected.

Thus the reality is that the systematic screening of the children in Fukushima has resulted in a significant 'noise' on the 'signal' that was originally to be measured: the excess of thyroid cancer (if any) in children as a consequence of the nuclear accident. Looking at the various scientific assessments, one can at least conclude that there is still an ongoing *scientific* discussion on possible thyroid cancer in children in Fukushima. That scientific discussion is relevant and needed, but one can understand that it would benefit from a serene and accommodating atmosphere – an atmosphere that is not present now, hindered as it is by power politics and distrust. Both hypotheses (excess thyroid cancer due to the accident/no excess thyroid cancer after the accident) are used in support of specific political, social and economic interests, and meanwhile, science, when asked for advice, will seemingly remain completely 'perplexed' for a time to come. Last but not least, one has to take into account the possibility that the 'truth' about whether there is more thyroid cancer in children in Fukushima due to the nuclear accident or not will never be revealed.

2 Science in the era of uncertainty

The post-accident crisis in Fukushima is not the only case in which science is 'faced with perplexity' today. In many common situations where science is expected to advise policy, it has difficulties doing so in an unambiguous way, as it has to deal with hypotheses that cannot (yet) be proven. Given that in public science is referred to as policy advice more than ever before, those scientific hypotheses are nowadays granted with a social, political or commercial function. They are prematurely released from the laboratory, without full support from empirical evidence, but with a specific task: to warn the world about dangerous situations or evolutions, or to inform about promising trends and capacities. And, whether in the area of environmental protection, economics, health or technology assessment, in many cases, they are produced as 'if-then' hypotheses upon explicit request from politics, civil society or the market. In the absence of evidence that would facilitate straightforward judgement, consensus and consequent action, these hypotheses have themselves become the 'end products' of science, and society has no other choice than to deal with them.

What kind of science are we talking about? It is science that matters for social well-being, in the sense that it is needed to inform and advise on policy concerned with societal challenges that directly or indirectly affect our social well-being. Understanding science as a problem- or solution-oriented process of knowledge generation that concerns social well-being- equals the understanding that the hypotheses that figure in this process directly or indirectly inspire or 'instruct' action in the interest of that social well-being. In other words, the scientific practices considered here involve 'science that directly matters for society'. It is a science that engages in the investigation of aspects of the natural environment and of the social realm, and that produces knowledge to be used 'in that social realm'. To illustrate this demarcation, researching the hypothesis of anthropogenic global warming (AGW) is of direct relevance for (and instructs action in) the social context, while researching the hypothesis of the Big Bang as the origin of the current universe, although relevant for a deeper understanding of nature and, in consequence, of humanity, is not of 'direct social relevance'. To put it in more literary terms, dealing with the AGW hypothesis informs an ethics of social conduct, while the Big Bang hypothesis inspires an aesthetics of the social world. However, the presentation of these examples does not suggest the existence of two unambiguously demarcated categories of scientific assessment, being directly 'relevant' versus 'irrelevant' for social well-being. The routes science can explore are unbounded, and scientific insights that would have no direct purpose or benefit at first sight may become relevant in the future, possibly in other contexts. In addition, it is known that techniques developed at the service of fundamental research, such as those performed in particle accelerators, often have secondary application possibilities in daily life.

The focus is thus on science that matters for social well-being. However, while science has the task to inform policy as mentioned earlier, it is also science that is confronted with the existence of knowledge-related uncertainty and with value pluralism with respect to its assessments or promises. There is uncertainty because scientific research has to deal with incomplete or speculative knowledge due to stochasticity, complex interrelations of cause and effect, the possibility of unknown phenomena or simply due to contingency in the future course of things. In addition, *regardless* of the uncertainty, laypeople as well as experts may have different or even conflicting value-based visions on the phenomena, practices or technologies that are topics of research, or on the policies for which science aims to provide guidance.

At first sight, this sophisticated description seems to only refer to a narrow kind of niche science. A critical look at the societal challenges we face, however, makes clear that the description concerns not only extreme cases such as understanding thyroid cancer in Fukushima, but almost the complete action field of contemporary science aiming to advise on the health risks we face in our daily life, either coming with specific human behaviour or as a consequence of technology application, industrial activity or urbanisation. Well-known examples are the health risks associated with mobile phones,[1] alcohol[2] and the herbicide Roundup.[3] In addition, there is the science concerned with our individual and collective physical, psychological and spiritual *condition humaine*; discussions on what makes up a healthy diet endure in popular discourse as well as in scientific circles; the question of whether chronic fatigue syndrome has physical rather than (or instead of only) social causes is still open (and everyone knows that either answer would have serious implications for health care); and the Diagnostic and Statistical Manual of Mental Disorders (especially its latest fifth edition (Kernberg American Psychiatric Association 2013)) seems today more a cause of public controversy than a source for medical guidance. What do the general description and the examples teach us? The Fukushima and Roundup cases are subject to controversy, fed by accounts of observed or suspected strategic alliances between science on the one hand and political, economic or civil society actors on the other. Science, in these cases, is said to violate its traditional criteria of objectivity and independence by strategically ignoring or manipulating 'its own truth', either 'at the service' of political or commercial interests or because it is put 'under pressure' by politics, regulators or the market to deliver evidence it (eventually) cannot deliver.

However, while (the risk of) misconduct in scientific research is obviously an issue to be taken into account, the matter envisaged here is of another, more fundamental, nature; on the one hand, facing uncertainty, this kind of science is unable to inform and advise policy in deciding on action in any straightforward and unambiguous scientific way. While on the other hand, policy in these situations 'cannot wait' until full scientific evidence is available, as it needs to decide on action in face of the societal challenges envisaged. The lack of full scientific evidence leaves room for interpretation (supportive belief, scepticism, disbelief) motivated and influenced by specific interests relevant to the societal challenge at stake. Meanwhile, science as a whole seems set to remain completely 'perplexed' at least for a time to come, and, in cases such as that of thyroid cancer in Fukushima, as mentioned in the introduction, one has to take into account the possibility that the 'truth' will never be revealed.

Thus the more fundamental problem with science that aims to advise policy today is not the problem of strategic manipulation of scientific advice by politics, civil society or the market (or by science itself) per se, but rather the challenge of dealing with the lack of evidence in situations where politics, civil society or the market 'need' that evidence to (eventually urgently) inform, criticise or justify specific actions or practices. All concerned actors, in these cases, are left with nothing more than underdetermined scientific hypotheses. And in the absence of evidence that would facilitate straightforward judgement, consensus and consequent action (as stated at the beginning of this section), these hypotheses have themselves become the 'end products' of science and society in general, and science, politics, civil society and the market in particular, have no other choice than to somehow deal with them in a responsible way.

At this point it may be necessary to emphasise that, despite of their mediating potential in the public social, economic or political sphere, the scientific hypotheses considered here are hypotheses produced in the context of 'serious' scientific practice – a practice that we could call 'scientific assessment'. Why 'assessment' instead of the traditional 'research'? The understanding of scientific assessment as a problem- or solution-oriented process of knowledge generation that concerns the wider social context while based on formal research methods suggests in itself already that scientific assessment is a practice of scientific inquiry that is embedded in (and in dynamic interaction with) the social, economic and political context that gives the particular assessment its meaning and relevance. Obviously, this has ethical implications for scientific assessment as a practice 'at the science-policy interface'. While in general these ethical implications would (only) refer to traditional understandings of research ethics, the need to deal with hypotheses not supported by full empirical evidence informs the need for a broader conception of ethics at the science-policy interface. One thing is certain: science, in these cases, can no longer justify itself as a simple and unencumbered quest for truth. Confronted with the need to deal with incomplete and speculative knowledge and value pluralism in making sense of environmental protection, economic policies or health issues, or of the promises of capacities and the acceptability of risks of technologies, the challenge of science in these cases is not the production of convincing proofs, but the construction of credible hypotheses.

In the following sections, I will explore the 'ethics of scientific assessment' for a society facing an unavoidable need to politically deal with scientific hypotheses that cannot (yet) be proven but that unquestionably matter for society. The idea is that this vision of the challenge of 'science in the era of uncertainty' inspires (or rather instructs) a new vision on the responsibility of policy that needs to rely on science. I thereby argue that these occurrences of 'scientific perplexity' are not only a concern for the scientific community, but first and foremost a challenge for democracy, and this from the perspective that 'proper' scientific policy advice is an intrinsic quality of democracy rather than of science itself.

3 Deliberating (the fact of) uncertainty

A scientific hypothesis, in a common understanding, is a tentative explanation about a phenomenon or a set of phenomena observed in the natural or social world. The explanation remains tentative until evidence of proof can be given that the proposed explanation is true or false. Dealing with a hypothesis means that, by definition, one is dealing with knowledge that is still incomplete and/or speculative. When proposing a scientific hypothesis, one proposes a 'possible reality', but, at the same time, one actually recognises the existence of specific 'occurrences' of scientific uncertainty that would need to be eradicated in order to find out whether that hypothesis indeed describes (or explains) that reality or not.

What is the scientific uncertainty at stake here? What *is* scientific uncertainty after all? Can it be recognised and assessed in terms of its nature and 'degree' in an objective way, or do we speak of scientific uncertainty only as a consequence of a lack of consensus within the scientific community? Or is the assessment of scientific uncertainty, either by an individual or as a collaborative action, always normative? And, if so, can one reach a consensus over its nature and 'degree', eventually even without an understanding of the natural and technical *phenomena* that play?

Different perspectives may result in different answers to these questions. Scientists would see uncertainty primarily as something to deal with in the research process itself. When trying to explain phenomena such as the origin of thyroid cancer in Fukushima, or the possible health effects that come with the use of Roundup, theory needs to be adequately matched with empirical data. Uncertainty can thereby relate to the difficulty in assessing whether or not a specific hypothesis is valid given a specific data set, leaving it unclear what phenomenon or phenomena one is actually observing. In addition, there is the uncertainty surrounding whether or not obtained data is actually 'valid enough', in the sense of whether it is 'representative enough' to support a proposed theory. Last but not least, there is the uncertainty that causes problems for the prediction of a future course of things, not only because one still has reasons to question the validity of underlying theories, but also simply due to contingency or to the fact that the interaction of different phenomena and processes is too complex to grasp and unravel. In these cases, it becomes clear that uncertainty is not only a concern of research itself, but also of policy that aims to deal with these phenomena and processes and that would need to rely on advice from science. An example to illustrate this is the 'Guide to SDG Interactions: from Science to Implementation' of the International Council for Science, which was written as advice for global and national policy concerned with the implementation of the sustainable development goals (SDG). The research aims to explore 'the nature of interlinkages between the SDGs', based on the premise that 'a science-informed analysis of interactions across sustainable development goals domains – which is currently lacking – can support more coherent and effective decision making and better facilitate the follow-up and monitoring of progress' (International Council for Science 2017: 7). The study highlights 'key uncertainties' causing problems for not only the assessment of 'what is at stake', but also the assessment of the effects of specific policy choices. For example, with respect to the interlinkage of SDG1 ('End poverty in all its forms everywhere') and SDG2 ('End hunger, achieve food security and improved nutrition, and promote sustainable agriculture'), the report states that:

> The main uncertainty is that pursuing SDG1 and SDG2 targets does not always reduce poverty and improve food and nutrition security everywhere and for everyone. As such, there is no guarantee that pro-poor agricultural development policies reduce poverty everywhere or that poverty-focused policies improve food security everywhere. To ensure that pro-poor policies are always conducive to enhanced food and nutrition security and sustainable agriculture requires a complex policy framework that differs by geography and status of development. There is no one-size fits all, which is why poverty reduction policies do not necessarily make everyone food secure.
>
> (International Council for Science 2017: 7)

Finally, in a broader understanding than only scientific, it is also common practice in research and policy concerned with health risk assessment to consider uncertainty in relation to 'risk' itself. In their article, 'The 4P Approach to Dealing with Scientific Uncertainty' (published in 1992), the authors recognised the phenomenon of 'contradictory' scientific assessments in the media, which are also highlighted here:

> One often sees contradictory stories in the news coming from 'reputable scientific sources' like: 'Global warming will occur and the results will be catastrophic unless something is done immediately' one day, followed by: 'There is no direct evidence for global warming and we should not waste money on something that may or may not happen' the next. Or one day: 'toxic chemical x causes cancer', followed by 'toxic chemical x occurs in too low a concentration in the environment to cause cancer'. These seemingly contradictory statements from the scientific community send our social decision making process into a tailspin.
>
> (Costanza and Cornwell 1992: 12)

The aim of the article, as the authors specify, is to 'develop an effective approach to dealing with uncertainty'. For this, they claim, it is important to make a distinction between 'risk' (which they call an event with a known probability, sometimes referred to as statistical uncertainty) and 'true uncertainty' (which, according to them is an event with an unknown probability, sometimes referred to as indeterminacy). They illustrate this in the following way:

> Every time you drive your car you run the risk of having an accident, because the probability of car accidents is known with very high certainty. We know the risk involved in driving because, unfortunately, there have been many car accidents on which to base the probabilities [. . .] If you live near the disposal site of some newly synthesized toxic chemical you may be in danger as well, but no one knows to what extent. No one knows even the probability of [. . .] getting cancer or some other disease from this exposure, so there is true uncertainty. Most important environmental problems suffer from true uncertainty, not merely risk.
>
> (Costanza and Cornwell 1992: 14)

Since the 1990s, the notion of uncertainty in relation to risk has become the subject of academic research in theory as well as in a wide variety of application contexts (see, among others, Renn 2008), but the understanding remains largely similar; specific occurrences of risk are 'calculable' because one can rely on scientific insights, simple forms of causality and, most important, reliable data from past experiences, while 'uncertainty' rather refers to insufficient scientific understanding, complex causality and/or incomplete or complete lack of data from the past.

In any case, whatever the nature and understanding of uncertainty, it seems scientists like to see it as something to 'reduce' or 'eradicate', and points of attention (and of scientific discussion) are the quality of data (accuracy, consistency, completeness), theory choice (taking into account the eventual influence of additional known or unknown factors) or the 'quality' of theory (with criteria such as reproducibility and falsifiability, but also non-empirical 'cognitive values' such as conservatism, simplicity, generality, consistency, broad scope, fruitfulness and testability) (Carrier, Howard, and Kourany 2014; Quine and Ullian 1978; Kuhn 1977). Even in the case of broad scientific consensus on a theory supporting evidence of a specific situation or trend, there may be uncertainty (and eventually, as a consequence, dissent) over whether *a specific phenomenon* is a proof of the theory being true (as is the case with specific occurrences of extreme weather in relation to the widely supported theory of human induced climate change).

Despite these 'struggles' with scientific uncertainty, the dominant idea within the scientific world is still that uncertainty can be tackled 'in an objective way', and it is known that scientists are not the only ones to take this position. Also, in the traditional popular understanding, science in general is seen as an objective and thus reliable source of knowledge. As the *Standard Encyclopaedia of Philosophy* puts it:

> The admiration of science among the general public, and the authority science enjoys in public life, stems to a large extent from the view that science is objective or at least more objective than other modes of inquiry.

> Understanding scientific objectivity is therefore central to understanding the nature of science and the role it plays in society.
>
> (Reiss and Sprenger 2017)

Known conceptions of objectivity are objectivity as 'faithfulness to facts', objectivity as 'absence of normative commitments' and objectivity as 'absence of personal bias' (Reiss and Sprenger 2017). Objectivity, so it seems, is generally not characterised as being 'faithful to uncertainty', in the sense of being vigilant to uncertainty and recognising specific occurrences of uncertainty. The possibility of objectivity as the absence of normative commitments or personal bias, on the other hand, has been subject to critical thinking for a few decades. Scientific studies have argued and shown that the social context in which scientists operate does have an influence on their thinking. In their interpretation of both theory and fact, scientists are biased due to influence from their 'practical' lifeworlds (the lab, the scientific discipline, the institute, the network) and by paradigmatic thinking maintained within these lifeworlds.

Since the end of the last century, the 'social constructivist' approach to the study of science (and technology) has become an academic discipline in itself (see, among others, Longino 1990; Bijker, Hughes, and Pinch 1987; Kukla 2000). The idea of 'influence', however, goes beyond a 'thin' psychological interpretation; science and the society wherein it operates are not separate worlds, but influence each other. In other words, influence does not only 'happen' in the mind of the scientists but is 'materialised' in the fabric of society where scientists and other people operate. As Sheila Jasanoff (2004: 2) puts it: 'The ways in which we know and represent the world (both nature and society) are inseparable from the ways in which we choose to live in it'. Science and 'the social order' do not only influence but rather 'co-produce each other':

> Co-production is symmetrical in that it calls attention to the social dimensions of cognitive commitments and understandings, while at the same time underscoring the epistemic and material correlates of social formations. Co-production can therefore be seen as a critique of the realist ideology that persistently separates the domains of nature, facts, objectivity, reason and policy from those of culture, values, subjectivity, emotion and politics.
>
> (Jasanoff 2004: 3)

What counts for nature, facts, objectivity, reason and policy also counts for 'the fact of scientific uncertainty'; *the way in which we know and represent scientific uncertainties are inseparable from the ways in which we choose to live with them*. In other words, the way in which and the 'degree' to which knowledge supporting a hypothesis is judged to be incomplete and/or speculative are relative, as they depend on 'the social dimensions of our cognitive commitments and understandings'. When an expert working for the International Agency for Research on Cancer (IARC) of the WHO says that glyphosate in Roundup is 'possibly carcinogenic to humans', and a scientific expert working for Monsanto claims that

Roundup is safe if used as prescribed, then the general public might think that one of the two is lying (most people will think the Monsanto expert is not telling the truth). The reality of course is that both sides propose a 'preferred' hypothesis that is difficult to prove (eventually, for the time being) and that neither of the two sides can prove that the other is wrong. Consequently, the IARC expert may claim that, acknowledging uncertainty, from a moral as well as from a pragmatic perspective, the precautionary principle should become the dominant criterion to instruct policy: the product should be taken off the market only because of the existence of suspicion of a possible negative health effect. The Monsanto expert, on the other hand, can refer to regulation still permitting Roundup to be sold.[4]

Taking into account what has been argued for/said before, it becomes clear that acknowledging the need for policy to deal with scientific hypotheses that cannot (yet) be proven comes down to accepting the existence of specific occurrences of scientific uncertainty that cannot (yet) be eradicated, but also accepting the existence of specific *interpretations* of these occurrences of scientific uncertainty and of the consequences thereof. As the Roundup case shows, the same body of incomplete and speculative knowledge on the health effects can even lead to opposing conclusions on the very existence and degree of those health effects. The idea of 'co-production' also supports the insight that 'specific interpretations' of the same body of incomplete and speculative knowledge should thereby not necessarily be understood as driven or shaped by clearly identifiable 'strategic acts'. From the philosophical perspective of 'value pluralism', one can also understand these interpretations to be shaped by the different value frameworks people might refer to, taking into account of course that these value frameworks are part of the overall process of 'co-production' themselves. Taking all this together, one can understand the way in which and the degree to which scientists and other observers are biased due to influence from social contexts or paradigmatic thinking itself as another emergence of scientific uncertainty.

In our contemporary society, living with low doses of glyphosate, radioactivity, electromagnetic radiation, fine dust, flame retardants, arsenic, food preservatives, hormone additives (as in contraceptive pills), trans fats, sugar and alcohol is living with the scientific uncertainty troubling the understanding and prediction of their true health effects. Of course, science needs to continue to strive for better understanding and prediction, but, meanwhile, its hypotheses should be taken care of instead of leaving them to lead an uncontrolled commercial or political life. Following what was said about scientific uncertainty previously, it becomes clear that, in the context of a specific issue in need of political action (like thyroid cancer in Fukushima or the use of Roundup), taking care of a scientific hypothesis (or multiple possible hypotheses) that cannot (yet) be proven comes down to acknowledging the existence of scientific uncertainty that cannot (yet) be eradicated and, ultimately, the need to deliberate *specific interpretations* of that scientific uncertainty. The overall motivation for this is not a care for the credibility of science itself, but a care for fairness and effectiveness and societal trust in policy dealing with these issues. In light of the previous, one may understand that this 'care' becomes a joint responsibility of policy, science and the stakeholders concerned with the specific issue. The justification of applications of science and technology with possible adverse effects is thereby not a simple exercise of 'balancing' the benefits of their use with the 'tolerable' health effects or burdens on the environment coming with their use. That justification is a complex problem in itself that, in principle, should be guided by ethical 'criteria' such as the precautionary principle and informed consent of the (potentially) affected (see, among others, Asveld and Roeser 2008; Meskens 2016). One could wonder how, in the context of a specific issue in need of political action, the precautionary principle could ever steer policy and consequent regulation if different interpretations of scientific uncertainty exist and are strategically maintained instead of deliberated.

We will come back to the precautionary principle in the conclusion of this chapter. In this phase of the reasoning, two questions need to be tackled. Firstly, what does it mean to care for fairness and effectiveness in policy dealing with applications of science and technology if science is 'perplex', in the sense that it is unable to deliver scientific evidence needed to unambiguously inform policy what to do? And, secondly, how can policy ever generate societal trust if political decision makers would need to acknowledge to the general public that there is no scientific evidence to unambiguously inform them of what would be the right thing to do? Scientific perplexity seems to leave open the playing field for the political and commercial strategic moves we observe today, and one doesn't need in-depth social studies to understand that there is very little public trust in the way contemporary politics is now dealing with issues such as Roundup, fine dust or the consequences of Fukushima on public health.

The main claim argued for in this chapter is that there is a way out. Science may be called perplex in these cases, but that doesn't mean it is paralysed. Despite the perplexity, it has a crucial role to play in striving for fair and effective policies and societal trust, but it cannot do it alone. As stated in the previous section, confronted with the need to deal with uncertainty due to incomplete and speculative knowledge and value pluralism in the context of issues in need of political action, the challenge of science is no longer the production of convincing proofs, it is the construction of credible hypotheses. And in the general interest of rendering hypotheses with credibility, science has no choice but to 'open up its method' towards society. What this could mean in theory and practice is the topic of the fourth section of this text.

4 Critical visions (on what science is and/or should be)

From the perspective presented in the previous sections, reflections on how to responsibly deal with 'the politics of hypothesis' could take two possible routes; they can develop from critical analysis of how scientific advice is currently produced and subsequently interpreted, steered and used by concerned political, social and commercial actors, or they can develop normative thought on what science actually can be and should be, taking into account the challenge of knowledge production with respect to our current complex social problems. Over the last few decades, various academic visions have been produced on what science 'should do', 'can do' or on what science 'actually is' today. They combine the two routes, although with a focus on values and normative thinking, which means that they should rather be seen as explorations in 'critical philosophy' or ethics rather than as 'objective' social science in themselves. One can recall, among others, Longino's 'science as social knowledge' and her idiom of 'contextual empiricism' (Longino 1990, 2001), the plea for 'post-normal science', relying on an 'extended peer community' consisting of all those with a stake in the dialogue on the issue (Funtowicz and Ravetz 2003), the arguments of Harré and Van Langenhove with respect to a necessary new ontology of the social sciences in the interest of their 'usability' in policy (van Langenhove 2007), the views of Kitcher on science and democracy and his concept of 'well-ordered science', (Kitcher 2011, 2014), the idioms of 'Mode-2 science' (Gibbons 1994), 'socially robust knowledge' (Nowotny, Scott, and Gibbons 2001), transdisciplinarity (Bernstein 2015, among others) and 'co-production of science and social order' (Jasanoff 2004). The context and scope of this text does not allow a broad and in-depth elaboration on these academic visions but, from a general perspective, one can say they have common elements in the way they draw attention to the unavoidable deliberative character of contemporary scientific knowledge production, but also that they typically emerged as critical views on modernity in general and with respect to occurrences of positivism, scientism and technocracy in policy of science and technology in particular. Important in the context of this chapter is to look at the motivations put forward to present and defend these new visions on science. The aim of this focus is to see what elements they can provide to understand and illustrate how to deal with the problem of scientific perplexity and 'the politics of hypothesis' as characterised previously.

The (academic) literature that deals with the question of what science 'should do', 'can do' or 'actually is' is already vast and still expanding. But one can identify two general lines of reasoning; on the one hand, there is the 'social constructionist' approach built on the argument that science is never 'objective' or 'value-free', in the sense that scientific research is always influenced by the value frameworks of the scientists involved.[5] On the other hand, there is the argument that the complexity of our contemporary challenges requires an 'advanced' kind of science able to 'grasp' that complexity. Understanding climate change, the effects of Roundup or what to do in Fukushima is not about 'isolating' natural, technical and social facts to objectively guide policy but about seeing and understanding 'the bigger picture' of interrelated problems and of the relations between nature, technology and society in these cases in the first place.[6] Important to note is that, in general, both lines of reasoning are developed out of a concern for the credibility of science, driven by a motivation to rethink but 'maintain' science in its role of provider of information and explanation towards society in general and towards (democratic) policy in particular. That concern is apparently needed; science is said to be 'in crisis' today, constantly in search of funding, meanwhile trying to withstand the academic pressure for publications and the commercial and political pressure to deliver evidence it may not be able to deliver.[7] Moreover, modern science has been accused of being biased in general (because of its 'typical' Western and/or masculine perspective) and suspected of 'commercial conspiracies' with big market players in multiple cases in recent history. Last but not least, important scientific achievements build up since the Enlightenment are now questioned again by religious and other cultural powers who see these scientific findings as disturbing for their own spiritual ideologies. As a result of all this, in the words of Philip Kitcher, the authority of science is 'eroding':

> During the twentieth century, governments became convinced of the wisdom of investing in scientific research, and citizens became accustomed to think of natural scientists as authorities on whose conclusions they could rely. In recent decades, however, a variety of challenges to particular scientific judgements has fostered a far more ambivalent attitude to the authority of the natural sciences. Many Americans do not believe that contemporary evolutionary theory offers a correct account of the history of life. Europeans are sceptical about scientific endorsements of the harmlessness of genetically modified organisms. Around the world, serious attention to problems of climate change is hampered by suspicions that the alleged 'expert consensus' is premature and unreliable.
>
> (Kitcher 2011: 15)

Can and should the authority of science be reinstalled? And what kind of authority would that be, taking into account the challenges described earlier? Especially in the interest of tackling the problem of bias, new approaches to research can aim to 'restore' scientific objectivity *within* the scientific world, or focus more on a new understanding of what science is and should be *in interaction with* policy and society at large.

The first approach is most known in the form of the work of Helen Longino. According to Longino's main philosophical claim, knowledge, and especially scientific knowledge is social (Longino 1990). By 'social' it is not meant that acts of knowledge generation are 'embedded in the social', but that knowledge generation happens through the social interaction of actors *concerned* with knowledge generation related to a specific topic. She calls this social interaction leading to knowledge 'transformative criticism', and this interaction, she claims, is unavoidable, but in the case of scientific knowledge generation it is at the same time that what can make it 'self-corrective' and therefore credible.[8] This 'self-correction' is done by what she calls 'the social account of objectivity':

> If scientific inquiry is to provide knowledge, rather than a random collection of opinions, there must be some way of minimizing the influence of subjective preferences and controlling the role of background assumptions. The social account of objectivity solves this problem. The role of background assumptions in evidential reasoning is grounds for unbridled relativism only in the context of an individualistic conception of scientific method and scientific knowledge. If our conception of the methods of knowledge construction in science is broadened to embrace the social activities of evidential and

> particularly conceptual criticism, we see how individual subjective preferences are minimized in the final products.
>
> (Longino 1990: 216)

In other words:

> Values are not incompatible with objectivity, but objectivity is analyzed as a function of community practices rather than as an attitude of individual researchers towards their material or a relation between representation and represented.
>
> (Longino 1990: 216)

Bringing together scientists with different 'backgrounds' (walks of life, cultures, regions, employers) can indeed ensure a 'levelling out' of individual subjective preferences. However, in this view, scientific knowledge generation can still happen in various 'non-overlapping' closed scientific communities concentrated around a specific issue, each of them disconnected from society. One could say that this is exactly what happens in the Roundup case, taking into account that both the positions of Monsanto and the World Health Organisation are not determined by two single scientists each driven by their 'individual subjective preferences', but precisely by 'community practices' of a 'Monsanto scientific community' and a 'WHO scientific community'. On the one hand, following Longino, one can understand that, on each side, the 'social account of objectivity' will have done its work in ruling out specific *individual* subjective preferences. On the other hand, one can say that the two communities are each characterised by a specific *shared* subjective preference determined by the social 'role' of the 'function' each scientific community is taking up (serving a private sector actor or advising a public service actor respectively).

Longino is 'aware' of this problem; scientists' background assumptions, she argues, are epistemically acceptable only if they have survived critical scrutiny in a discursive context characterised by four 'quality criteria': (1) there must be publicly recognised forums for the criticism of evidence, of methods and of assumptions and reasoning; (2) there must be uptake of criticism, in the sense that there must be preparedness within the community to take criticism seriously and to 'learn' from it; (3) there must be publicly recognised standards by reference to which theories, hypotheses and observational practices are evaluated and by appeal to which criticism is made relevant to the goals of the inquiring community and (4) communities must be characterised by 'equality' of intellectual authority (Longino 2001). However, while the first criterion suggests the need for interaction with the wider spectrum of societal stakeholders (including citizens), Longino specifies that 'criticism of research ought to be articulated in the same standard and public venues in which 'original research' is presented: journals, conferences, and so on' (Longino 2001: 129). In other words, the public venues that could serve as forums for critical scrutiny remain nonetheless within the scientific world, a world that is known to be rarely opened towards or visited by citizens or even civil society actors concerned with issues such as public health. The scientific claim that one can observe a rise in thyroid cancer among children in Fukushima has been scientifically criticised in the same scientific journal ('Epidemiology') in which the original research was published, and one can understand that it is not evident for the citizens of Fukushima to get access to these discussions (if only because they are in English). In addition, if scientists discuss a particular occurrence of scientific uncertainty in those 'publicly recognised forums for the criticism of evidence, of methods and of assumptions and reasoning', then one can assume that the collective background assumption of the community is that the only meaningful challenge for science is the 'reduction' or 'eradication' of the uncertainty in that case, and not necessarily the recognition of (temporary) scientific perplexity and the consequent formulation of a scientifically underpinned promotion of the precautionary principle to guide policy.

In summary, one can conclude that, for Longino, critical scrutiny of scientific knowledge remains a scientific and not a 'democratic' act. Philip Kitcher, on the other hand, is known to have developed a view on science in its direct interaction with (and responsibility towards) democracy. For Kitcher, in a democratic society, science should serve the formation of 'public knowledge', taking into account that public knowledge can be understood as knowledge existing 'whenever and wherever there are channels of communication through which information is transmitted from some organisms in a social group to others' (Kitcher 2011: 86). In developing his argument, the chief aim is:

> to offer an account of how this broad system of public knowledge, with science as a prominent part, functions to promote our values, how it contributes to and is constrained by the goals of democracy, and where our contemporary version of it might be amended to advance those values and goals.
>
> (Kitcher 2011: 86)

The question for him, then, is how democratic values might affect what is taken as public knowledge. In the traditional view, for science, it is the system of peer review that will 'certificate' specific scientific ideas and findings to appear in peer-reviewed journals and, in this way, 'promote' these ideas and findings to become public knowledge available for society in general and for policy in particular. In that sense, peer review can also be seen as a way to control whether the research has dealt with scientific uncertainty in a proper way. In general, however, scientific papers are not written and published with the aim to characterise and 'recognise' (for the time being) a persistent occurrence of scientific uncertainty. Rather, they aim to 'relativise' scientific uncertainties in the defence of a specific hypothesis about the natural or social reality. Therefore, for Kitcher, this system of certification should be open for scrutiny in itself, claiming that: 'we should consider whether there are serious possibilities that processes of certification can sometimes go awry':

> Are there general features of the sciences, as they are practiced, making it likely that, in some particular areas, particular 'findings' are wrongly certified,

> inscribed 'on the books' even though an ideal deliberation would determine certification premature or even illegitimate?
>
> (Kitcher 2011: 140)

His answer is a yes, and he claims that:

> It is easy to think there might be, to imagine instances in which a particular ideological agenda or pervasive prejudice inclines members of a scientific subcommunity to favor particular hypotheses, to overrate certain kinds of evidence, or to manufacture evidence.
>
> (Kitcher 2011: 141)

In support of his claim, Kitcher mentions, among other examples, the strategies of the tobacco industry to 'prove' the harmlessness of tobacco,[9] but one can easily look at the case of Roundup in a similar sense. For Kitcher, the 'ideal deliberation that would determine certification premature or even illegitimate' (Kitcher 2011: 140) cannot take place 'within' the scientific community itself. That deliberation should be organised as a form of 'public reason' in which non-scientists also play a role in the certification of scientific claims, and that, ideally, would comply with two 'quality criteria'; as a process of scientific deliberation, it should be 'well-ordered' and conducted in 'ideal transparency'. For Kitcher, science is well-ordered 'when its specification of the problems to be pursued would be endorsed by an ideal conversation, embodying all human points of view, under conditions of mutual engagement' (Kitcher 2011: 106). In doing so, scientific and other presuppositions can be made explicit and can be exposed to a wider discussion. Consequently, he argues, there is also an epistemic argument for democratisation in processes of certification:

> Representation of a broader set of perspectives within the scientific community has the potential to expose ways in which the methods used by that community are less reliable than they are supposed, and may thus lead to improvements in certification.
>
> (Kitcher 2011: 150)

In addition, as a second quality criterion, a system of public knowledge is 'ideally transparent' 'just in case all people, outsiders as well as researchers, can recognise the methods, procedures and judgments used in certification (whether they lead to acceptance or rejection of new submissions) and can accept those methods, procedures and judgments' (Kitcher 2011: 151).[10]

Kitcher recognises that the ideal based on these two criteria impose extremely strong conditions unattainable in practice. However, imagine, in the case of Roundup, facing the need to make a policy decision on whether it should be taken off the market or not, it *would* be possible to organise this ideal conversation in practice. In other words, imagine that the science of the health effects of Roundup would be subject to a process of well-ordered certification conducted in ideal transparency, what would one then actually come to *know*? And if the case of thyroid cancer in children in Fukushima would be treated in the same way, what would one then actually come to know? It may be clear that the resulting knowledge would not be the 'truth' about the health effects of Roundup or of the Fukushima nuclear accident respectively. Rather, in both cases, the 'knowledge' would be the joint acknowledgement and understanding that there is scientific uncertainty related to these health effects that cannot be cleared out (yet). In addition, in the Fukushima case, the ideal conversation would endorse an uneasy insight about our human nature, namely the fact that many people live with forms of thyroid cancer that remain largely undiscovered.

Longino and Kitcher present views on what science is and should be taking into account one should always remain vigilant to the possibility of scientific bias. In addition, for Kitcher, the need to 'open up' the scientific method for public participation and 'public reason' is motivated on ethical grounds; if values (scientific and others) come to play a role in scientific research, then it is important to stress that 'there are no ethical experts, only the authority of the conversation' (Kitcher 2011: 57, 2014). And for Kitcher, that conversation is or should be a 'democratic' conversation.

Moving on to other views on what science today should be or actually is, it is important to note that calls for a more participatory form of science have been developed in other routes of thought, and for different reasons.

Another vision on science relevant in the context of this paper is that on the need for 'post-normal science' developed by Funtowicz and Ravetz. In their article, 'A New Scientific Methodology for Global Environmental Issues', they claim that: 'The extreme uncertainty of the methods used to address the disturbed global environment limits the application of traditional scientific methodologies to current problems' (Funtowicz and Ravetz, cited in Costanza 1991: 137). They suggest the need for an advanced kind of science, called 'second order science'. For second order science, they argue, ' facts are uncertain, values in dispute, stakes high and decisions urgent. Such sciences are important when, paradoxically, "hard" policy decisions depend on "soft" scientific inputs'(Funtowicz and Ravetz, cited in Costanza 1991: 137). In follow-up research, they further elaborate on this advanced form of science, now called 'post-normal science', being a kind of science that 'focuses on aspects of problem solving that tend to be neglected in traditional accounts of scientific practice: uncertainty, value loading, and a plurality of legitimate perspectives' (Funtowicz and Ravetz 2003: 1). For Funtowicz and Ravetz, post-normal science is science that *includes* value judgements and even ethical reflection as 'scientific' aspects to be taken into account. Considerations on possible adverse effects of applications of science and technology are traditionally not seen as belonging to 'applied science', but they can be part of what Funtowicz and Ravetz call 'professional consultancy'. They see professional consultancy as an extended form of science in cases where both systems' uncertainty and decision stakes are higher. However, they argue, considerations on the *fairness* of the fact that these adverse effects affect specific people or populations are, in turn, not seen as elements to be taken into account in professional consultancy (allowed to stand in traditional scientific research). According to Funtowicz and Ravetz, these considerations belong to the realm of post-normal science.[11] Post-normal science does not dispute the idea that science can provide reliable knowledge or 'exclusive expertise in its legitimate contexts'. Rather, the idea is that the *quality* of science as policy advice depends on whether or not considerations on environmental, social and ethical aspects are included in that advice (Funtowicz and Ravetz, cited in Costanza 1991: 148). In practice, post-normal science differs from traditional applied science and professional consultancy in two ways: it makes use of 'extended peer communities' and it takes into account 'extended facts'. For Funtowicz and Ravetz, peer communities representing the traditional 'certified expertise' (called the 'insiders') are 'manifestly incapable of providing effective conclusive answers to many of the problems they confront', and therefore 'the outsiders are capable of forcing their way into dialogue'. Those outsiders should be 'other scientists and experts, technically competent but representing interests outside the social paradigm of the official expertise' but also the lay public including 'community activists, lawyers, legislators and journalists' and 'those whose lives and livelihood depend on the solution of the problems', given that these last have 'a keen awareness of how general principles are realized in their "back yards"' (Funtowicz and Ravetz, cited in Costanza 1991: 149). However, including local citizens in 'post-normal' scientific knowledge production is not only motivated by 'fairness' (enabling their 'right' to participate in knowledge generation and decision making on issues that might negatively affect them) but also based on the idea that they will contribute to the production of 'better knowledge'. According to Funtowicz and Ravetz, not only is there a need for extended peer communities, but also a need to 'enrich' the cognitive basis of post-normal science with 'extended facts'. These extended facts include 'the beliefs and feelings of local people', bearing in mind that 'When such testimonies are introduced into scientific debate, and subject to some degree of peer review before reporting or acceptance, they approach the status of scientific facts'. Not only their beliefs and feelings should be taken into account, but also their 'experiences with a deep knowledge of a particular environment and its problems' (Funtowicz and Ravetz, cited in Costanza 1991: 150).[12] While citizens' beliefs, feelings and 'indigenous' local knowledge might be collected and analysed by social science researchers, for post-normal science, combining its two criteria (extended peer communities and extended facts), it is clear that citizens should not (only) be subject of study but also that they should be able to participate themselves in knowledge production to advice policy.

In summary, when there is a need to deal with scientific uncertainty and values in issues in need of political action, those like Kitcher, also Funtowicz and Ravetz call for a 'democratisation' of the generation of knowledge for policy advice, 'not merely in mass education but in enhanced participation in decision making for common problems'. To make that possible, they argue, 'The task is to create the conceptual structures, along with the political institutions, whereby a creative dialogue may be developed' and 'For this, post-normal science is a foundational argument' (Funtowicz and Ravetz, cited in Costanza 1991: 150–151). It is important to recognise here that the challenge of science envisaged by Funtowicz and Ravetz is not the scientific uncertainty troubling the generation of knowledge about a specific natural or technical phenomenon (such as the health effects of Roundup) but rather the understanding and prediction of a set of interrelated phenomena, *including social phenomena*, making up a complex issue. Global environmental issues (which was their original focus) such as climate change or the loss of biodiversity are indeed complex issues, in the sense that they are made up of complex interactions of natural, technical and social phenomena. Understanding global environmental issues therefore requires an understanding of their overall complexity, or thus of *how* all natural, technical and social phenomena that play a role interact. The challenges for science in this case seem to be greater than in the case of Roundup or thyroid cancer in Fukushima, given the extended range of uncertainties due to the interaction of multiple processes, all complex in themselves, and the possibility of multiple value-laden 'legitimate perspectives'. Nevertheless, their plea for post-normal science is relevant in the context of this paper, as also in the case of Roundup or Fukushima, one can say that 'facts are uncertain, values in dispute, stakes high and decisions urgent'. More important is the insight that, just as in the case of Kitcher, the argumentation of Funtowicz and Ravetz in favour of the democratisation of science is *ethical*, in the sense that there is no 'hard evidence' or 'proof' for the need for post-normal science, or thus for the need for public participation in research that would also consider 'extended facts'. The opinion that certified experts are 'manifestly incapable of providing effective conclusive answers to many of the problems they confront' (as Funtowicz and Ravetz have put it) is a critical opinion most likely not shared by those experts themselves, and neither by the political authorities and private sector actors who employ those experts to defend their own stakes and support their own strategies.

5 Conclusion: the idea of reflexivity as a quality of the science-policy interface

The context of this chapter does not allow further consideration of relevant academic views on what science is or should do in the context of governance of the complex policy problems of today. On the other hand, the views of Kitcher, Funtowicz and Ravetz provide us with the necessary elements to understand and illustrate how to deal with the problem of scientific perplexity and 'the politics of hypothesis' as characterised in sections 2 and 3. After all, 'scientific perplexity', facing the need to deal with scientific uncertainty and the need to take into account values while being asked for advice on issues in need of political action, is just another way to describe the challenge of science as understood in the academic visions considered earlier. In other words, the case of Roundup or of thyroid cancer in Fukushima is in need of a democratisation of science as described by Kitcher or Funtowicz and Ravetz. However, an issue obviously recognised but not specifically emphasised by them is the fact that 'extended peer review' (through the organisation of transdisciplinarity and public participation) may generate new knowledge, but not necessarily 'reduce' or 'eradicate' the scientific uncertainty hindering unambiguous policy advice in the first place. Whether in the understanding of Kitcher, Funtowicz and Ravetz or from any other view, in these cases, *a fully democratised process of knowledge generation would still be left with a scientific hypothesis that cannot (yet) be proven*. The fate of the scientific hypotheses such as those about the health effects of Roundup or about thyroid cancer in Fukushima, but also the one related to human-induced climate change, is that they cannot be but subject of discursive evaluation in the public and political sphere. They are useless when kept in the laboratory and become meaningful only when released into the public as a subject of concern for a democratic society. Once in the public and political sphere, they remain loaded with scientific rigour and responsibility, but fulfil at the same time a social and political mediating function. Organised as well-ordered or post-normal science, the construction of scientific hypotheses could become a full participatory process in itself, involving those with political responsibilities and commercial interests related to the phenomenon or activity the hypothesis is trying to characterise, but also and primarily involving those potentially affected by the phenomenon or activity. Paradoxically, even in case of controversy, societal trust can emerge with the joint acknowledgement and fair description of scientific perplexity, and for the general public, acknowledging for itself the existence of scientific uncertainty troubling the understanding and prediction of health effects coming with specific practices could be a source of trust in science as such. Consequently, the joint recognition of scientific uncertainty would become a first democratic act in itself, and deliberating specific interpretations of that uncertainty would make scientific advice *reflexive*, as it would enable the discussion and negotiation of the various stakeholders' cognitive commitments and understandings, whether or not driven by strategic interests. The process of deliberation would be emancipatory and confrontational at the same time, also for the participating potentially affected members of the general public. As a result, the hypotheses that cannot be proven (yet) have been proven and that, as a consequence, would still have a social and political function, would not gain credibility in society by way of anticipated or promised empirical evidence, but by the critical-reflexive and democratic method that would be used to (re)formulate them. The final aim of this kind of deliberation is not to come to a consensus on knowledge related to the issue at stake, but the very act of deliberation itself. The reason is that it is the only 'authoritative place' that would allow a discussion and promotion of ethical values such as the precautionary principle, equality, sustainability and the protection and empowerment of the weak as principles to inspire and steer policy.

So what are the ethics of scientific assessment as a practice 'at the science-policy interface'? The discussion of what science is, what constitutes reliable scientific knowledge and how it should and could be generated and used, will remain a theoretical challenge inherent to any modern 'reflexive' society. This is not a fatalistic conclusion but an expression of hope. In parallel, however, the problem of what science is, what constitutes reliable scientific knowledge, and how it should and could be generated and used can be 'solved' in practice in any situation where concrete scientific advice would be needed in decision making today. As argued previously, occurrences of 'scientific perplexity' are not only a concern for the scientific community, but first and foremost a challenge for democracy, and this from the perspective that 'proper' scientific policy advice is an intrinsic quality of democracy rather than of science itself. Since half a century ago, critical academic research has suggested that science as 'proper' policy advice would primarily need to be understood as a democratic and reflexive process of knowledge generation. Meanwhile, 'bottom-up' citizens actions have started to challenge the traditional structures and institutions of scientific knowledge production and political decision making; citizen-led activism confronts authorities with the shortcomings of their policies, civil society lead initiatives assist in 'unlocking' local indigenous knowledge for policy, and 'citizen science' initiatives scrutinise or complement knowledge produced by 'official expertise'. However, these initiatives will remain only 'practices of resistance' as long as there is no reform of those traditional structures and institutions of scientific knowledge production and political decision- making that would allow 'reflexivity' to emerge as a quality of the science-policy interface. If, in our contemporary society, scientific assessment is to be understood as a practice of scientific inquiry that is embedded in (and in dynamic interaction with) the social, economic and political context that gives the particular assessment its meaning and relevance, then the ethics of scientific assessment imply ethical virtues for everyone concerned with that assessment. The preparedness to, in the words of Funtowicz and Ravetz, 'create conceptual structures, along with the political institutions, whereby a creative dialogue may be developed' (Funtowicz and Ravetz, cited in Costanza 1991: 150) and the preparedness to take the outcome of that dialogue seriously, may primarily be called a political virtue, but once the structures and institutions are created, the possibility of that creative dialogue depends on the preparedness to adopt and foster one common virtue by everyone concerned – reflexivity as an ethical attitude with respect to the own position, interests, strategies, hopes, hypotheses, beliefs and concerns, and this in any formal role or social position (as a scientist, engineer, politician, manager, civil society representative, activist or citizen). The views of Kitcher and Funtowicz and Ravetz on how to organise 'good science for better policy making' are practical but may still be called utopian and idealistic. On the other hand, the possibility to organise 'reflexivity' as a quality of the science-policy interface does not require utopian reform on all levels. For the time being, the existing traditional structures and institutions of scientific knowledge production and political decision making may hinder reflexivity as a 'quality of our society' in general sense, but they do not hinder the organisation of 'creative' transdisciplinary and inclusive dialogue around *concrete* issues or the political preparedness to take the outcome of that dialogue seriously *in principle*. Whether in the case of Roundup or of thyroid cancer in Fukushima, all the required actors are *present* and available. What is needed is the political will to bring them together. Meanwhile, the 'bottom-up' citizens actions mentioned earlier may contribute to social empowerment by raising awareness of the issues within the general public, including awareness of the fact that, even in cases where science has a central role in getting to know the issue, one does not necessarily need scientific evidence to guide policy for the betterment of society.

Notes

1 The World Health Organisation states that 'radiofrequency electromagnetic fields' produced by mobile phones are possibly carcinogenic to humans (World Health Organisation 2014a).

2 According to the World Health Organisation, there is now 'an extended knowledge of the causal relationship between alcohol consumption and more than 200 health conditions', (World Health Organization 2014b). The organisation advocates strategies to 'reduce the harmful use of alcohol' (World Health Organisation 2010) while other policies suggest that there exists something like a 'responsible consumption of alcohol' (e.g. the EU Alcohol Strategy (European Commission n.d.)), eventually expressed a specific maximum number of 'units' per day for man and women (see, among others, (US Gov MedlinePlus Medical Encyclopedia n.d.). There remains, however, uncertainty over whether there is an actual level of 'responsible use' below which there is no effect detectable as compared to not drinking at all.

3 The chemical glyphosate is an ingredient in Monsanto's weed killer product 'Roundup'. The International Agency for Research on Cancer (IARC) of the World Health Organisation (WHO) concluded in 2015 that glyphosate is 'probably carcinogenic to humans' (Guyton et al. 2015, p. 490). That conclusion has been scientifically contested (see for example, Williams et al. 2016), but the overall uncertainty remains (see, among others, Cressey 2015). The issue became even more complicated when the Food and Agriculture Organisation (FAO) of the United Nations, together with the World Health Organisation, claimed that glyphosate was 'unlikely to pose a carcinogenic risk to humans from exposure through diet, thereby contradicting the assessment of the WHO's own International Agency for Research on Cancer (Neslen 2016). Also, the European Food Safety Authority contradicted the IARC assessment (European Food Safety Authority (EFSA) 2015).

4 The question of whether and how the precautionary principle is influencing policy and regulation of health and environmental risks in general, and in Europe and the US in particular, is a topic of ongoing discussion. (See, among others, Wiener and Rogers 2002; Garnett and Parsons 2017).

5 In one line of academic thought, the 'social constructionist' approach is said to have a 'modest' and a 'strong' version. In the modest version, social interests (of scientists) 'only' influence their choice of research areas and scientific problems. In the 'strong' version, not only the autonomy but also the epistemological integrity of science is questioned, in the sense that social interests may also determine theory choice and the acceptance of scientific hypotheses (Longino 1990; Barnes and Bloor 1982). From this perspective, one can understand the reflections on possible interpretations of scientific uncertainty in section 2 of this paper as being more aligned with the 'strong' version. Worthwhile to note also is that the philosophical debate on the validity of the social constructionist approach is still continuing (see, among others, Hacking 2000).

6 I wrote about the character of complexity of our 'complex social problems' and about what that would imply for science in general in Meskens (2017).

7 See Saltelli and Funtowicz (2017) for a general reflection on 'the crisis of science' today.

8 The context and scope of this paper do not allow for further elaborations on the *philosophical* discussion between Longino and her critics. Her defence of the philosophical claim that 'knowledge, especially scientific knowledge, is social', is aimed as a way to overcome the 'rational-social dichotomy', or thus the idea that cognitive rationality and sociality are mutually exclusive, or dichotomous (Longino 2001, p. 203).

She calls this dichotomy as maintained by 'mutual caricatures', being the idea that scientific inquiry is fully rule-governed calculation versus the idea that scientific inquiry is fully (or only) determined by social interest and power. According to Philip Kitcher, Longino's view 'collapses into relativism', in the sense that 'truth' is apparently only possible as some type of 'acceptance', or thus as a form of knowledge that doesn't provide researchers with a basis from which they can make principled judgements (Kitcher, Philip, "Contrasting Conceptions of Social Epistemology", in Schmitt 1994: 122).

9 For this, since the 1950s, the tobacco lobby did not present scientific research in itself, but rather 'sophisticated public relations approaches' to undermine and distort the emerging 'compelling peer-reviewed scientific evidence of the harms of smoking' (Brandt 2012, p. 63).

10 Kitcher primarily introduces the criterion for science to be 'well-ordered' as a needed quality of science *policy* rather than of the scientific method itself, stating that: 'A society practicing scientific inquiry is well-ordered just in case it assigns priorities to lines of investigation through discussions whose conclusions are those that would be reached through deliberation under mutual engagement and which expose the grounds such deliberation would present' (Kitcher 2011, p. 114). In a second perspective, he argues, also the certification of scientific ideas and findings within a specific line of investigation would benefit from an ideal or thus 'well-ordered' conversation.

11 One of the original cases considered by Ravetz was the construction of large hydropower dams, wherein he put forward the question whether people can possibly be compensated for the loss of their 'homes, farms and religious monuments' drowned by the artificial lake: 'Dams, once seen as a completely benign instrument of human control over raw nature, have come to be seen as a sort of predatory centralism, practiced by vast impersonal bureaucracies against local communities and the natural environment. When such issues come into play, we are beyond professional consultancy and in the realm of post-normal science' (Ravetz 1971: 333; Functowicz and Ravetz, in Costanza 1991: 147).

12 As an example, Funtowicz and Ravetz refer to a well-known study of Brian Wynne showing that the sheep farmers of Cumbria in England had a better understanding of the ecology of radioactive deposition (from the Chernobyl fallout) in the environment than the 'official' scientists. Their understanding is based on their 'knowledge by experience' related to drainage characteristics of specific kinds of soil and to the way these characteristics depend on the constitution of the soil and on the way of and degree to which the soil is affected by the wind pattern in the region (Wynne 1992).

References

Asveld L., Roeser S. (eds.) (2008) *The Ethics of Technological Risk*. London and Sterling, VA: Routledge.

Barnes B., Bloor D. (1982) 'Relativism, Rationalism and the Sociology of Knowledge', in: *Rationality and Relativism*, edited by Hollis M., Lukes S. Oxford: Blackwell.

Bernstein J. H. (2015) 'Transdisciplinarity: A Review of Its Origins, Development, and Current Issues', *Journal of Research Practice*, 11(1), 1.

Bijker W. E., Parke Hughes T., Pinch T. J. (1987) *The Social Construction of Technological Systems: New Directions in the Sociology and History of Technology*. Cambridge, MA: MIT Press.

Brandt A. M. (2012) 'Inventing Conflicts of Interest: A History of Tobacco Industry Tactics', *American Journal of Public Health*, 102(1), 63–71. doi:10.2105/AJPH.2011.300292.

Carrier M., Howard D., Kourany J. (eds.) (2014) *The Challenge of the Social and the Pressure of Practice: Science and Values Revisited*. Pittsburgh: University of Pittsburgh Press.

Costanza R. (1991) *Ecological Economics: The Science and Management of Sustainability*. New York, NY: Columbia University Press.

Costanza R., Cornwell L. (1992) 'The 4P Approach to Dealing With Scientific Uncertainty', *Environment: Science and Policy for Sustainable Development*, 34(9), 12–42. doi:10.1080/00139157.1992.9930930.

Cressey D. (2015) 'Widely Used Herbicide Linked to Cancer', *Scientific American*. Available at www.scientificamerican.com/article/widely-used-herbicide-linked-to-cancer/.

Dreger S., Pfinder M., Christianson L., Lhachimi S. K., Zeeb H. (2015, September) 'The Effects of Iodine Blocking Following Nuclear Accidents on Thyroid Cancer, Hypothyroidism, and Benign Thyroid Nodules: Design of a Systematic Review', *Systematic Reviews*, 4. doi:10.1186/s13643-015-0106-3.

European Commission (n.d.) 'Alcohol Policy', *Public Health*. Available at https://ec.europa.eu/health/alcohol/policy_en. Date Accessed: 1 April 2017.

European Food Safety Authority (EFSA) (2015) 'Conclusion on the Peer Review of the Pesticide Risk Assessment of the Active Substance Glyphosate', *EFSA Journal*, 13(11). doi:10.2903/j.efsa.2015.4302.

Funtowicz S., Ravetz J. (2003) 'Post-Normal Science', in: *Online Encyclopedia of Ecological Economics*, edited by International Society for Ecological Economics. Available at https://scholar.google.com/citations?user=GlE0bhkAAAAJ&hl=en.

Garnett K., Parsons D. J. (2017) 'Multi-Case Review of the Application of the Precautionary Principle in European Union Law and Case Law', *Risk Analysis*, 37(3), 502–16. doi:10.1111/risa.12633.

Gibbons M. (1994) *The New Production of Knowledge: The Dynamics of Science and Research in Contemporary Societies*. Los Angeles, CA: Sage Publication.

Guyton K. Z., Loomis D., Grosse Y., Ghissassi F. E., Benbrahim-Tallaa L., Guha N., Scoccianti C., Mattock H., Straif K. (2015) 'Carcinogenicity of Tetrachlorvinphos, Parathion, Malathion, Diazinon, and Glyphosate', *The Lancet Oncology*, 16(5), 490–1. doi:10.1016/S1470-2045(15)70134-8.

Hacking I. (2000) *The Social Construction of What?* Cambridge, MA: Harvard University Press.

IAEA (2015) *The Fukushima Daiichi Accident*. Vienna: International Atomic Energy Agency. Available at www-pub.iaea.org/books/IAEABooks/10962/The-Fukushima-Daiichi-Accident.

International Council for Science (2017) 'A Guide to SDG Interactions: From Science to Implementation', *International Council for Science – ICSU 2017*. Available at www.icsu.org/publications/a-guide-to-sdg-interactions-from-science-to-implementation.

Jasanoff S. (ed.) (2004) *States of Knowledge: The Co-Production of Science and the Social Order*. London: Routledge.

Kernberg American Psychiatric Association (2013) *Diagnostic and Statistical Manual of Mental Disorders Dsm*. Washington, DC: American Psychiatric Association.

Kitcher P. (2011) *Science in a Democratic Society*. Amherst, NY: Prometheus Books.

Kitcher P. (2014) *The Ethical Project*. Cambridge, MA: Harvard University Press.

Kuhn T. S. (1977) 'Objectivity, Value Judgment, and Theory Choice', in: *The Essential Tension*, 320–39. Chicago, IL: University of Chicago Press.

Kukla A. (2000) *Social Constructivism and the Philosophy of Science*. London and New York: Psychology Press.

Langenhove L. van (2007) *Innovating the Social Sciences: Towards More Useable Knowledge for Society*. Vienna: Passagen Verlag.

Longino H. E. (1990) *Science as Social Knowledge: Values and Objectivity in Scientific Inquiry*. Princeton, NJ: Princeton University Press.

Longino H. E. (2001) *The Fate of Knowledge*. Princeton, NJ: Princeton University Press.

Meskens G. (2016) 'Ethics of Radiological Risk Governance: Justice of Justification as a Central Concern', *Annals of the ICRP*, 45(1 Suppl), 322–44. doi:10.1177/0146645316639837.

Meskens G. (2017) 'Better Living (in a Complex World): An Ethics of Care for Our Modern Co-Existence', in: *Ethics of Environmental Health*, 115–36. Routledge Studies in Environment and Health. London and New York: Routledge.

Neslen A. (2016) 'Glyphosate Unlikely to Pose Risk to Humans, UN/WHO Study Says', *The Guardian*, May 16. Available at www.theguardian.com/environment/2016/may/16/glyphosate-unlikely-to-pose-risk-to-humans-unwho-study-says.

Nowotny H., Scott P. B., Gibbons M. T. (2001) *Re-Thinking Science: Knowledge and the Public in an Age of Uncertainty*. London: Polity.

Quine W. V., Ullian J. S. (1978) *The Web of Belief*. New York, NY: McGraw-Hill Education.

Ravetz J. (1971) *Scientific Knowledge and Its Social Problems*. New Brunswick, NJ: Routledge.

Reiss J., Sprenger J. (2017) 'Scientific Objectivity', in: *The Stanford Encyclopedia of Philosophy*, edited by Zalta E. N., Metaphysics Research Lab. Stanford University. Available at https://plato.stanford.edu/archives/spr2017/entries/scientific-objectivity/.

Renn O. (2008) *Risk Governance: Coping With Uncertainty in a Complex World*. London: Earthscan.

Saltelli A., Funtowicz S. (2017, August) 'What Is Science's Crisis Really About?', *Futures, Post-Normal Science in Practice*, 91, 5–11. doi:10.1016/j.futures.2017.05.010.

Schmitt F. F. (1994) *Socializing Epistemology: The Social Dimensions of Knowledge*. Lanham, MD; London: Rowman & Littlefield.

Takamura N., Orita M., Saenko V., Yamashita S., Nagataki S., Demidchik Y. (2016) 'Radiation and Risk of Thyroid Cancer: Fukushima and Chernobyl', *The Lancet Diabetes & Endocrinology*, 4(8), 647. doi:10.1016/S2213-8587(16)30112-7.

Tsuda T., Tokinobu A., Yamamoto E., Suzuki E. (2016) 'Thyroid Cancer Detection by Ultrasound Among Residents Ages 18 Years and Younger in Fukushima, Japan: 2011 to 2014', *Epidemiology*, 27(3), 316. doi:10.1097/EDE.0000000000000385.

US Gov MedlinePlus Medical Encyclopedia (n.d.) *Responsible Drinking*. Available at https://medlineplus.gov/ency/patientinstructions/000527.htm. Date Accessed: 1 April 2017.

Vaccarella S., Franceschi S., Bray F., Wild C. P., Plummer M., Dal Maso L. (2016) 'Worldwide Thyroid-Cancer Epidemic? The Increasing Impact of Overdiagnosis', *New England Journal of Medicine*, 375(7), 614–17. doi:10.1056/NEJMp1604412.

Wakeford R., Auvinen A., Nick Gent R., Jacob P., Kesminiene A., Laurier D., Schüz J., Shore R., Walsh L., Zhang W. (2016) 'Re: Thyroid Cancer Among Young People in Fukushima', *Epidemiology*, 27(3), e20. doi:10.1097/EDE.0000000000000466.

Wiener J. B., Rogers M. D. (2002) 'Comparing Precaution in the United States and Europe', *Journal of Risk Research*, 5(4), 317–49.

Williams D. (2015a) 'Do the Thyroid Cancer Findings After Fukushima Represent a Radiation Related Increase or the Normal Incidence Uncovered by Screening?', *Presentation Delivered During an Internal Workshop in November 2015 on Thyroid Cancer in Fukushima*.

Williams D. (2015b) 'Thyroid Growth and Cancer', *European Thyroid Journal*, 4(3), 164–73. doi:10.1159/000437263.

Williams G. M., Aardema M., Acquavella J., Sir Colin Berry, Brusick D., Burns M. M., Viana de Camargo J. L. et al. (2016) 'A Review of the Carcinogenic Potential of

Glyphosate by Four Independent Expert Panels and Comparison to the IARC Assessment', *Critical Reviews in Toxicology*, 46(Suppl 1), 3–20. doi:10.1080/10408444.2016.1214677.

World Health Organisation (2010) *Global Strategy to Reduce the Harmful Use of Alcohol*. Available at www.who.int/substance_abuse/publications/global_strategy_reduce_harmful_use_alcohol/en/.

World Health Organisation (2011) *Use of Potassium Iodide for Thyroid Protection During Nuclear or Radiological Emergencies*. Available at www.who.int/ionizing_radiation/pub_meet/tech_briefings/potassium_iodide/en/.

World Health Organisation (2014a) *Electromagnetic Fields and Public Health: Mobile Phones*. Available at www.who.int/mediacentre/factsheets/fs193/en/.

World Health Organization (2014b) *Global Status Report on Alcohol and Health*. World Health Organization. Available at http://www.who.int/topics/alcohol_drinking/en

Wynne B. (1992) 'Misunderstood Misunderstanding: Social Identities and Public Uptake of Science', *Public Understanding of Science*, 1(3), 281–304. doi:10.1088/0963-6625/1/3/004.

Yamashita S., Suzuki S., Suzuki S., Shimura H., Saenko V. (2018) 'Lessons From Fukushima: Latest Findings of Thyroid Cancer After the Fukushima Nuclear Power Plant Accident', *Thyroid*, 28(1), 11–22. doi:10.1089/thy.2017.0283.

Part III

The role of vested interests in environmental health research

7 Science, policy, and the transparency of values in environmental health research

David B. Resnik

1 Introduction

Environmental health research often has implications for policy decisions that impact moral, political, social, and economic values and interests.[1] For example, research sponsored by a pesticide manufacturer on the safety of one of its products may lead to regulatory decisions permitting the sale and use of the product under certain conditions, which may impact that company's profits, public health, and the environment. Government-sponsored research on the effects of ozone on respiratory function may support a decision to lower ambient air quality standards for ozone, which may impact economic development and public health. Research on global climate change may lead to laws and treaties that limit carbon emissions and impact the economy, public health, and the environment (Resnik 2012).

Because environmental research can impact values, members of the public, scientists, and policymakers may be concerned about the potential for bias. For example, scientists working for a chemical company may make decisions related to experimental design or data analysis or interpretation which tend to produce outcomes favorable to the company's interests in marketing the chemical. Conversely, scientists working for an environmental group may make research decisions producing outcomes that could prevent the company from marketing the chemical. Both sides in a debate about the safety of the chemical may accuse the other of biasing science to promote values (Elliott 2011; Elliott and Resnik 2014).

In this chapter, I discuss how values may impact environmental health research, and argue that transparency can play a crucial role in addressing biases in environmental health research. Transparency involves honestly and openly disclosing one's methods, materials, and data as well as financial, political, and other values or interests that may impact one's research.

2 Science and values

To understand the relationship between science and values, it is important to distinguish between values related to the process of developing scientific knowledge, i.e., epistemic values, and extra-scientific values, i.e., social, political, moral, economic, or personal values (Longino 1990; Elliott 2011). Most philosophers and scientists acknowledge that epistemic values, such as honesty, testability, simplicity, rigor, generality, originality, and explanatory power are important in scientific judgment and decision-making (Resnik and Elliott 2016). For example, if two different hypotheses both fit the data equally well, scientists could choose to accept the simpler of the two (Kuhn 1977; Giere and Bickle 2005). A principle of simplicity (or parsimony) can be justified in scientific judgment and decision-making because simpler hypotheses, theories, or models are easier to understand and test than more complex ones (Giere and Bickle 2005). Accordingly, when I examine the relationship between science and values, I have extra-scientific values in mind.

There are two basic questions concerning the relationship between science and extra-scientific values. The first is descriptive: "Do values impact scientific judgments and decisions?" The second is prescriptive: "Should values impact scientific judgments and decisions?" These are distinct questions because one might acknowledge that values often affect scientific judgments and decisions but maintain that scientists ought to take steps to minimize the impact of values on their work (Resnik 2007, 2009).

Logical empiricism is the philosophical paradigm most closely associated with the view that values do not impact scientific judgments and decisions. Philosophers and scientists who held this position viewed science as an abstract thought process that uses deductive and inductive reasoning to draw inferences from statements concerning observations, experiments, or tests, i.e., the data (Ayer 1952; Popper 1959; Nagel 1961; Hempel 1965). The logical empiricists held that human knowledge should stem from empirical evidence or from logical or mathematical relationships, and they sought to rid science of statements that could not be supported in this manner, i.e., metaphysics (Kitcher 1993). They distinguished between science and non-science (or pseudo-science) and articulated formal methods for scientific testing, confirmation, and explanation.

During the 1960s and 1970s, philosophers, historians, sociologists, and other scholars developed a variety of objections to logical empiricism's philosophy of science. While I do not have sufficient space to review these objections here (see Kitcher (1993, 2001) and Haack (2003) for further discussion), I can make the general observation that most of the problems with logical empiricism's philosophy of science stem from its failure to account for the practical realities of inquiry, such as the social, psychological, political, economic, and moral aspects of science (Kuhn 1970, 1977; Kitcher 1993, 2001; Resnik 1996; Haack 2003; Douglas 2009; Elliott 2011). Science is a human activity, not a logical or mathematical system.

As a human activity, science reflects the values, interests, biases, and beliefs of those who engage in it. Values can impact scientific judgments and decisions at the following stages of inquiry (Resnik 1996, 1998, 2007; Douglas 2009; Elliott 2011, 2017):

- **Selecting problems or topics**. Since most scientists require funding for their work, the problems/topics they select often reflect their sponsors' values

(Elliott 2011). For example, a chemical company may decide to fund a research project that can help it obtain regulatory approval for one of its products. A company may also defund a study that is not generating results that will benefit it financially. A government health research agency may set its funding priorities based on the public's values, e.g., U.S. funding agencies may allocate more money to breast cancer research than malaria research because more U.S. citizens care about treating breast cancer than malaria.

- **Designing research**. Values can influence the design of a study. Researchers usually gather data on outcomes they are interested in investigating. A toxicologist working for a chemical company may want to know whether a chemical increases the risk of certain adverse outcomes, such as liver toxicity or nausea. An epidemiologist funded by a government health research agency may want to know whether a disease is associated with gender, race, ethnicity, education, or income. Values play a fundamental role in the design of studies involving humans or animals, since it would be considered unethical to cause unnecessary harm to either (Shamoo and Resnik 2015). For example, if there is already an effective treatment for a serious illness, a researcher may conduct a clinical trial that compares an experimental treatment to an effective treatment (instead of a placebo) to ensure that patients receive some form of therapy. Researchers may also place limits on the design of animal experiments to minimize pain or suffering. Some researchers may bias a study design to obtain a specified result. Although this is not considered ethical, it happens (Resnik 2007). For example, a toxicologist working for a chemical company may under-power[2] a study so that it is not likely to yield statistically significant results related to toxic effects of a chemical manufactured by the company.
- **Collecting and recording data**. Values can influence how data are collected or recorded. A scientist who faces pressure to obtain results to advance his or her career might fabricate or falsify data. Again, this is not considered ethical, but it happens (Shamoo and Resnik 2015). In research on humans, researchers may remove information from data which could personally identify the participants to protect their confidentiality.
- **Analyzing data**. Values can influence data analysis because there is often more than one way to analyze the data, and different approaches may yield different results (Elliott 2017). For example, in a clinical trial of an experimental drug, researchers working for a pharmaceutical company may decide to use an on-study analysis plan, rather than an intent-to-treat plan. In an on-study analysis, researchers analyze the data only from participants who have complied with the protocol and have not been withdrawn from the study. In an intent-to-treat analysis, researchers analyze data from all participants who have enrolled in the study. While the on-study analysis may provide more accurate information about effectiveness, the intent-to-treat analysis provides better information on safety and risk because it includes data on people who have been removed from the study to protect them from harm (Resnik and Elliott 2016).

- **Interpreting data**. When researchers interpret their data, they draw inferences related to the scientific and social significance of their results. Values often influence data interpretation because the inferences that researchers make often depend on background assumptions, which often reflect value commitments (Elliott 2011, 2017). For example, an investigator conducting a clinical trial for a pharmaceutical company may conclude that the data show that the company's new drug is superior to drugs which are already on the market, even though the company's drug is more expensive than competitors. Other medical researchers may disagree with this interpretation, however, because they think the cost is an important factor to consider when evaluating a drug. Interpreting the outcome of this study would depend on how one defines "superior treatment," which is a value judgment. In the environmental health arena, scientists working for industry and researchers working for government agencies may disagree on how to interpret data related to the acceptability of the risks of a chemical (Elliott and Resnik 2014). Their disagreement may depend, in large part, on how one defines "acceptable risk," which is also a value judgment.
- **Disseminating data, results, and methods**. Values can influence decisions related to publishing and sharing data, results, and methods. Scientists conducting research for a chemical company may decide not to publish data showing that a chemical increases cancer risk. Virologists conducting experiments on genetic modifications of a deadly virus may decide not to publish their research because terrorists could use it to make a bioweapon (Resnik and Elliott 2016). Clinical investigators studying adverse effects related to drug interactions may decide to publish their work before submitting it to a peer-reviewed journal to protect consumers from harm. Chemists working on a polymer coating with potential applications in manufacturing may decide not to publish or share data until they receive a patent on the product (Resnik 2007).
- **Accepting hypotheses and theories**. Finally, values can influence decisions concerning hypothesis and theory acceptance. One of logical empiricism's chief critics, Richard Rudner, argued that scientists often must make value judgments when they establish the level of evidence needed to reject a hypothesis or theory, because they must consider the consequences of making a mistake (Rudner 1953). Rudner argued that scientists may require a higher level of evidence to accept a hypothesis with important implications for human health or safety than to accept one without such implications, because the consequences of making a mistake are more serious when public health or safety is at stake. For example, scientists may require a higher level of evidence to accept the hypothesis "drug X is safe" than to accept the hypothesis that "drug X has a molecular weight of 800 Daltons." It is also important to note that history includes numerous examples of hypotheses and theories that were rejected or accepted for social or political reasons. For example, the Soviet Union prohibited scientists from teaching or conducting research on Mendelian genetics, because the theory conflicted with

the Communist Party's ideology. Thousands of scientists were executed or imprisoned for teaching or studying Mendelian genetics. The official theory of genetics, Lysenkoism (named after Trofim Lysenko), served the Party's political objectives because it held that hereditary factors play a minor role in shaping human behavior, which supported the Party's claim that selfishness would not undermine the communist state (Resnik 2009). In the seventeenth century, Galileo Galilea was placed under house arrest and forced to recant his views concerning astronomy, because his heliocentric theory of the planetary motion conflicted with the Catholic Church's official doctrine concerning man's place at the center of the universe (Resnik 2009).

Although many of the arguments concerning the impact of values on science draw upon historical cases and sociological and philosophical theories, an increasing number of empirical studies have demonstrated statistical associations between financial interests and sources of funding and research outcomes. For example, Friedberg et al. (1999) found that 95% of articles with industry funding reported positive results for cancer treatments as opposed to 62% without such funding. Ridker and Torres (2006) found that 65% of articles with industry funding reported favorable results for new cardiovascular drugs as opposed to 39.5% without industry funding. Friedman and Richter (2004) found that articles published in top medical journals which disclosed a financial conflict of interest (COI) were more than twice as likely to report positive results concerning a treatment being investigated than articles that did not disclose a financial COI. Friedman and Friedman (2016) found that studies reporting a financial COI were more than four times as likely to report negative results concerning the health risks of a commercial product than studies without such disclosures. Sismondo (2008) conducted a systematic review of studies examining the relationship between sources of funding and research outcomes in pharmaceutical research and found a strong statistical association between industry funding and outcomes favorable to industry. Bes-Rastrollo et al. (2013) conducted a systematic review of studies on the relationship between consumption of sugar-sweetened beverages and weight gain or obesity. They found that studies with industry funding were less likely to report an association between consumption of sugar-sweetened beverages and weight gain or obesity than those without industry funding.

What are plausible explanations of relationship between sources of funding and financial interests and research outcomes? If we consider the different ways that values can impact scientific decision-making (discussed earlier), we can see that several different hypotheses can help to explain the effects of funding and financial interests (Krimsky 2003; Resnik 2007; Lexchin 2012). First, some of these effects probably stem from funding decisions made by companies, since companies may make these decisions with an eye toward promoting their financial interests. Second, some of these effects may be related to publication decisions, because companies may decide to publish research they regard as favorable to their interests and not publish research viewed as unfavorable. Third, in some cases investigators with industry funding or financial COIs may deliberately bias their data collection, research design, or data analysis to produce desired results (Krimsky 2003; Resnik 2007; Lexchin 2012).

Fourth, in many cases values may subconsciously influence judgment and decision-making (Resnik 2007; Resnik and Elliott 2013; de Winter 2016). Studies have shown that even small gifts can influence physicians' prescribing practices (Katz, Caplan, and Merz 2003). Physicians often claim they can accept a gift from a drug company without allowing it to affect their clinical practice, but the evidence suggests they are unaware of how the gift has influenced their judgment and decision-making (Katz, Caplan, and Merz 2003). Psychological research on the influence of subconscious biases on judgments and decisions concerning risk-taking, visual perception, and social interactions (Kahneman 2011; Greene 2013) supports the view that value influences in science often operate subconsciously. For example, a scientist may decide to include (or not include) a variable related to a toxicology study without realizing that his or her decision resulted from a value judgment concerning the importance of that variable. A scientist may choose a data analysis plan with little awareness of how values have impacted his or her thought process. Because values often operate subconsciously, it is important for scientists to try to become aware of how values can impact their own judgment and decision-making and to disclose sources of funding and financial and other interests. I will take up this point again when I discuss the value of transparency.

3 Value-neutrality

Now that we have reviewed some of the evidence and arguments showing that values often influence scientific judgment and decision-making, the next question to address is whether they should have this effect. There are three different ways of answering this prescriptive question, which I will refer to as value-neutrality, value-partiality, and limited value-neutrality.

The value-neutrality view holds that science ought to be neutral with respect to extra-scientific values (Douglas 2009; Pielke 2007). Scientists should follow methods, rules, and procedures that control for bias and promote objectivity.[3] A study of an industrial chemical, for example, should not promote the values of industry or the values of public health advocates: it should be neutral with respect to these opposing values. The main argument for the value-neutrality view is that we need scientists to provide facts and expert opinions to inform policy debates (Pielke 2007; Resnik 2009). Science functions as a neutral arbiter when we are considering public policies. If we did not have some agreed upon facts and expert opinions to serve as a basis for public policy, it would be even more difficult to resolve these debates, given the disagreements we are likely to have about how to prioritize competing values. For example, when citizens, political leaders, and regulators are attempting to decide whether to restrict the use of a pesticide in agriculture, it is important for them to have facts at their disposal concerning the role of the pesticide in controlling pests, and the risks that it poses to human health and the environment (Resnik 2012). Expert opinions concerning the likely consequences of different policy options for human health, the environment, agriculture, and the economy can also help decision-makers choose the best course of action. Without some agreed upon facts and expert opinions concerning the pesticide, the policy debate would boil down to an intractable conflict between competing values, such as public health vs. industry and economy, food production vs. environmental protection, etc. Some of our recent environmental policy debates, such as the controversy concerning global climate change, are difficult to resolve not only because people disagree about how to prioritize competing values but also because they disagree about the scientific facts (Pielke 2007; Resnik 2012).

There are some pertinent objections to the value-neutrality view, however. One of them is that it is not humanly possible for scientists to be completely value-neutral, especially since values often have subconscious influences on judgment and decision-making (Elliott and Resnik 2014). The best course of action is for scientists to disclose their value commitments and discuss how these assumptions may be influencing their judgments and decision-making concerning such issues as research design, data analysis, and data interpretation (Elliott and Resnik 2014). It is better to be transparent about one's values rather than to hide them or disingenuously claim that they have no impact on one's thought processes.

The second objection is that scientists should not be value-neutral because some values should influence science (Kitcher 2001; Elliott 2011). For example, one might argue that scientists should explicitly adopt certain values, such as public health and environmental protection, and allow them to influence decisions related to experimental design, data analysis, data interpretation, and other aspects of research. Science ought not to be value-neutral, one might argue, because the purpose of conducting research is not only to acquire knowledge but also to improve the human condition. Science has epistemic and practical goals (Resnik 1998; Kitcher 2001; Elliott and McKaughan 2014). An ancillary argument for this second objection appeals to Rudner's (1953) insight (discussed previously) that scientists must consider the consequences of making a mistake when establishing the level of evidence needed to accept a hypothesis or theory. The assessment of these consequences depends on the values that one has in mind. For example, a public health advocate would want to avoid a mistake that could threaten public health, whereas an agent for industry would want to avoid a mistake that could harm industry interests (Elliott 2011).

Taken together, these two objections form the basis of the argument for value-partiality: scientists should allow values to influence their work because it is impossible to be value-neutral and because certain values (such as public health or environmental protection) should influence research. There are some pertinent objections to the value-partiality, view, however. The first is that people may disagree about the values that science should promote: a public health advocate would argue that it should promote public health, whereas an industry leader might argue that it should promote technological development and economic growth (Elliott 2011). The second is that a thoroughgoing value-partiality would distort and corrupt science. Science conducted to explicitly promote an ideological, moral, or economic agenda would completely lose its neutrality, objectivity, and reliability and no longer be science at all: it would be politics by other means (Resnik 2009; Douglas 2009). Lysenkoism (discussed earlier) is a striking example of what can happen when scientists and political leaders abandon value-neutrality as a goal.

Objections to the value-partiality view lead to a compromise position which I call limited value-neutrality. According to this view, scientists should strive to maintain value-neutrality but should sometimes allow values to affect their judgment and decision-making and they should explicitly acknowledge these influences (Elliott 2011; Elliott and Resnik 2014; Resnik and Elliott 2016). To prevent science from degrading into politics by other means, one could argue that some aspects of science should be as value-neutral as is humanly possible. Values should influence problem selection, because sponsors of scientific research should have substantial input concerning the choice of topics they are deciding to fund. Values should also influence the design of research involving human or animal subjects to protect them from harm. Values may sometimes influence publication decisions if disseminating the results of research is likely to have adverse impacts on national security or other social values.

In other areas of scientific decision-making, values influences should be minimized. One could argue that epistemic values, such as honesty, rigor, testability, and the like, should take precedence over extra-scientific questions in study design (when human or animal subjects are not involved), data collection, data analysis, and data interpretation (Resnik 2009; Douglas 2009; Elliott 2011). For example, scientists should never fabricate or falsify data to promote extra-scientific values because this would be contrary to the value of honesty. Likewise, scientists should not manipulate statistical analyses to promote extra-scientific values because this would violate their commitment to rigor. Extra-scientific values can come into play in these areas only when they do not undermine epistemic ones. For example, if two or more interpretations of the data from a study on the safety of chemical equally satisfy epistemic criteria, a scientist could choose an interpretation that best promotes public health (Elliott 2011).

The limited value-neutrality view has its own problems, however. The first is that proponents of this view have not provided enough guidance about how to apply it to concrete problems involving science and values. Proponents have sketched out their position, but they owe us more details concerning the conditions under which extra-scientific values should be allowed to influence science (Elliott and McKaughan 2014). While this problem is important, it does show that the limited value-neutrality view is fundamentally flawed. Since the view is relatively new, proponents may need more time to flesh out the details of their position.

The second problem, which is potentially more serious than the first, is that the limited value-neutrality view still does not answer the question of whose values should have a limited influence on science. This is a fundamental issue in moral and political philosophy with no clear answers. Different constituencies (e.g., public health advocates, environmentalists, industry scientists, academic scientists, and liberals, conservatives, feminists, etc.) are likely to assert that their values should influence science. While we may achieve agreement on some acceptable value influences in science, such as protections for human or animal research subjects, we may disagree about other influences. For example, a public health advocate might claim that public health values should influence data interpretation related to chemical safety, while a scientist working in industry might assert the opposite view. Given the high degree of value pluralism in most countries, perhaps the best way of responding to this problem is to encourage competing parties to voice their disagreements in the public arena and address them through democratic political processes. For example, suppose that a government regulatory agency is deciding how to regulate a chemical used in manufacturing plastics. The company that manufactures the chemical, an environmental group, and an independent government organization could all sponsor studies on the safety of a chemical and offer their interpretations of the data. The regulatory agency, as well as concerned citizens, scientists, and political leaders, could then examine the data and interpretations and form their own assessments of the chemical's safety and the acceptability of the risks it poses to human health and the environment. Transparency concerning values would seem to play a key role in assessment of the science conducted by these different groups. For example, it would be important for the regulatory agency (and citizens and others) to know who sponsored a study of the chemical and whether there are any financial conflicting interests.

4 Value transparency

As noted earlier, transparency plays an important role in the limited value-neutrality approach to the relationship between science and values. In this section, I define transparency, explain why it is important in science, and discuss some of its shortcomings.

Transparency in science involves full (i.e., honest, open, and complete) disclosure of methods, materials, data, assumptions, ethics approvals, and other informational items that can impact the outcome of research (Shamoo and Resnik 2015). Since values can affect research outcomes, disclosure should also include institutional affiliations; sources of funding; financial interests, such as stock, intellectual property, or consulting or speaking arrangements with corporate sponsors; as well as non-financial interests that could impact research, such as relationships with organizations with political or social agendas (Elliott and Resnik 2014).[4] Disclosure may occur in the body of a manuscript submitted for publication, appendices, or supporting documents. Most scientific journals require authors to disclose sources of funding and conflicting financial and non-financial interests, and many also require reviewers and editors to disclose conflicting interests (Resnik, Konecny, and Kissling 2017). Transparency applies not only to submitting articles for publication, but also to other aspects of research, such as submitting research proposals to funding agencies, reviewing proposals for agencies, serving on a committee that oversees research with human beings or animals, and providing expert testimony (Shamoo and Resnik 2015). Most academic institutions have policies that require a faculty to disclose their financial conflicts of interest (Shamoo and Resnik 2015).

Transparency is important in scientific research for several reasons. First, transparency provides editors, reviewers, and scientists with information needed to reproduce the research (Resnik and Shamoo 2017). It can be nearly impossible to reproduce the results of a study if one does not have access to information concerning its design and methods. Reproducibility is one of the hallmarks of good (i.e., objective, reliable) science (Resnik and Shamoo 2017). Lack of transparency has been one of the factors behind some of the recent problems with reproducibility in science (Resnik and Shamoo 2017).

Second, transparency provides editors, reviewers, scientists, and other concerned parties with information relevant to evaluating the rigor, reproducibility, integrity, credibility, and trustworthiness of research (Resnik and Elliott 2013). A scientist who learns that the manufacturer of a chemical has sponsored a study on its safety may doubt the objectivity or credibility of the results, given this potential source of bias. The scientist need not assume that the researchers have deliberately fabricated, distorted, or manipulated the data, design, or analyses, since biases may subconsciously influence scientific judgment and decision-making (Resnik and Elliott 2013). A scientist who learns about a potential bias related to a funding source (or other relevant value related to the research) may decide to subject the study to more scrutiny than he or she would otherwise.

Third, transparency helps to promote the trustworthiness of the research by reassuring scientists and the public that information pertinent to a study is out in the open (Resnik 2007; Shamoo and Resnik 2015). Transparency also helps prevent the loss of trust that can occur when a researcher's financial or other interests are uncovered after a study has been published. When this occurs, scientists and members of the public may feel that the researcher has tried to hide some important information that could affect their evaluation of the study and they may become suspicious of the research. Trust plays an essential role in collaboration, publication, peer review, and other aspects of research in which scientists work together toward common goals, because scientists must trust that colleagues they interact with will behave professionally and ethically. Trust is also important for fostering the public's support of research, since people are less likely to allocate government funds toward activities that they view as untrustworthy. People are also less likely to participate in research studies if they do not trust the investigators or their institutions or sponsors (Shamoo and Resnik 2015). Trust plays a very important role in policy-relevant science, since political leaders and the public may reasonably expect that information used to make policy decisions is reliable and accurate.

Although transparency is widely recognized as an important principle for promoting the integrity, objectivity, credibility, and trustworthiness of research, some have argued that it has a limited ability to deal with the negative impacts of values on science. Elliott (2008) argues that transparency is often ineffective because (1) people often do not read disclosure statements; (2) some researchers may believe that disclosure gives them a "moral license" to behave unethically (see also Loewenstein,

Cain, and Sah 2011); and (3) disclosure does not address the underlying source of potential bias (see also Krimsky 2003; Resnik 2007). It is also worth noting that most scientific journals do not have policies related to enforcing their COI and funding disclosure policies (Resnik, Konecny, and Kissling 2017). Thus, an unscrupulous researcher could easily evade a journal's disclosure rules without fear of reprisal.

While transparency is no panacea, most would agree that it plays an essential role in managing the impacts of values on science, since one cannot address a potential problem that remains hidden. Moreover, there are steps that journal editors, scientists, and others can take to increase the effectiveness of transparency. First, journals can adopt policies for enforcing their disclosure policies. If editors learn that an author has an undisclosed source of funding or conflict of interest after his or her article is published, they could retract or correct the article or impose a penalty on the author (Resnik, Konecny, and Kissling 2017). Funding agencies and academic institutions could also take steps to enforce their disclosure policies.

Second, to discourage "moral licensing," journals should clearly describe and effectively enforce their policies related to ethics and integrity, including policies pertaining to misconduct, authorship, and research involving human or animal subjects.

Third, in some cases scientists should discuss how their values impact research design, data analysis, or data interpretation. For example, a toxicologist who conducts a systematic review of published data related to the risks of an industrial chemical and concludes that it is safe should discuss value assumptions relevant to making this inference, such as the definitions of "risk," "safety," and "acceptable risk" used in his or her analysis (Elliott and Resnik 2014). A pharmaceutical researcher that uses the on-study approach to data analysis should provide a justification for employing this method that refers to value assumption, e.g., "We used the on-study approach to better understand the drug's efficacy." Discussing possible relationships between one's values and one's research results can help reviewers, scientists, and other concerned parties to understand the reasoning process involved in the production of one's data, results, or interpretations (Elliott and Resnik 2014).

In some situations, however, disclosure may not be sufficient to control biases related to problematic relationships or interests. In these cases, it may be best to prevent conflicts from occurring (Shamoo and Resnik 2015). For example, most U.S. research funding agencies prohibit scientists from reviewing proposals submitted by colleagues working at the same institution, current collaborators, or former advisors or students (within five years) (Shamoo and Resnik 2015). Committees that oversee research with human or animal subjects prohibit members from reviewing studies with which they are associated (Shamoo and Resnik 2015). Some journals will not publish editorials written by authors with financial conflicts of interest or research funded by tobacco companies (Resnik, Konecny, and Kissling 2017). Many universities try to minimize institutional conflicts of interest by segregating financial operations (such as management of grants, contracts, intellectual property, and investments) from non-financial operations (such as review of research involving humans or animals or development of the curriculum).

5 Conclusion

Transparency helps to promote the integrity, reproducibility, objectivity, and trustworthiness of environment health research by providing scientists and members of the public with information concerning materials, methods, data, and analyses, as well as sources of funding, financial interests, and other values that may influence the scientific judgment and decision-making of the researcher. Transparency is especially important in research with implications for public policy, because opposing sides related to controversial issues may be concerned about the potential for bias. Although transparency does not prevent bias, it helps to mitigate it by enabling reviewers, investigators, policymakers, and concerned citizens to understand the values and interests that may impact scientific data, results, and interpretations. Additional research on the impact of values on scientific research and the effectiveness of disclosure statements may help investigators and the public to understand how to promote transparency in science.

Acknowledgments

This research was supported, in part, by the Intramural Program of the National Institute of Environmental Health Sciences (NIEHS), National Institutes of Health (NIH). It does not represent the views of the NIEHS, NIH, or the U.S. government.

Notes

1 In this chapter, I use the term "value" to describe something regarded by a person or community as good or worthwhile, such as life, health, happiness, wealth, freedom, or virtue. I use the term "interest" as something good for a person, institution, organization, or larger group. For the sake of brevity, I use the term "values" to include "values and interests."
2 A study is under-powered if the sample size is not large enough to obtain statistically significant results.
3 Different scientific disciplines employ different methods for controlling bias. For example, double-blinding and randomization help to control bias in clinical trials.
4 Although most of the conflict of interest debate in scientific research has focused on financial interests, non-financial interests are also becoming an important concern in research. For example, citizens who help researchers collect data on the environmental impacts of the natural gas industry may have an interest in banning certain techniques used to extract gas from the ground (Resnik, Elliott, and Miller 2015). Groups opposed to genetically modified foods may sponsor studies on the health risks of these products (Resnik 2015).

References

Ayer A. J. (1952) *Language, Truth, and Logic*. 2nd ed. New York, NY: Dover.
Bes-Rastrollo M., Schulze M. B., Ruiz-Canela M., Martinez-Gonzalez M. A. (2013) 'Financial Conflicts of Interest and Reporting Bias Regarding the Association Between Sugar-sweetened Beverages and Weight Gain: A Systematic Review of Systematic Reviews', *PLoS Medicine*, 10(12), e1001578.

de Winter J. (2016) *Interests and Epistemic Integrity in Science*. Lanham, MD: Rowman & Littlefield.
Douglas H. (2009) *Science, Policy and the Value-Free Ideal*. Pittsburgh, PA: University of Pittsburgh Press.
Elliott K. C. (2008) 'Scientific Judgment and the Limits of Conflict-of-interest Policies', *Accountability in Research*, 15(1), 1–29.
Elliott K. C. (2011) *Is a Little Pollution Good for You? Incorporating Societal Values in Environmental Research*. New York, NY: Oxford University Press.
Elliott K. C. (2017) *A Tapestry of Values: An Introduction to Values in Science*. New York, NY: Oxford University Press.
Elliott K. C., McKaughan D. J. (2014) 'Non-epistemic Values and the Multiple Goals of Science', *Philosophy of Science*, 81(1), 1–21.
Elliott K. C., Resnik D. B. (2014) 'Science, Policy, and the Transparency of Values', *Environmental Health Perspectives*, 122(7), 647–50.
Friedberg M., Saffran B., Stinson T. J., Nelson W., Bennett C. L. (1999) 'Evaluation of Conflict of Interest in Economic Analyses of New Drugs Used in Oncology', *Journal of the American Medical Association*, 282(15), 1453–7.
Friedman L. S., Friedman M. (2016) 'Financial Conflicts of Interest and Study Results in Environmental and Occupational Health Research', *Journal of Occupational and Environmental Medicine*, 58(3), 238–47.
Friedman L. S., Richter E. D. (2004) 'Relationship Between Conflicts of Interest and Research Results', *Journal of General Internal Medicine*, 19(1), 51–6.
Giere R., Bickle J. (2005) *Understanding Scientific Reasoning*. 5th ed. Belmont, CA: Wadsworth.
Greene J. (2013) *Moral Tribes: Emotion, Reason, and the Gap Between Us and Them*. New York, NY: Penguin Press.
Haack S. (2003) *Defending Science With Reason*. New York, NY: Prometheus Books.
Hempel C. (1965) *Aspects of Scientific Explanation and Other Essays in the Philosophy of Science*. New York, NY: Free Press.
Kahneman D. (2011) *Thinking, Fast, and Slow*. New York, NY: Farrar, Straus, and Giroux.
Katz D., Caplan A. L., Merz J. F. (2003) 'All Gifts Large and Small: Toward an Understanding of the Ethics of Pharmaceutical Industry Gift-giving', *American Journal of Bioethics*, 3(3), 39–46.
Kitcher P. (1993) *The Advancement of Science*. New York, NY: Oxford University Press.
Kitcher P. (2001) *Science, Truth, and Democracy*. New York, NY: Oxford University Press.
Krimsky S. (2003) *Science in the Private Interest: Has the Lure of Profits Corrupted Biomedical Research?* Lanham, MD: Rowman & Littlefield.
Kuhn T. S. (1970) *The Structure of Scientific Revolutions*. 2nd ed. Chicago, IL: University of Chicago Press.
Kuhn T. S. (1977) *The Essential Tension*. Chicago, IL: University of Chicago Press.
Lexchin J. (2012) 'Those Who Have the Gold Make the Evidence: How the Pharmaceutical Industry Biases the Outcomes of Clinical Trials of Medications', *Science and Engineering Ethics*, 18(2), 247–61.
Loewenstein G., Cain D. M., Sah S. (2011) 'The Limits of Transparency: Pitfalls and Potential of Disclosing Conflicts of Interest', *American Economic Review: Papers and Proceedings*, 101(3), 423–8.
Longino H. (1990) *Science and a Social Activity*. Princeton, NJ: Princeton University Press.
Nagel E. (1961) *The Structure of Science*. New York, NY: Harcourt, Brace, and World.

Pielke R. (2007) *The Honest Broker: Making Sense of Science in Policy and Politics*. Cambridge: Cambridge University Press.
Popper K. (1959) *The Logic of Scientific Discovery*. London: Hutchinson.
Resnik D. B. (1996) 'Social Epistemology and the Ethics of Research', *Studies in the History and Philosophy of Science*, 27(4), 565–86.
Resnik D. B. (1998) *The Ethics of Science*. New York, NY: Routledge.
Resnik D. B. (2007) *The Price of Truth: How Money Affects the Norms of Science*. New York, NY: Oxford University Press.
Resnik D. B. (2009) *Playing Politics With Science: Balancing Scientific Independence and Government Oversight*. New York, NY: Oxford University Press.
Resnik D. B. (2012) *Environmental Health Ethics*. Cambridge: Cambridge University Press.
Resnik D. B. (2015) 'Retracting Inconclusive Research: Lessons From the Séralini GM Maize Feeding Study', *Journal of Agricultural and Environmental Ethics*, 28(4), 621–33.
Resnik D. B., Elliott K. C. (2013) 'Taking Financial Relationships Into Account When Assessing Research', *Accountability in Research*, 20(3), 184–205.
Resnik D. B., Elliott K. C. (2016) 'The Ethical Challenges of Socially Responsible Science', *Accountability in Research*, 23(1), 31–46.
Resnik D. B., Elliott K. C., Miller A. K. (2015) 'A Framework for Addressing Ethical Issues in Citizen Science', *Environmental Science and Policy*, 54, 475–81.
Resnik D. B., Konecny B., Kissling G. E. (2017) 'Conflict of Interest and Funding Disclosure Policies of Environmental, Occupational, and Public Health Journals', *Journal of Occupational and Environmental Medicine*, 59(1), 28–33.
Resnik D. B., Shamoo A. E. (2017) 'Reproducibility and Research Integrity', *Accountability in Research*, 24(2), 116–23.
Ridker P. M., Torres J. (2006) 'Reported Outcomes in Major Cardiovascular Clinical Trials Funded by For-profit and Not-for-profit Organizations: 2000–2005', *Journal of the American Medical Association*, 295(19), 2270–4.
Rudner R. (1953) 'The Scientist Qua Scientist Makes Value Judgments', *Philosophy of Science*, 20(1), 1–6.
Shamoo A. E., Resnik D. B. (2015) *Responsible Conduct of Research*. 3rd ed. New York, NY: Oxford University Press.
Sismondo S. (2008) 'Pharmaceutical Company Funding and Its Consequences: A Qualitative Systematic Review', *Contemporary Clinical Trials*, 29(2), 109–13.

8 The role of vested interests and dominant narratives in science, risk management and risk communication

Colin L. Soskolne

1 Introduction

With the mission of science being to advance knowledge in the pursuit of truth, the professional obligation of scientists is to conduct themselves in support of this mission. The pursuit of truth then becomes the aspirational goal and special interest of anyone who considers him/herself a member of the family of scientists.

In practice, however, there are many drivers that determine a scientist's professional conduct in any of its numerous branches, specialty, and subspecialty fields; from among the most well-intentioned aspiring scientist to the well-established. Not least important among the drivers of professional conduct is the influence of dominant narratives, including the methodological paradigms of science. Without understanding these as upstream influencers, the scientific enterprise is rendered less capable of fulfilling its mission. Its ability to serve the public interest is thus undermined and diminished.

Epidemiology as an applied science

Epidemiology is the applied science of population health. The results from epidemiological research are used to inform evidence-based policy. Its utility comes from linking findings from toxicological and animal experimentation in the controlled laboratory setting with human health studies conducted in communities. The latter are studies appropriately applied in real-world settings.

Epidemiologists study the distribution and determinants of disease in populations and apply the knowledge gained to the control of health problems. The focus is on preventing harm to populations (i.e. morbidity; premature mortality, and well-being). Practically speaking, epidemiology is the science that informs rational health policy by bridging laboratory findings to the human response to toxicants and other hazardous exposures.

The analysis and interpretation of epidemiological data and reports can result in controversy. Reports based on poor science, or misleading reports from special interest groups (ideologically and/or financially driven), can foment uncertainty, confuse the public and policy-makers, and lead to delayed or damaging policies that negatively impact people (Ruff 2015; Ruff 2017) and the living systems on which they depend.

As defined in *A Dictionary of Epidemiology* (Porta 2008), epidemiologists study a health problem in a community with a view to applying the knowledge gained to control the problem. The logical upstream determinant of control *per se* lies in rational, well-formulated, evidence-based policy. While science advances through an iterative process of falsifiability and refutation (Popper 1963; Maclure 1985), this process has been corrupted by special interests that run counter to the mission of science (Michaels 2008).

The approach taken in this chapter

The goal in this chapter is to expand on the chapter entitled "Global, regional and local ecological change: ethical, aspects of public health research and practice" (Soskolne 2017), by narrowing the focus to the role of vested interests and dominant narratives in science as these pertain to risk management and risk communication. Two recent case studies are provided to achieve this goal.

Throughout the case studies, the need for ethical analysis is evident, particularly as we emphasize the need to expose those interests being served in policy choices by asking the question: "who carries the burden of risk and who derives the benefit from a policy action or, indeed, from inaction?" In other words, when we translate knowledge into action by using science to inform policy, whose interests are being served? And, whose interests are being served when no action is taken in the face of independent evidence?

In 1965, Hill provided what has become the foundation for rational approaches to using science to inform policy. Because uncertainty is inherent to all scientific knowledge, those in the applied science of epidemiology have embraced Hill's concluding remarks in which he posits:

> All scientific work is incomplete – whether it be observational or experimental. All scientific work is liable to be upset or modified by advancing knowledge. That does not confer upon us a freedom to ignore the knowledge we already have, or to postpone the action that it appears to demand at a given time (p. 300).

The need for action is required in the face of knowledge. In this chapter, I deconstruct what delays action in the face of ideological and moneyed influence.

2 Historic snippets of scientific misconduct and dishonesty

Misconduct and dishonesty in science have been known since the times of Galileo and Newton in the basic and physical sciences (Broad and Wade 1982). In their book, many examples of misconduct and dishonesty are provided, including:

- Ptolemy, who took the credit from another Greek astronomer, Hipparchus;
- Galileo, father of empiricism, whose experiments defied replication; and

- Newton who, from his lofty seat as president of the Royal Society, accused Leibniz of plagiary while doctoring supporting measurements to make his own *Principia* more persuasive.

The book argues that the conventional wisdom of science being a strictly logical process, with objectivity the essence of scientists' attitudes, errors being speedily corrected by rigorous peer scrutiny and replication, is a mythical ideal and an idealized construct.

And, since the advent of applied health sciences, like epidemiology, the opportunities for misconduct and dishonesty have grown. Today, the driver of these is more likely the financial incentives, unlike in former days when job security or glory may have been more what motivated such misconduct. Human frailty appears to be operating as much today as it was in the past. Continuing problems include inadequate safeguards and research oversight (Ruff 2015; Ruff 2017)

3 Navigating that which tempts us from the pursuit of truth

The work of epidemiologists involves navigating through all types of bias that can influence research in public health. Hence, epidemiology training must bring attention to all of the kinds of bias so that epidemiologists can better fulfil their mission as the scientists and practitioners of community health. Because it is possible to manipulate experimental and control groups in ways that introduce bias and thus fail to serve the public interest through the pursuit of truth (as expected of scientists), it is ever more recognized that ethical training and oversight are crucial.

Our ethics and values determine in large part our behaviours and the choices that we make as scientists, accepting that scientists are also humans and subject to human frailties. The four fundamental principles of bioethics, none being more important than the other, are (Beauchamp and Childress 2008):

- *Respect for autonomy* – requires respect for individual rights and freedoms
- *Beneficence* – requires doing good
- *Non-maleficence* – requires doing no harm
- *Social and distributive justice* – requires fair and equitable allocation of risks and benefits to all without discrimination.

All biomedical studies must consider, in advance of any study, the impact of the study being proposed from the vantage point of these four principles. In public health research, additional principles apply and also must be considered, including the need to:

- *Protect the most vulnerable*
- *Engage with the community*
- *Apply the Precautionary Principle*, and
- *Conduct oneself with integrity.*

Given the many competing interests involved in population and community health research, we must not be naïve about the forces at play that influence both science and policy.

Great vigilance and personal integrity are required to counter the influence of financially interested parties and corrupt/morally bankrupt governments. In particular, the seduction by moneyed interests in using academics to downplay or deny the seriousness of hazards must be recognized. These are the studies that will infiltrate the scientific literature to cast doubt and foment uncertainty (Michaels 2008). So infamous are some examples of these misdeeds that books and documentary movies are accessible that have explored and exposed them. The epidemiologist made aware of these misdeeds will be better equipped to recognize their recurrence in other contexts.

4 Some examples of bias

Biases that can be introduced into applied research, either wittingly or unwittingly, and that are counter to the public interest are:

- *Publication bias* – selected material infiltrates the literature
- *Suppression bias* – questions that upset powerful interests are suppressed
- *Repression bias* – questions that we know might upset powerful interests we refrain from asking
- *Funding bias* – only that which powerful interests want studied will be studied.

These and other biases, if allowed to go unchallenged, present the policy-maker with a conundrum. By increasing uncertainty, confusion results, and the policy-maker's ability to implement health policy is made all the more difficult. The tobacco example is perhaps the best known in that it took some 50 years with many sick people and premature deaths along the way, before policies could be introduced to more effectively control people's access and exposure to tobacco.

It has been demonstrated through freedom of information just how the industry mounted disinformation campaigns, lied, manipulated, and deceived both the public and policy-makers, and how they co-opted or appropriated scientists to lie (Oreskes and Conway 2010). The real tragedy is that, while business relentlessly pursues its goal of financial profit, scientists accept their money and then proceed to please their sponsor.

5 How manipulation operates

Equipped with the tools of epidemiology, epidemiologists can introduce bias in subtle and influential ways. Applied health scientists, studying diseases where they arise, can discover a finding that does not support the *status quo*, going contrary to the interests of a powerful stakeholder. In such instances, the epidemiologist must be prepared to face the "Four D's," which are applied with the intent of avoiding rational policy action. The scientist can be confronted with:

- *Deny* – denial that the findings could be correct
- *Delay* – in that more research will be called for
- *Divide* – in that commissioned work will result in biased findings
- *Discredit* – if the scientist persists, he/she will be discredited.

This paradigm (i.e. the "Four D's") was applied many times over in the case of each of the following substances before public policy was changed:

- Tobacco
- Nickel
- Benzene
- Lead
- Asbestos
- Climate Change

For those card-carrying epidemiologists who wittingly (and for usually large sums of money) allow themselves to cast aside their scientific values of pursuing truth in the public interest, a toolkit of techniques is available to them to skew results and produce junk science (Cranor 2011; Soskolne 2017) through applying the following techniques that usually operate in the application of the methods of the discipline:

- Under-powered studies
- Inadequate follow-up methods
- Inadequate follow-up time
- Inappropriate biomarkers of exposure
- Contaminated controls
- Unbalanced discussion
- Selective disclosure of competing interests
- Biased/selective interpretation
- Mechanistic information is ignored for inferring effects
- Exaggerated differences are made between human and toxicology studies, the insistence being on separating effects seen in animals from effects in humans
- Molecular structures predicting hazard potential are ignored
- The insistence on first demonstrating effects in local populations of exposed people, despite demonstrated effects in humans elsewhere
- The failure to make explicit the implicit value judgements that go into deciding appropriate standards of evidence for drawing policy-relevant conclusions (i.e. suppressing dominant interests and values).

These techniques are more fully explicated in Cranor (2011), and in Soskolne (2017). Let us see how some of these techniques operate in practice by examining two case studies.

Case studies vis-à-vis vested interests and dominant narratives

In Soskolne (2017), many forces are shown to be at play when epidemiologists work to inform policy in order to maintain and improve population/community health. "Ideology" was shown as one class of such drivers, and "financial conflicting interests" was shown to be another. On examining the empirical evidence around delays in policy action to protect public health from, for instance, the hazards of tobacco, lead, asbestos, and fossil fuel exploitation, both classes were shown to be foundational to the scientist's contextual narrative. Let us now see how vested interests and dominant narratives manifest in the following two case studies.

Case study #1: the Fukushima Daiichi nuclear power plant accident in 2011

In a 2016 article published by Tsuda et al., elevated thyroid cancer rates were reported among residents aged 18 years and younger in Fukushima, Japan. The scientific question was entirely appropriate if epidemiology was to be applied to help in the recovery from the 2011 accident at the Fukushima Daiichi nuclear power plant. Essentially, an elevation in thyroid cancer rates would be an expected outcome from community exposures to radiation fallout as experienced after the accident. By demonstrating the effect locally, interventions then could be justified and designed to minimize the more severe manifestations of radiation exposures.

In a cultural setting where respect for authority is valued more highly than respect for personal autonomy, Tsuda et al. (2016) have been faced with pressures to dismiss their findings. All kinds of scientific arguments have been invoked to encourage such a step. More surprising, however, coming from the International Agency for Research on Cancer (IARC) was an article by Vaccarella S. et al. (2016). Vested interests and dominant narratives exerting influence aside, the article (from this author's reading of it), misquotes Tsuda et al. (2016) on thyroid ultrasound screening among children in Fukushima, stating that a 30-fold increase was observed within a few months after the screening began; Tsuda et al. (2016) had stated that it was within 4 years.

Further, the IARC authors, in attributing Fukushima's thyroid cancer excess to over-diagnosis, also overlooked clinical details in the Fukushima cases. More importantly, childhood thyroid cancer has rarely been detected among unexposed populations, even by ultrasound screening. These authors went on to attribute an increased worldwide incidence of thyroid cancer to over-diagnosis from "new diagnostic techniques." They disregard the impact of worldwide nuclear testing. In the US alone, 86 atmospheric nuclear tests contributed to an estimated increase of 49,000 cases (95% confidence interval: 11,300–212,000). Finally, Iodine-131 exposure is a highly efficient carcinogen for thyroid cancer, leading to both cumulative and lifelong risk.

It appears that Vaccarella et al. (2016) might rather have confined their analysis to adults to avoid the pitfalls identified above. In summary, their article ignores

Tsuda et al. on the question of the over-diagnosis hypothesis, their population was not one of 0–18 year-olds but middle-aged, and the different pathophysiology of the lesions found in adults has little relevance to children. Among adults, they do acknowledge a more or less 2–3-fold increase in incidence, but prior to the accident (1988–2007). Their projected incidence rates based on modelling are at best speculative. Attempts to publish the above concerns as a letter-to-the-editor resulted in its rejection, and it was never published. What interests were at play and what was so contrary to the dominant narrative (either at IARC and/or on the editorial board of the journal) that would have resulted in the suppression of such concerns?

Case study #2: aircraft cabin contamination: fume events and aerotoxic syndrome

For decades, the airline industry has denied any connection between contaminated aircraft cabin air through so-called fume events, and the harms experienced by susceptible flight attendants, pilots, and possibly also passengers. When evidence of harm mounts, becoming irrefutable, and denial continues to dominate, the responsible role for applied health scientists is to defend those harmed and to prevent future harms. That role is one of pursuing truth and advocating for independent public interest research.

By pursuing truth, all parties could win, including those parties directly and indirectly harmed. Such action would result in improved safety and health for affected communities where problems are demonstrated; potential crises mid-flight could be averted. Other implicated parties include those dominating policy usually with a financial interest; responsible action from them would result in enhanced reputation with commensurate business advantages; it also would result in reduced economic burdens through inevitable compensatory damages. Those with responsibility for aircraft maintenance and insurance also would be spared cost overruns. Human rights and justice would prevail.

However, the airline industry, like other industries, focuses on short-term profits, and history repeats itself; lessons learned from policies ultimately introduced to prevent harm from tobacco, lead, asbestos, and other controllable polluting substances must, inevitably, be applied in the airline industry. This will prevent ongoing harms.

Narrow thinking

To understand influence and its impact, we must recognize that we all exist and operate in the framework of:

- A contextual narrative
- A dominant paradigm

With this recognized, what role could impartial science play in the public interest? Suppressing studies or designing studies such that the questions needing to be asked could not be addressed have been seen to apply. Why? Because permitting questions then obligates those privy to the answers/results to act.

Regarding engine and aircraft fluids – consisting of tricresyl phosphate (TCP), other hazardous substances, including by-products of pyrolysis – along with cases of fume events reported to date, and illness reports proximate to these events with observed long-term sequelae, the Precautionary Principle would seem warranted: Where there is a risk from a certain agent, the presence of uncertainty shall not be used as a reason for postponing cost-effective measures to prevent such exposure.

6 Deconstructing the "FOUR D's" applied to air cabin air quality

Not only is the European Aviation Safety Agency (EASA) in denial, they are also delaying action by sponsoring further research. They deny any health effects from fume events, despite the reality of sick people resulting from such events with acute illness proximate to exposure events, and with longer-term effects likely in some cases; they altogether dismiss "aerotoxic syndrome" as even possible. Their linear reductionist approach, invoking the argument of low-level OPC in cabins, appears to provide them the basis for ruling out any human health effects from fume events, and also from low-level chronic exposure to cabin air even in the absence of acute fume events.

Their bias toward finding no-effect is apparent in their project description using words such as "misguided" in ruling out alternative hypotheses in their study. One is left wondering if, with their approach, they will measure the most relevant exposures and endpoints.

Recent wisdom shared from Greenberg (2017) indicates that, under the Precautionary Principle,

> the discharge of gases and fumes into an aircraft cabin can be justified only after prior investigation finds the practice to be innocuous. The chemical cocktails to which passengers and crew are exposed will vary qualitatively and quantitatively, so that, even if a standard examination methodology has been employed, their effects need not be identical between incidents.

The obligation of the industry is to avoid supply-air contaminating cabin air. With the design of one aircraft more recently, the problem has been largely avoided. Given what is already known, while more research may be of interest to advance knowledge with greater precision in our estimates of effect, we have sufficient experience to act now to protect cabin crew, pilots, and passengers by engineering the problem out and acknowledging previous harms caused.

The German Airline Association's Trade Group (BDL), among others, was invited to participate in a 2017 seminal conference on the topic in London, England. Their own position statement claims:

> Regarding the topic of cabin air, it has repeatedly been stated in the past few years whether the health of the passengers and crews as well as the safety of the flight could be endangered by the penetration of burned oil residues into the cabin air. It is therefore important to the airlines to know whether there are actually reliable findings from scientific investigations that confirm these statements and whether there is a problem that necessitates changes in flight operations or the maintenance or manufacture of aircraft (BDL 2017).

If the BDL had seen a glaring inconsistency between its decision to not participate in the 2017 conference and with the above words, they may have aligned their actions with their words by sending a representative and some of the German aviation industry to participate in the conference. Instead, by boycotting or shunning an opportunity to have a seat at the table, the opportunity to advance science is denied. Science advances through transparent, open discussion, and access to data.

The question now is: When will cabin air quality be rationally addressed, given that it has long been subjected to the "FOUR D's"?

7 The International Joint Policy Committee of the Societies of Epidemiology (IJPC-SE)

The *International Joint Policy Committee of the Societies of Epidemiology* (IJPC-SE) works at the interface of research and policy. The IJPC-SE strives to bring clarity to the science of epidemiology, paving the way to rational evidence-based policy. It works to promote and protect public health by serving as an ethical and effective counterweight to the misuse of epidemiologic evidence.

The challenge in pursuing truth is in recognizing how evidence is generated and how junk science infiltrates the literature and confuses decision-making bodies. The IJPC-SE, with its global volunteer professional base of epidemiologists, can help in instances where science is being misused. Through its collective efforts, the IJPC-SE brings the benefit of a unified professional voice in the public interest. Other industries have been compelled to clean up their acts. With evidence in hand, the airline industry too would be compelled to relent.

The IJPC-SE is a not-for-profit consortium of 23 national and international volunteer, professional epidemiology organizations, spanning six continents, that have joined together to ensure health for all through ethical, independent, and transparent science. It works collaboratively and transparently to address health-related issues and minimize harm. It hosts forums and develops position statements and policy briefs with recommendations to protect and improve public health. Through its collective efforts, the IJPC-SE brings the benefit of a unified professional voice in the public interest.

Ultimately, rational policy will be influenced by evidence. The generation of evidence by trained scientists is expected to follow scientific and ethical principles such that valid science *will* result.

By persistently holding corporate leaders' feet to the fire on their obligation to protect worker and passenger safety and health based on valid evidence, decency, common sense, and rational policy should eventually prevail.

8 The way forward

True democracy, through a well-informed public, underscored by an improved government science, technology, and innovation strategy should:

- Offer incentives to non-profit professional organizations in support of capacity-building to expose junk science, particularly where applied science works at the nexus of policy
- Introduce disincentives (i.e. regulatory penalties) for those engaging in producing junk science

We must also recognize that academia is a multi-billion dollar industry that fails to adequately address conflicting interests. At the end of the day, ethics is key to science and to public health. Without a serious and effective system of ethical oversight, evidence and public policy are being easily corrupted by vested interests. Overwhelming evidence of this has been provided by the tobacco industry, the asbestos industry, the fossil fuel industry, the chemical industry, the fast food industry, the mining industry, the sweetened beverage industry, and the lead industry; the list is long.

9 Concluding messages

- We all lose when the trajectory on which we find ourselves is flawed and unsustainable.
- A WIN – WIN – WIN outcome is most likely when the pursuit of truth is sought with a mind open to adapting to empirical realities.
- Powerful interests relentlessly manoeuver their way onto review panels, influence boards of our professional associations, and infiltrate the literature with junk science.
- Systemic, institutionalized bias enables science to conform to the dominant paradigm.
- Expert witness tensions arise between the plaintiff and defence sides of the argument in tort actions where the rubber hits the road concerning policy decisions.
- Uncertainty is inherent to science.

- Science strives to be value-neutral or value-free, but the human instrument is not.
- We must look first to ourselves when examining the current trajectory of influence in science, because causal inference is a function of who it is that is making the inference which, in turn, is a function of how we apply our scientific methods.

Disclosure

I strive for professional service in the public interest.

I served for a few years and until 2012 as an expert witness in litigation on behalf of plaintiffs, monies from which generally went into a University-managed research account.

As a professional legacy, I bankrolled the IJPC-SE as a voluntary professional society for the years between 2011 and 2016, hoping that it might become an enduring counterbalance to ideological and moneyed influence in policies impacting health.

The IJPC-SE was one of the endorsers of the 2017 Aircraft Cabin Air Quality Conference.

I helped Dr Tsuda with editing his 2016 publication on thyroid cancer in relation to the Fukushima 2011 accident.

Postscript

The International Joint Policy Committee of the Societies of Epidemiology (IJPC-SE) is, at time of going to press, undergoing a name-change to the International Network for Epidemiology in Policy (INEP). Re-branding will take place thereafter.

References

BDL. (2017) *Progress Report. Quality of the Cabin air in Commercial Aircraft*. Available at https://gcaqe.org/wp-content/uploads/2017/11/BDL_progress-report-English-Mar2017.pdf

Beauchamp T. L., Childress J. F. (2008) *Principles of Biomedical Ethics*. Oxford: Oxford University Press.

Broad W., Wade N. (1982) *Betrayers of the Truth: Fraud and Deceit in the Halls of Science*. New York, NY: Simon & Schuster.

Cranor C. F. (2011) *Legally Poisoned: How the Law Puts Us at Risk From Toxicants*. Boston, MA: Harvard University Press.

Greenberg, M. (2017) Personal communication.

Hill A. B. (1965) 'The Environment and Disease: Association or Causation?', *Proceedings of the Royal Society of Medicine*, 58, 295–300.

Maclure M. (1985) 'Popperian Refutation in Epidemiology', *American Journal of Epidemiology*, 121, 343–50.

Michaels D. (2008) *Doubt Is Their Product: How Industry's Assault on Science Threatens Your Health*. New York, NY: Oxford University Press.

Oreskes N., Conway E. M. (2010) *Merchants of Doubt: How a Handful of Scientists Obscured the Truth on Issues From Tobacco Smoke to Global Warming*. New York, NY: Bloomsbury Press.

Popper K. (1963) *Conjectures and Refutations: The Growth of Scientific Knowledge*. London: Routledge.

Porta M. (ed.) (2008) *A Dictionary of Epidemiology*. 5th ed. New York, NY: Oxford University Press.

Ruff K. (2015) 'Commentary: Scientific Journals and Conflict of Interest Disclosure: What Progress Has Been Made?', *Environmental Health*, 14, 45. doi:10.1186/s12940-015-0035-6 (8 pages).

Ruff K. (2017) 'Serving Industry, Promoting Skepticism, Discrediting Epidemiology', Chapter 7 in: *Corporate Ties that Bind: An Examination of Corporate Manipulation and Vested Interest in Public Health*, edited by Walker M. J., 119–35; 482–5. New York, NY: Skyhorse Publishing.

Soskolne C. L. (2017) 'Global, Regional and Local Ecological Change: Ethical, Aspects of Public Health Research and Practice', Chapter 1 in: *Ethics of Environmental Health*, edited by Zölzer F., Meskens G. Routledge Studies in Environment and Health. London and New York, NY: Routledge, Taylor & Francis.

Tsuda T., Tokinobu A., Yamamoto E., Suzuki E. (2016) 'Thyroid Cancer Detection by Ultrasound Among Residents Aged 18 Years and Younger in Fukushima, Japan: 2011 to 2014', *Epidemiology*, 2016(27), 316–22.

Vaccarella S., Franceschi S., Bray F., Wild C. P., Plummer M., Dal Maso L. (2016) 'Worldwide Thyroid-cancer Epidemic? The Increasing Impact of Overdiagnosis', *The New England Journal of Medicine*, 375, 614–17.

9 Tragic failures

How the law and science fail to protect the public

Carl F. Cranor

1 Introduction

How science is utilized in the law can facilitate or frustrate public health protections from chemical creations via preventive administrative institutions.[1] The law needs scientific tools and findings in order to implement protections within legal requirements, and it matters when and how those tools are used.

The interaction between law and science is an important ethical issue and merits discussion for two reasons: (a) in the United States (U.S.) for 40 years we have followed policies that poorly protect the public from chemical creations entering commerce (the choice of *when science should be used* for public protections), and (b) there has been a temptation to demand too much scientific evidence to withdraw risky substances once they are in commerce (the choice of *how much and what kind of science* should be used for this purpose).

2 The legislative choice about when science should be used to protect the public

Laws to protect the public from exposures to toxic substances were, by and large, created on the model of other laws designed to protect the public from legal violations. For instance, in the criminal law, typically but not quite invariably, we are quite concerned that a person not be apprehended and charged with a crime until he or she has violated the law and caused harm.[2] Occasionally, movies or science fiction scenarios suggest that the criminal law could be designed differently by discerning or trying to discern those who *would* violate the law in certain circumstances and detain them before they do so. This would be something of a pre-violation test to support intervention in order to prevent criminal harm to others.

Similar approaches also guide the tort law. To be held accountable in torts, the plaintiff (the injured party) must show that a defendant violated the law by causing harm to the plaintiff in a manner that is legally compensable under the law. There are some exceptions in torts for injunctions if the threat of potential harm is sufficiently great and imminent. The closest tort law examples of such laws are nuisance laws that provided much of the inspiration for environmental and environmental health legislation (Rodgers 1994; Cranor 2017). These were post-exposure, post-violation laws that are part of the tort or personal injury law.

Common to both the criminal law and torts (and there are other examples) is that before a legal violation occurs with the possibility of sanctions for a defendant, typically someone (or perhaps an institution) must be harmed in some manner or other (depending upon the area of the law).

At some risk of using an abstract characterization that may mislead readers we might say that a significant body of U.S. law is only enforced after harm (or perhaps risks) occur. Of course, the law must have a violation provision – a law must be violated – before legal authorities can intervene in someone's life. However, laws could be written in order to make many different activities violations – intending to harm others for which there is no criminal or tort liability, planning to harm others on one's own (some statutes make this a crime), planning with others to harm someone, e.g., rob a bank (which is a conspiracy punishable by the criminal law with analogous activities subject to tort liability).

3 Environmental health law

This provides background for environmental health laws. If legislators approach protection of the public from toxic substances in the same manner as they approach protection of the public from criminal or tortious activities, they would tend to design major laws like those that have dominated the U.S. legal system since the mid-1970s. With a few major exceptions the public has been "protected" (hardly the correct word) from chemical creations that might cause harm by what are called "postmarket" laws. Let me explain.

The major law that governed the vast majority – about 80–90% – of chemical creations, the 1976 Toxic Substances Control Act (TSCA), is a postmarket law in two senses. First, chemical creations could enter commerce without any routine toxicity testing being conducted about them. Second, products remain in commerce until there is sufficiently good scientific evidence that poses an "unreasonable risk to human health or the environment" or actually is documented as causing harm. With these provisions it resembles other areas of the law; (a) there are few or no constraints for engaging in an activity, such as creating a new chemical substance and marketing it; and (b) some form of harm or risk must be shown after it occurs and before there is a legal violation and intervention.

TSCA only required the submission of a premarket "notification provision" (PMN) before a proposed new product could be commercialized. A company proposing a new chemical creation needed only to "notify" the EPA that it sought to manufacture it by submitting a document with certain minimal information about it. The information must include "all available data on chemical identity, production volume, by-products, use, environmental release, disposal practices, and human exposures" (U.S. Environmental Protection Agency, "New Chemicals Program"). Missing from this description is information about necessary toxicity data requirements and any tests conducted on the product.

Companies could voluntarily choose to test (or not to test) any new substances and be in full compliance with TSCA's PMN requirement. However, if in fact they tested their creations, they were legally obliged to report this; this is especially required if the assessment reveals that it has toxic features. However, this provision has poorly protected the public.

First, the law itself created ignorance about the chemical universe because it grandfathered 62,000 substances as safe in 1976 (Schierow 2007). Another 22,000 entered commerce subject only to PMN provisions and few companies tested their products (Schierow 2007). Moreover, although the U.S. EPA could require testing of a product, it had to have evidence that it posed some "unreasonable risk to humans or the environment" before doing so. Together these two features created a universe of about 84,000 chemical inventions about which little was known (more later).

Second, the use of PMNs *invited additional ignorance*. If a company tested a product but found no toxic effects, it was presumptively free from legal requirements. However, if tests showed the substance was toxic, the company was required to report that result to the EPA. (Also, companies do not necessarily comply with this aspect of the law [Lerner 2015a]). The agency in turn would then have some scientific data suggesting that the product "may pose an unreasonable risk to health or the environment," potentially triggering an EPA order for more test data (such data would also be subject to discovery in the tort law). Thus, voluntary testing of a product potentially invites additional legal problems.

Third, competitive incentives additionally undermine testing. If one company tests its products but another does not, then the first company's cost structure is higher than the second. Consequently, both companies have competitive incentives not to test their products. Unfortunately, this incentive structure likely motivated major chemical companies to eliminate their often quite good toxicology departments (Eastmond 2012; Melman 2012).

Considerable toxic ignorance resulted from this law: 70–75% of all chemicals lacked sufficient data to conduct adequate risk assessments. (National Research Council 1984) This was unchanged as of the early-1990s and even little changed as of 1997 (Bingham 2004; Bailar 2004).

Consequently, one major shortcoming of "old" 1976 TSCA concerns *when* scientific data is utilized to discern whether or not a product is toxic.

In contrast, under premarket laws that require a battery of tests for toxicity and then scientific review of that data at an administrative agency before the proposed product may be commercialized, science is utilized before the public is exposed. This approach much better protects the public from harm because toxicants have a good chance to be identified before the public is exposed. Premarket laws governing pharmaceuticals and pesticides had been enacted before Congress passed TSCA in 1976, but these models were not followed (Cranor 2017).

TSCA's postmarket provisions have had some obvious substantial adverse consequences for employees and members of the public. Consider, for example, the case of DuPont and its production of perfluorooctanoic acid (PFOA), also known as C8, the main ingredient in Teflon, Gore-Tex, and stain-resistant fabrics, *inter alia.*

Jeremy Darling, a DuPont employee riding his bicycle in a large warehouse, fell on its crossbar and hurt his groin. The pain did not go away and he was ultimately diagnosed with testicular cancer, known to be associated with C8 (Barry, Winquist, and Steenland 2013). His treatment was expensive, costing $75,000, which in turn forced him into bankruptcy (Lerner 2015a).

Co-worker Ken Wamsley, a lab analyst, worked with C8, and was clearly aware of fine powder in the air that felt like soap. He contracted ulcerative colitis, known to be associated with C8 exposure, and ultimately rectal cancer – a commonly associated disease (Lerner 2015a; Steenland et al. 2013).

Carla Bartlett lived near a DuPont plant, drank tap water contaminated with C8, and later developed kidney cancer. A tort law jury awarded her 1.6 million dollars for her disease, known to be associated with C8 exposure (Balibouse 2015). Other individuals were also harmed. David Freeman contracted testicular cancer from drinking water containing C8 and received $5.6 million plus punitive damages in the tort law (Rinehart 2016).

Wilbur Tennant sold a parcel of land to DuPont to be used for trash from its plant, but was instead used as an illegal toxic waste dump. C8 migrated from the dump into a nearby stream from which Tennant's cattle drank. They died from the exposures and were part of the initial motivation for a lawsuit against DuPont (Lerner 2015b).

We know of these results because all resulted from jury verdicts or tort law settlements facilitated by a scientific panel formed as a result of litigation that identified these typical adverse effects from C8. This suit authorized a scientific advisory panel to survey all those in the vicinity of the Ohio plant who had been exposed to C8 and then to conduct human epidemiological studies to determine if there were any patterns of toxic harm resulting from C8 exposures. The panel identified at least six different diseases traceable to C8, which in turn facilitated the above suits or associated settlements (Barry et al. 2013).

A class action lawsuit developed from these initial findings by people who alleged that they had been harmed by C8 exposures. This produced the tort law verdicts described earlier. Because these sentinel cases indicated that DuPont was likely to lose many cases where plaintiffs had characteristic diseases traceable to C8, the company chose to settle for $671 million to cover damages affecting 3,550 plaintiffs and their communities (Mancini 2017).

Two major considerations led to these people being injured by C8. Without required premarket toxicity testing provisions, DuPont was not required to conduct toxicity tests before manufacturing the substance. In addition, because it failed to follow reporting requirements of TSCA, this added to the problems.

Before TSCA was passed, DuPont did in fact conduct toxicity tests that revealed toxic effects on rats, dogs, and rabbits, killing some of them. Shortly after TSCA was enacted it also had evidence that it adversely affected their employees. Once TSCA was implemented, the company was required to inform the EPA of toxicity results and adverse effects on its employees. It only belatedly did so in violation of the law (Lerner 2015b). In addition, it almost certainly violated the law by dumping potentially toxic materials into the ground and rivers near its plants. This killed Mr. Tennant's cattle and contaminated the water supplies of about 80,000 people in Southern Ohio and West Virginia. A DuPont lawyer in an email to his son referred to C8 as "the material 3M sells us that we poop into the river and into drinking water along the Ohio River" (Lerner 2015b).

The shortcoming of TSCA should be clear at this point. *When* science is used to determine toxic effects is an important social/ethical decision. Premarket laws use the tools of science to try to identify toxic products before they enter commerce. This gives scientists an opportunity to review the data and decide whether or not the risks are sufficiently serious to justify preventing public exposures. Thus, they much better protect the public, and children in particular, from harm.

Postmarket laws such as TSCA are especially problematic. In general they largely call on science well after exposures, risks, and potential harms have occurred. Thus, they poorly protect the public.[3] Failure to have routine premarket toxicity testing under TSCA almost guaranteed that the toxicity of chemicals would not be identified until after they were already in commerce.

These failings are even more critical for an important subpopulation – children. During their development from fertilized eggs to embryos to fetuses to newborns to teenagers, before reaching adulthood they are particularly susceptible to toxicants. I do not develop these points in detail here because I have done so elsewhere, but some of them merit summarizing (Cranor 2011).

Children are more susceptible to toxicants because their bodies are developing and creating new tissues and organs that make these biological processes more vulnerable to disruption or damage.

They have greater exposures per body weight via umbilical cord blood and breast milk. Pregnant women can harbor up to 43+ toxicants that would be shared with developing children *in utero* (Woodruff, Zota, and Schwartz 2011; American College of Obstetricians and Gynecologists 2013). A pregnant woman's contamination is shared with developing children in utero. There is "no placental barrier per se: the vast majority of chemicals given to the pregnant animal (or woman) reach the fetus in significant concentrations soon after administration" (Schardein 2000: 5). And, confirming this effect, babies have been born contaminated with toxicants (Miller et al. 2002)). Once they are born they have higher metabolism, breathing, absorption, circulation rates, along with higher fluid and food intake rates per body weight (Miller et al. 2002). Finally, as they become mobile they play close to ground/floor, "mouth" everything in sight, ingesting more dust and anything with which it is contaminated.

Children typically have lesser defenses than adults to toxic invaders (Grandjean et al. 2008; Dietert and Piepenbrink 2006). Quite importantly, children have a longer lifespan for diseases to develop. If someone my age experiences an exposure that could trigger a cancer in 20 years, I might not be around to contract it. However, if a newborn or young child has the same exposure she has a much longer period of life for cancer to appear. Adverse effects to the brain and immune system appear irreversible; a developing child has only one chance for the organ to "get it right" (Grandjean 2013).

The upshot of this brief reference to children is that postmarket laws are completely inadequate for protecting them from toxicants.

There are several more general shortcomings of postmarket laws:

(1) If consumers and businesses have concerns about products being toxic, they cannot choose between more toxic and less toxic alternatives. There is no economic market that would allow consumers to choose between less toxic alternatives, because so little is known about the vast majority of chemical creations.

For example, after British Petroleum's Deepwater Horizon explosion and oil spill, BP sought to use a common oil dispersant to break up large oil slicks into droplets. Was it safe? Top EPA officials were aware it had some ecological and human risks. When asked about alternatives to this product and whether they were safer, they could not offer any guidance because they knew nothing about the risks of alternative dispersants (Demarini 2012).

Bisphenol A (BPA) illustrates an analogous problem. By now this is a well-known endocrine disrupter that is being discontinued because of scientific concerns and public pressure. However, companies continue to have needs that BPA fulfilled; what chemical creations should they use? Apparently, they have opted for one or two products quite similar to BPA: Bisphenol S (BPS) or Bisphenol F (BPF). Do they pose risks? For the most part the scientific assessment is still out, but both seem to have the same order of estrogenic potency as BPS or estradiol (Rochester and Bolden 2015).

(2) Toxic ignorance hampers responses to chemical emergencies or spills. When West Virginians were threatened by the spilling of 4-methylcyclohexane methanol, or MCHM, was it risky, dangerous, or safe? Scientists did not know because by entering commerce under TSCA, there was no toxicity data about it. Only now, long after people have been exposed to MCHM in their water, is a scientific body of data being developed, but not much is yet known about this product.

(3) Importantly, because few scientific data are produced simultaneously with commercialization, research likely starts from scratch to determine any toxicity after products are in commerce. Thus, once investigators suspect a substance may be toxic because of early testing, they likely have a sparse scientific from which to work. One can compare these effects with premarket testing and approval laws: substantial toxicity research has already been done and there are publicly accessible data about the product (at least to the agencies that approved it) and there may also be adverse reaction reports sent to the administrative agency, especially for pharmaceuticals. Consequently, researchers can turn to both sources to glean whatever toxicity information may be in the record. Moreover, there may be clues to toxicity that were missed during premarket review that can be understood after new tests suggest toxic effects.

Under postmarket laws even if wise, conscientious, well-motivated scientists committed to protecting the public's health begin research as soon as toxicity is suspected, having cumulative scientific studies to support improved health standards can take substantial time. Scientific studies march to their own drummers. Actually fully implementing health protections can take much longer as they are frequently frustrated by companies' intransigence against losing valuable products (more later).

One set of public health shortcomings of postmarket laws might be summarized as follows. People are not protected simultaneously with commercialization of a product either because it was grandfathered as safe, or, because a new substance entered with little or no toxicity data. Members of the public have no knowledge of its toxicity properties so they cannot protect themselves by choosing less toxic rather than more toxic products. And, once a product seems to pose adverse health effects, it can take much longer to create a cumulative scientific case to reduce risks or remove the product from commerce than likely would be the case under premarket laws.

The consequences of slow removal of products are readily apparent. At the EPA's Integrated Risk Information System risk assessments, needed risk assessment steps to protect the public's health, have been painfully slow. For example, trichloroethylene (TCE) at different levels and circumstances of exposures is known to cause cancer, birth defects, and Parkinson's disease. Yet its assessment at IRIS has been under review for more than 20 years, precluding further agency action to protect the public during that time (Government Accountability Office 2008).

Dioxin, a known carcinogen, likely transgenerational toxicant and endocrine disruptor, has been under consideration at IRIS for 17 years (Government Accountability Office 2008). Perchloroethylene, a probable carcinogen, contributor to neurological diseases, and groundwater contaminant, has been in the queue for 13 years (Government Accountability Office 2008). And, formaldehyde, a known human carcinogen, causing nasopharyngeal, sinonasal, and myeloid cancers, along with other disorders, has been under review for at least 17 years (assessments were begun, halted, then restarted) (Government Accountability Office 2008).

Sluggish activity at IRIS has consequences not only for TSCA, but also for other laws that utilize risk assessments. C8 or PFOA, the main ingredient in Teflon, is toxic, but there are no drinking water or clean air standards for it under the Safe Drinking Water Act or the Clean Air Act. Even though DuPont and 3M have ceased manufacturing it, as a persistent substance, it will remain in the environment and drinking water for decades, with a substantial latency period before it even shows up in some water systems (Bartell 2016).

Finally, after hundreds of studies by independent scientists and an administrative record of 45,000 pages of legal and scientific justification, the EPA was not permitted by a court to remove the extremely toxic substance asbestos from commerce (General Accounting Office 2005; *Corrosion Proof Fittings v. Environmental Protection Agency* 1991).

Why are health protections so slow?

Answering this question takes us to the second important law-science issue in this paper: *how much and what kind of scientific evidence* should be needed to reduce the risks of products once they are in commerce?

A background issue is that environmental health agencies have the legal burden of proof to change the status quo ante and must find or generate needed data (often from scratch) and justifications for improved health protections. Multiple studies must be funded and conducted, but these have their own pace as already noted. Because of the latency of some diseases, they must have time to appear. In this legal context companies need only play *defense*, and they have become good at it.

Consequently, how much and what kinds of studies are used to protect the public are important social or moral decisions. If conducting, compiling, assessing the science, and acting on it are too slow, people can become seriously ill or die from exposures permitted and diseases not prevented. This happened to Sandy Guest.

She was a hairdresser, who in her job used Brazilian Blowout. This product was "loaded with formaldehyde." Because of her frequent exposures she became sick and eventually died of leukemia, a known outcome of formaldehyde exposure (Morris 2015). Why does my claim seem plausible?

In 1981 the U.S. National Toxicology Program (NTP), the main US agency that identifies substances that are toxic, classified formaldehyde as a likely human carcinogen (National Research Council 2014) Thirty years later it upgraded its assessment: formaldehyde is a "known human carcinogen." Between those dates more than 17 studies revealed that people were contracting cancers "of the nasopharyngeal region, sinonasal cavities, and myeloid leukemia" (National Research Council 2014), the disease from which she died, as well as other adverse effects. Animal experiments reinforced the human data.

From these findings researchers concluded that formaldehyde is carcinogenic to humans. That in turn would have informed a community of experts. Public health officials almost certainly knew of formaldehyde's toxicity. Yet, no public, nationwide legal standards or restrictions on its use had been set that would have protected Sandy Guest. Inordinately slow assessments of substances that turn out to be toxic, thus, can kill those exposed.

4 Demanding ideal or "doubt-free" science

Two defense strategies adopted by companies slow improved health protections from products already in commerce. One is to use "doubt" arguments, pioneered by the tobacco industry, and the other utilizes demands for "ideal" science as suggested by Arthur Furst, a well-known and broadly educated toxicologist (now deceased).

Most companies, it appears, now follow the earlier lead of the tobacco industry as set out in an early memo to guide their thinking: "Doubt is our product since it is the best means of competing with the 'body of fact' that exists in the minds of the general public. It is also the means of establishing a controversy" (Brown and Williamson 1969; Michaels 2012: 275).

Creating doubt about the science utilized to identify toxicants and guide improved health standards is a typical company or industry strategy to protect commercial products. A company's strategy is to attack early drafts of health assessments shortly after their posting. Next, they try to force new reviews. Usually, they would introduce industry-funded studies or industry-favorable interpretations of existing studies, often when public health protections are nearly final. Agencies typically must take them into account (Sass and Rosenberg 2011; Michaels 2012; Michaels and Montforton 2008) Even after their own studies are incorporated, they may continue to slow the process.

Before the process is over, they may enlist key politicians with political leverage to further delay health protections. For instance, the formaldehyde industry sought the political intervention of Louisiana Senator David Vitter to slow the formaldehyde assessment. He held President Barack Obama's administrative appointments hostage in the U.S. Senate until the President agreed to have the formaldehyde health protections reviewed by the National Academy of Sciences (NAS). This would take at least two more years, delay health protections, and continue companies' income from such products. Ultimately the NAS reported that the EPA correctly found that formaldehyde causes three different cancers in people, the main point of contention (NRC 2014b). However, even a reasonably successful NAS review does not ensure that new protections are implemented because the EPA may still have to update and modify its health standards before they can be finalized. Once they become law there will be a further phase-in period to give companies an opportunity to modify their products or workplace practices to comply.

While all these defensive efforts were occurring, Sandy Guest was exposed to a hairspray for her clients that was "loaded" with formaldehyde. She paid for company intransigence and regulatory delay with her life.

A second seemingly more scientific strategy that can slow health protections would be for companies to demand "ideal" science before administrative agencies institute better health protections. After all, companies have invested in their products and these should not be casually modified or withdrawn from commerce without good scientific reasons. However, as I argue later, agencies need not have ideal science before having *sufficiently good science* to protect the public.

One suggestion of what might be considered ideal science was articulated by Arthur Furst, a broadly educated toxicologist. He is now deceased, but his views provide a useful foil with which to contrast more reasonable approaches.

As a scientist he asked what evidence would be needed to ensure that a substance was a human carcinogen. He was not making proposals either for regulatory agencies or for the tort law.

> As an absolute minimum, there should be a close agreement between conclusions from well-designed epidemiological studies of exposed populations,

> with conclusions drawn from good and valid animal bioassays (using appropriate routes of exposure and reasonable exposure levels and with an end point in which a cancer has been induced, one similar to that of the exposed human). Some corroboration from short-term tests will strengthen the association. If the biotransformation of the agent under consideration is similar in humans and on active animal species, there are more reasons to consider this agent a human carcinogen. The limitation is that the mechanism of action of the agent in inducing an animal cancer does not undergo a process or require an organ for which there is no human counterpart.
>
> (Furst 1990, 12)

According to his view, a serious mistake is to judge a substance as a carcinogen when some of his recommended evidence is missing (he likely would regard this as a false positive). In contrast, he risks not concluding that a substance is a carcinogen, when a substantial, but not ideal, body of evidence shows it is (a scientific false negative). An opposite mistake would be to require so little evidence that some substances would be judged as carcinogens, when a more robust body of data would show that they were not (scientific false positives).

I submit that the correct answer lies between his quite demanding recommendations and the opposite mistake. Demanding copious and highly certain data about each substance before health agencies take regulatory action precludes quicker assessment of that product and quicker evaluation of others in commerce but not yet evaluated. This would leave an agency, scientists, and the public ignorant about a large universe of substances not yet assessed and at risk for any that are toxic.

There are also important practical consequences of Furst's suggestion. To the extent that he recommends that certain lines of evidence must be *necessary conditions for inferring toxicity*, this will leave overall toxicity assessments about particular substances in limbo until all the necessary conditions are satisfied.

For example, he appears to believe that human epidemiological data (and several such studies) must be present before a substance can be judged a human carcinogen. While human studies can be and are scientifically relevant and important data, they have several limitations that preclude their being necessary conditions of carcinogenic or other toxicity assessments.

Sample sizes can be too small and statistically underpowered to reliably detect a risk even if it is present. When this occurs it can result in a mistaken "no effect" or false negative results; namely, there is no evidence that exposure causes an adverse effect. For example, benzene exposure clearly causes acute promyelocytic leukemia (APL), as found by the scientific community and by a federal court in the U.S. However, an epidemiological study would rarely detect it because it only occurs in about one per million people. In a U.S. legal case at the time of plaintiff's trial, there were *no human studies* showing benzene could cause APL. Yet, scientists were highly certain, based on other lines of evidence, that benzene could cause this rare disease (I return to this later).

More generally, epidemiological studies "are not sufficiently sensitive to identify a carcinogenic hazard (or other hazards) except when the risk is high or involves an unusual form of cancer" (Cogliano et al. 2004; Cogliano et al. 2011). This would be true for very common diseases, such as breast or prostate cancers (in which circumstances it is difficult to separate one cause of these common cancers from another), or quite rare diseases, such as APL.

Human studies must allow for a sufficient latency period after exposure for the disease to appear. Because the latency period between exposure to asbestos and the appearance of mesothelioma is 40 or more years (Straif 2011), studies conducted 20 years after exposure might find few or no cases of the disease. Yet, according to the International Agency for Research on Cancer (IARC), "all forms of asbestos cause mesothelioma and cancers of the lung, larynx and ovary" (IARC 2012: 294). Similarly, the latency period for females exposed *in utero* to diethylstilbestrol (DES) before they contract cervical/vaginal cancer is about 20 years. Thus, studies conducted 10 years after exposures will likely not reveal any disease effects from exposure to DES.

Often there can be "insufficient human experience with the agent to determine its full toxicological potential" (Huff and Rall 1992). While the Greeks and Romans were quite familiar with some toxicity properties of lead, scientists only recently discovered some of lead's subtle effects in contributing to impulsive and ultimately antisocial behavior (Canfield et al. 2003). Human studies must also have accurate exposure data, but often this can be difficult to document. In addition, in order to use human studies people must become sick or have died in order to conduct the study; this is a high price to prevent disease for others.

Professor Furst also recommended requiring animal data. Again, while this can be important and relevant scientific evidence pointing to human harm, it too should not be "required" because on some occasions and for some period of time such studies did not reveal that arsenic and benzene were carcinogenic in animal studies.

The International Agency for Research on Cancer, for example, does not require human data to identify known human carcinogens. Without human epidemiological data it identified as known human carcinogens: the anticancer drug 1-(2-chloroethyl)-3-cyclohexyl-1-nitrosourea ("CCNU"), neutron radiation, a substance used in the plastics industry, 4,4'-methylenebis (2-chloroaniline) ("MOCA"), and some benzidine-based dyes that threaten workers (IARC 2016). More recently, IARC identified eight other known human carcinogens without having good human epidemiological data (Cogliano et al. 2011).

In addition, IARC identified 64 substances or groups of substances as *probable human carcinogens*. For 35 of the 64 probable human carcinogens, IARC had *no human epidemiological data* at all (Cranor 2017, 2013). For the vast majority, the overall classification is based on sufficient evidence in animal studies complemented by "mechanistic and other relevant data," typically genetic or chromosomal damage in animals and sometimes similar damage in cultured human or nonhuman cells (IARC 2016).

When IARC classifies substances that are either known or probable human carcinogens, it regards both categories as "*equally compelling cancer hazard[s]*; IARC's classification system simply distinguishes whether the data on which that conclusion is based include strong evidence in exposed humans" (Cogliano et al. 2008: 103, emphasis added).

5 Having sufficient data for health protections

As I have presented elsewhere for public health protections, administrative agencies should recognize the importance of different combinations of data and how they can show chemical creations can harm humans.

> Sometimes there will be good human studies, sometimes not. Sometimes there will be good animal data and few or no human data. Sometimes good mechanistic data is available that can serve instead of animal or human data, and so on. Researchers and agencies should consider the total body of scientifically relevant evidence that is readily available to determine how it does or does not 'fit together' to credibly assess the toxicity of a chemical creation. If missing data are needed to complete the scientific picture, they should seek it out or develop it. . . . [T]hey should free themselves from a priori and necessary kinds of evidence [as proposed by Furst and as often urged by companies defending their products] in order to better and more quickly assess toxicants to protect the public. Indeed, these are current policies at research agencies such as the IARC and the [National Toxicology Program] NTP, along with regulatory agencies such as the U.S. and the California Environmental Protection Agencies (EPAs).
>
> (Cranor 2017: 152)

It is worth adding that mechanistic data – "data on preneoplastic lesions, tumor pathology, genetic and related effects, structure – activity relationships, metabolism and toxicokinetics, physicochemical parameters and analogous biological agents" – has become increasingly important at IARC (IARC 2006: 15). This can importantly substitute "for conventional epidemiological studies when there is less than sufficient evidence in humans, [and] for conventional [animal] bioassays when there is less than sufficient evidence in experimental animals" (Cogliano et al. 2008: 104).

Moreover, it is important to note that in contrast to some suggestions by companies whose products may be considered for regulation because of risks they pose that the National Research Council has cautioned against some fixed framework for assessing the toxicity of product: "It seems impossible and undesirable to build a scientifically defensible framework in which evidence is integrated in a completely explicit, fixed, and predefined recipe or algorithm" (NRC 2014a: 86).

In order to better protect the public from chemical creations in our midst, at the outset of this paper I posed two important social or moral issues about the use of science in the law: "*When* should science be utilized to protect the public from risks of toxicants," and "How much and what kind of science should be utilized to reduce risks or remove the products so that people are not exposed?"

The answer to these questions can now be succinctly given:

(1) The public is better protected when scientific studies are used to understand any toxic effects *before* products enter commerce as they are under U.S. laws

for pharmaceuticals and pesticides and as they are under Europe's REACH legislation. While not a cure-all (even toxic pharmaceuticals and pesticides emerge from premarket testing and review to expose the public), this works far better than postmarket laws and is especially important for protecting children from toxic exposures. It also provides an initial body of science to which experts can later return to help determine whether or not a product in commerce is toxic, which exposures need to be reduced, or perhaps whether or not the products need to be withdrawn.

(2) The public is also better protected once products are in commerce and have to be withdrawn or have risks reduced, if agencies do not succumb to "ideal" or "doubt-free" science before taking health-protective actions. As noted previously, "Researchers and agencies should consider the total body of scientifically relevant evidence that is readily available to determine how it does or does not 'fit together' to credibly assess the toxicity of a chemical creation." (Cranor, 2017: 152)They should have a conception of a body of evidence that is *sufficient* for taking action to protect the public and not be tempted to require ideal or doubt-free science.

6 A new law to better protect the public

The U.S. Congress in the last year moved to require a premarket toxicity review of chemical creations entering commerce under a "New" TSCA, The Frank R. Lautenberg Chemical Safety for the 21st Century Act, which amends the 1976 TSCA. The law has several important provisions.

It requires that the EPA "must make an affirmative finding on the safety of a new chemical or significant new use of an existing chemical before it is allowed into the marketplace" (U.S. EPA 2016). In doing so it must "consider risks to susceptible and highly exposed populations [these may include infants, pregnant women, children, and workers] and ensure a substance does not pose an "unreasonable risk" (U.S. EPA 2016).

Moreover, there are mandated schedules and procedures to review commercially "active" products in the market. The EPA must give priority to chemicals that are persistent, bioaccumulative, and are known human carcinogens or otherwise have high toxicity (Dennison 2016). There are also numerous other provisions that I have sketched elsewhere and others have detailed, but lack of space precludes saying more about them in this venue (Cranor 2017). Congress clearly addressed one issue that I have raised for many years – the need for premarket toxicity testing and scientific review of products before entering commerce. How this is implemented is also an important moral/social issue. If the EPA administrator make an "affirmative finding about the safety of a chemical creation" but without sufficient evidence to properly justify the finding, premarket review will be a sham. Will new chemicals be properly reviewed for safety – supported by good toxicity testing with in-depth review – or will they only receive a cursory review with little/no testing? The preliminary bad news is that cursory reviews are being adopted. Since January 2017 the EPA has approved 600 new products to enter commerce, an unheard of rate and quite different from reviews of pharmaceuticals and pesticides. Did the agency have sufficient data on each substance so it could make a well-informed assessment of its toxicity, and did it carefully evaluate each product for its safety? These possibilities seem unlikely.

The Lautenberg Act also required expediting reviews of potentially toxic products already in commerce, but whether or not this will be successful is a much more open question. Even if the EPA could conduct risk assessments and improve health protections for 20 substances in commerce per year, an unheard of rate, it would take 1,500 years to review the likely commercially 30,000 "active" substances meriting review. However, the history of EPA actions (especially at IRIS) and of industry intransigence raises concerns about the likely success of these requirements. At the actual mandated rate of 6–7 years per 20 substances, the legacy chemicals that have already entered commerce from the "old TSCA" will exist for centuries.

7 Conclusion

When and *how* legislators choose to use science in administrative health laws is an important social/ethical decision that the U.S. legal system ignored for 40 years for new chemical creations, except for pharmaceuticals and pesticides. Premarket toxicity testing and review laws are vastly superior morally to postmarket laws. The U.S. has finally moved to join Europe with premarket laws for new chemical products with the Lautenberg Act.

How much and what kind of evidence should be required in order to reduce risks from products in commerce and the public is exposed is a second major social/moral decision. Researchers and public health agencies should not accede to company efforts to insist on "ideal" or "doubt-free" science; this will fail to protect the public.

EPA administrators could distort the recent Lautenberg Act by permitting new products into commerce with little or no testing and then insisting on quite detailed and "doubt-free" evidence before removing them for health risks. Neither would protect the public well. The affected public will have to be aware of the possibilities to ensure they are better protected than under the "old" TSCA.

Notes

1 The administrative law is not the only institution that serves to protect the public from risks posed by toxic substances, but I do not pursue these issues here. The tort or personal injury can also assist to some extent, although tort law injury actions typically occur after someone has been harmed.

2 There are some categories of violations that permit police officers to intervene before a major violation has occurred that actually causes harm to a person, such as conspiracies, attempts or preparations to commit crimes, although the borderline between these crimes and actual completed crimes that harm others may be contested.

3 TSCA is not the only postmarket law. Legal protections from toxicants under the Safe Drinking Water Act, the Clean Air Act, the Clean Water Act, and the Occupational Safety and Health Act are all postmarket.

Bibliography

American College of Obstetricians and Gynecologists Committee on Health Care for Underserved Women, American Society for Reproductive Medicine Practice Committee, with the assistance of the University of California at San Francisco (UCSF) Program on Reproductive Health and the Environment (2013, October) 'Committee Opinion: Exposure to Toxic Environmental Agents', *Committee Opinion* 575.

Bailar J. C. (2004) 'Personal Communication', Collegium Ramazzini.

Balibouse D. (2015) 'Teflon on Trial: Ohio Woman Wins $1.6mn Lawsuit Alleging DuPont Chemical Led to Cancer', *Reuters*, October 8. Available at www.rt.com/usa/318032-dupont-chemical-cancer-lawsuit/.

Barry V., Winquist A., Steenland K. (2013) 'Perfluorooctanoic Acid (PFOA) Exposures and Incident Cancers Among Adults Living Near a Chemical Plant', *Environmental Health Perspectives*, 121(11–12), 1313–18.

Bartell S. M. (2016) *Personal Communication on the Latency Period Between Dumping C8 Into the Ground and Its Appearing in Drinking Water*. Irvine, CA: University of California Press.

Bingham E. (2004) 'Personal Communication', Collegium Ramazzini.

Brown & Williamson Tobacco Company (1969) 'Smoking and Health Proposal', *Brown & Williamson Document 680561778-1786*. Available at https://industrydocumentslibrary.ucsf.edu/tobacco/docs/#id=jryf0138 (also cited in Michaels D. (2012) *Doubt Is Their Product: How Industry's Assault on Science Threatens Your Health*. New York: Oxford University Press).

Canfield R. L., Kreher D. A., Cornwell C., Henderson C. R. Jr. (2003) 'Low-Level Lead Exposure, Executive Functioning, and Learning in Early Childhood', *Child Neuropsychology*, 9(1), 35–53.

Cogliano V. J., Baan R. B., Straif K., Grosse Y., Lauby-Secretan B., El Ghissassi F., Bouvard V. et al. (2011) 'Preventable Exposures Associated With Human Cancers', *Journal of the National Cancer Institute*, 103(24), 1827–39.

Cogliano V. J., Baan R. B., Straif K., Grosse Y., Secretan M. B., El Ghissassi F. (2008) 'Use of Mechanistic Data in IARC Evaluations', *Environmental and Molecular Mutagenesis*, 49(2), 100–9.

Cogliano V. J., Baan R. B., Straif K., Grosse Y., Secretan M. B., El Ghissassi F., Kleihues P. (2004) 'The Science and Practice of Carcinogen Identification and Evaluation', *Environmental Health Perspectives*, 112(13), 1269–74.

Corrosion Proof Fittings v. Environmental Protection Agency, 947 F.2d 1201 (Fifth Circuit, 1991).

Cranor C. F. (2011) *Legally Poisoned: How the Law Puts Us at Risk From Toxicants*. Cambridge, MA: Harvard University Press.

Cranor C. F. (2013) 'Milward v. Acuity Specialty Products: Advances in General Causation Testimony in Toxic Tort Litigation', *Wake Forest Journal of Law and Policy*, 105–39.

Cranor C. F. (2017) *Tragic Failures: How and Why We Are Harmed by Toxic Substances*. New York, NY and Oxford: Oxford University Press.

Demarini D. (2012) *Personal Communication*.

Dennison R. (2016) 'Historic Deal on TSCA Reform Reached, Setting Stage for a New Law After 40 Years of Waiting', *Environmental Defense Fund*. Available at blogs.edf.org/health/2016/05/23/historic-deal-on-tsca-reform-reached-setting-stage-for-a-new-law-after-40-years-of-waiting/#more-5276.

Dietert R., Piepenbrink S. (2006) 'Perinatal Immunotoxicity: Why Adult Exposure Assessment Fails to Predict Risk', *Environmental Health Perspectives*, 114(4), 477–83.

Eastmond D. (2012) 'Personal Communication', University of California, Environmental Toxicology Program.

Furst A. (1990) 'Yes, But Is It a Human Carcinogen?', *Journal of the American College of Toxicology*, 9(1), 1–18.

Grandjean P. (2013) *Only One Chance: How Environmental Pollution Impairs Brain Development – And How to Protect the Brains of the Next Generation*. New York, NY: Oxford University Press.

Grandjean P., Bellinger D., Bergman A., Cordier S., Davey-Smith G., Eskenazi B., Gee D. et al. (2008) 'The Faroes Statement: Human Health Effects of Developmental Exposure to Chemicals in Our Environment', *Basic & Clinical Pharmacology & Toxicology*, 102(2), 73–5.

Huff J., Rall D. P. (1992) 'Relevance to Humans of Carcinogenesis Results From Laboratory Animal Toxicology Studies', in: *Maxcy-Rosenau-Last Public Health & Preventive Medicine*, edited by Last J. M., Wallace R. B., 433–40, 453–7. Norwalk, CT: Appleton & Lange.

International Agency for Research on Cancer (IARC) (2006) 'Preamble', *IARC Monographs on the Evaluation of Carcinogenic Risks to Humans*. Available at http://monographs.iarc.fr/ENG/Preamble/CurrentPreamble.pdf.

International Agency for Research on Cancer (IARC) (2012) 'Asbestos (Chrysotile, Amosite, Crocidolite, Tremolite, Actinolite, and Anthophyllite)', *Special Issue: Arsenic, Metals, Fibres and Dusts. IARC Monographs on the Evaluation of Carcinogenic Risks to Humans 100C*, 219–309. Available at http://monographs.iarc.fr/ENG/Monographs/vol100C/index.php.

International Agency for Research on Cancer (IARC) (2016) *List of Classifications*. Available at http://monographs.iarc.fr/ ENG/Classification. (Last updated 22 February 2016).

Lerner S. (2015a) 'The Teflon Toxin: DuPont and the Chemistry of Deception', *The Intercept*, August, 11. Available at https://theintercept.com/2015/08/11/dupont-chemistry-deception/.

Lerner S. (2015b) 'The Teflon Toxin: The Case Against DuPont', *The Intercept*, August 17. Available at https://theintercept.com/2015/08/17/teflon-toxin-case-against-dupont/.

Lerner S. (2015c) 'The Teflon Toxin: How DuPont Slipped Past the EPA', *The Intercept*, August 20. Available at https://theintercept.com/2015/08/20/teflon-toxin-dupont-slipped-past-epa/.

Mancini J. (2017) 'DuPont Reaches C8 Settlement Agreement for $670M', *The Parkersburg News and Sentinel*, March 24. Available at www.newsandsentinel.com/news/local-news/2017/02/dupont-reaches-c8-settlement-agreement-for-670m/.

Melman M. (2012) 'Personal Communication', Collegium Ramazzini.

Michaels D. (2012) *Doubt Is Their Product: How Industry's Assault on Science Threatens Your Health*. New York, NY: Oxford University Press.

Michaels D., Monforton C. (2005) 'Manufacturing Uncertainty: Contested Science and the Protection of the Public's Health and Environment', *American Journal of Public Health*, 95, S39–S48.

Miller M. D., Marty M. A., Arcus A., Brown J., Morry D., Sandy M. (2002) 'Differences Between Children and Adults: Implications for Risk Assessment at California EPA', *International Journal of Toxicology*, 21(5), 403–18.

Morris J. (2015) 'She Loved Making People Feel Great: Sandy Guest, 55, Hairdresser', *Center for Public Integrity*, June 29. Available at www.publicintegrity.org/2015/06/29/17533/she-loved-making-people-feel-great.

National Research Council (NRC) (1984) *Toxicity Testing: Strategies to Determine Needs and Priorities*. Washington, DC: National Academies Press.

National Research Council (NRC) (2014a) *Review of EPA's Integrated Risk Information System (IRIS) Process*. Washington, DC: National Academies Press.

National Research Council (NRC) (2014b) *Review of Formaldehyde Assessment in the National Toxicology Program 12th Report on Carcinogens*. Washington, DC: National Academies Press.

Rinehart E. (2016) 'DuPont Loses Another "Bellwether" C8 Law Suit', *The Columbus Dispatch*, Wednesday, July 6. Available at www.dispatch.com/content/stories/local/2016/07/06/DuPont-C8-litigation.html.

Rochester J. R., Bolden A. L. (2015) 'Bisphenol S and F: A Systematic Review and Comparison of the Hormonal Activity of Bisphenol A Substitutes', *Environmental Health Perspectives*, 123(7).

Rodgers W. H., Jr. (1994) *Environmental Law*. 2nd ed. St. Paul, MN: West.

Sass J., Rosenberg D. (2011) *The Delay Game: How the Chemical Industry Ducks Regulation of the Most Toxic Substances*. New York: Natural Resources Defense Council. Available at www.nrdc.org/sites/default/files/IrisDelayReport.pdf.

Schardein J. L. (2000) *Chemically Induced Birth Defects*. 3rd ed., rev. and expanded. New York, NY: Marcel Dekker.

Schierow L. J. (2007) 'The Toxic Substances Control Act (TSCA): Implementation and New Challenges', *CRS Report for Congress RL34118*. Washington, DC: Congressional Research Service, Library of Congress.

Steenland K., Zhao L., Winquist A., Parks C. (2013) 'Ulcerative Colitis and Perfluorooctanoic Acid (PFOA) in a Highly Exposed Population of Community Residents and Workers in the Mid-Ohio Valley', *Environmental Health Perspectives*, 121(8), 900–5. doi:10.1289/ehp.1206449.

Straif K. (2011) 'Carcinogens in the Workplace: State of the Art and Future Challenges', *Presentation in New Delhi, India*, March 23, 2011.

US Environmental Protection Agency. *EPA's New Chemicals Program Under TSCA: The Basics*. Available at www.chemalliance.org/topics/?subsec=27&id=689.

US EPA (2016) *Assessing and Managing Chemicals Under TSCA: Highlights of Key Provisions in the Frank R. Lautenberg Chemical Safety for the 21st Century Act*. Available at www.epa.gov/assessing-and-managing-chemicals-under-tsca/highlights-key-provisions-frank-r-lautenberg-chemical.

US General Accounting Office (2005) 'Chemical Regulation: Options Exist to Improve EPA's Ability to Assess Health Risks and Manage Its Chemical Review Program', GAO-05-458. Washington, DC: US General Accounting Office.

US Government Accountability Office (GAO) (2008, March) 'Chemical Assessments: Low Productivity and New Interagency Review Process Limit the Usefulness and Credibility of EPA's Integrated Risk Information System', GAO-08-440. Washington, DC: US Government Accountability Office.

Woodruff T. J., Zota A. R., Schwartz J. M. (2011) 'Environmental Chemicals in Pregnant Women in the United States: NHANES 2003–2004', *Environmental Health Perspectives*, 119(6), 878–85.

Part IV

Decision-making tools for environmental health

10 Ethical tools for decision-makers in environment and health

Peter Schröder-Bäck and Joanne Vincenten

1 Introduction

While writing these lines, the public authorities of the district in Germany where one of the authors lives – Aachen – has started an iodine tablets distribution programme to citizens, to reduce the risk of thyroid cancer in the case of a nuclear power plant accident. The (perceived) risk in Aachen is particularly large. Two older Belgian nuclear power plants (Tihange and Doel) which are 65 km and 140 km away respectively from Aachen, are seen to be a risk for the population health, given micro-cracks in some reactor units and other safety concerns.[1] Is such a programme the right intervention? Ethical issues arise here: for example, if this is an effective intervention doing more good than harm, if the distribution scheme is fair to all and everyone has the same chances for protection, if the underlying decision-making is evidence-based and transparent. In a different context, Zölzer (2015) has asked how to evacuate in case of a nuclear power plant accident and raises ethical questions in the context of when to evacuate and whom to evacuate. He calls for the inclusion of ethical considerations, such as how to weigh benefits and harm, make fair plans and prioritise justly, in the preparation and implementation of evacuation guidelines.

Indeed, these are just some examples on how policy-makers have to take complex decisions in the context of environment and health, when drafting policies, developing or applying guidelines, or taking decisions in emergency situations. Very often moral norms and values are at stake. Criteria of environmental justice, aspects of individual autonomy and questions of the common good, to mention only a few, are to be balanced in complex decisions. Often, the normative-ethical aspects of the decisions are hidden and go unnoticed by decision-makers in practice. Ethical tools can be sensitising decision-makers for normative-ethical aspects of their decisions and can support, but not replace, ethical reasoning.

This paper will introduce the concept of ethical tools for decision-making and will present such a tool. The paper discusses what opportunities and challenges there are for further developing and introducing such tools for the practice of decision-making in the context of environment and health.

2 Ethics in environment and health

First, we have to define what ethics is. Ethics is to be understood as the discipline that reflects systematically on moral norms and values. As such, ethics can also be understood in this practical sense as the discipline to advise on decision-making criteria, grounded in philosophical reflection and theory, when "tough decisions" are to be made. The discipline of ethics

> develops ethical principles, rules, and ideals that spell out standards of good and bad, right and wrong. Normative ethics tries to offer a substantive, albeit general answer to the question: What should I do? Normative ethics also tries to spell out reasons why a rational person ought to accept the answer it gives.
>
> (Jennings 2003: 2)

The academic discipline of ethics, as developed and conducted by philosophers, has developed theories that ground, develop or criticise moral values and norms. So-called "applied ethics" tries to break down ethical norms and values so that they become practically guiding in professional contexts or policy fields. Indeed, ethical knowledge needs to be "carried over" to decision-makers.

Indeed, there is empirical evidence that ethics in the practice of public health, to which we would also include environment and health, has growing demands within the decision-making process. The need for ethical reflection and support of ethicists, to facilitate ethical reflection for practice, has been identified by researchers. Ruth Gaare Bernheim discovered in a focus group study in the USA that,

> [p]ublic health practitioners at all levels of practice reported that they must confront numerous ethical choices, both explicitly and implicitly, in their professional roles every day. They often feel ill-prepared to make the "ethical trade-offs" and perceive a need for more education and support to make these decisions.
>
> (Gaare Bernheim 2003: 105)

Further, the need for reflection was specifically raised when asking staff of schools of public health in the European region. In the staff screening surveys, it became clear that schools of public health wanted to include an increased amount of ethical training in their educational programmes to ultimately improve the practice of public health (Aceijas et al. 2012). Yet at this time, ethics curricula are still in their infancy. There is also not much time and resources available to include ethical training in an already full curricula.

Despite the need for enhanced ethical training, a key question remains: How to support ethical reflection in training and, ultimately, practice? It is not helpful to recommend to decision-makers that they read the "Critique of Practical Reason" of Immanuel Kant or John Rawls's "A Theory of Justice." These works are foundational in ethics, but do not directly give advice or support criteria that are "ready to use." When thinking of health and ethics, one could also consider the Oath of Hippocrates, a concrete codification of norms and values for the health profession. However, "Hippocrates had nothing to say about public health" (Darragh and Milmoe McCarrick 1998: 1). As such, the Oath is certainly not sufficient as a normative guiding tool. Accordingly, some have argued, an extra framework for public health is needed. Nancy Kass famously formulated at the beginning of this millennium, when the discipline of public health ethics was further formed:

> A framework of ethics analysis geared specifically for public health is needed, both to provide practical guidance for public health professionals and to highlight the defining values of public health, values that differ in morally relevant ways from values that define clinical practice and research.
>
> (Kass 2001: 1776)

Again, it is reemphasized that "practical guidance" is needed. Professionals and other decision-makers – scientists, policy-makers, civil servants and so on – need support to identify moral issues in their practice and can reason about their action (or inaction) while meaningfully applying ethical insights, norms and values, to come to ethically justifiable decisions regarding (in)action.

Decision-makers are to take decisions and be able to publicly justify them. It is not sufficient to say: "I thought this was the best decision!" or to say, "I followed my intuition!" Rather, one has to be able to show that one did not only take evidence-based and evidenced-informed decisions, but also showed an awareness of values and norms and weighing these values. For example, knowing that an intervention was effective *and* the outcome was just and fair and refrained from stigmatisation and discrimination would be better than an alternative action or inaction that was not.

Still, there remains a dilemma. For thousands of years the body of ethical research has grown and is systematically and coherently being further developed. Yet, an ethical world formula, or a fully convincing "ready to use" ethical algorithm, has not been identified. Ethics always was and remains a discipline in which one strives for justification by giving reasons and developing argumentations based on moral norms and values. However, developing convincing argumentations is not easy, and philosophers might argue that for convincing argumentations a rich and comprehensive body of scholarship needs to be considered. Despite this, decision-makers cannot be fully trained in philosophy before taking decisions, and not every policy-making body can have an ethical advisory board to reflect on decisions or concrete guidelines.

Thus, what to do? One way to proceed could be "ethical tools" including guidance for their use. Ethical tools support a way to reflect actions and inactions systematically without going back to the complex original philosophical works, and yet are specific enough for concrete practical challenges (e.g. within public health and environment and health) to support reflection for decisions. The solution we want to offer and put forward for discussion is that it is helpful to familiarise decision-makers with ethical tools prepared by experts of ethics, together with experts and professionals of field-specific disciplines, which are therefore tools anchored in both rich theory and experience.

3 What are ethical tools?

Ethical tools, as we understand them and want to propose as helpful instruments, are approaches to reduce complexity and support the application of ethical norms and values for decision-makers. However, they are to be seen as a starting point for ethical reflection – not as sufficient for making ethical decisions. No algorithm is offered by ethical tools to find the right and best answer in situations of moral dilemmas. Ethical tools can indeed help to raise ethical awareness of decision-makers. First, by bringing ethical tools to the table of debate, or in the context of decision-making, it is made clear that decisions in public and concretely in environment and health are never taken in a vacuum of moral norms and values. Indeed, the very endeavour of pursuing health with public means manifests certain values – such as "health" and its importance and relevance for the public, so that even public means and structures and not only private initiatives are to be used for maintaining and furthering this value. Second, moral aspects and conflicting norms and values can be identified and made explicit with the help of ethical tools. For example, that it is not only the value "health" that is important and relevant, but also how it is distributed (aspects of fairness and justice), or how health is potentially traded off (e.g. against other goods such as "liberty" or "autonomy"). Lastly, the identification of these underlying moral norms and values, and their potential conflicts and so forth, can lead to explicit, balanced and differentiated judgements. Thus, ethical justification is supported.

Ethical tools are seen to be decision aids and starting points for justifications of actions or inactions – they are not to be confused with world formulas or easy to use algorithms (Borchers 2016). They offer a systematic set of criteria to structure, systematise, support, "simplify" and harmonise (ethically relevant) decision-making. The way ethical tools are developed is to be a specific decision aid for a specific context (e.g. an ethical tool from medical ethics should probably not be simply used for public health ethics). Ethical tools are developed and have to be developed concretely with specific questions in mind, such as: Who is to be addressed? (Borchers 2016).

To summarise, our own definition of ethical tools is that: Ethical tools are philosophically founded, normative instruments, built on field-specific, ethical frameworks, to guide, inform and facilitate decision-making in practice.

There have been many different forms of ethical tools discussed (Borchers 2016), among them are sets of principles or sets of questions, procedural protocols on how to make judgements based on values and norms (or such principle sets). These are the ones we focus on in this paper. However, other institutionalised processes are also discussed in the context of public health and specifically environment and health, e.g. consensus conferences in which citizens – as lay persons – are brought together to reflect commonly about chances and challenges of new technologies

(Beekman and Brom 2007). However, these reflection processes do not necessarily need to be based on or evolve around ethical standards and moral norms and values. Consensus conferences often leave the discussion open to the participating citizens to approach and debate the topic, and specific normative frameworks are not necessarily being prescribed for use.

These ethical tools, as we refer to them, can also be seen as offering "common ethical standard" and "minimal consensus" (Borchers 2016), because these ethical tools describe certain norms and values that are accepted to be minimal benchmarks. Indeed, these ethical tools offer norms and values that are widely accepted to be at least of relevance for making decisions in this context. This is not to say that these ethical tools with their norms and values are sufficient (for this context) and, particularly, these tools do not necessarily include methods to show how conflicts among norms and values are to be resolved. Another critical point is that these ethical tools could be said to be biased: by offering certain pre-selected normative criteria, certain perspectives are prescribed. Therefore it is important that ethical tools are well developed and validated, as we will discuss in the next section.

In either case, these ethical tools aim at finding a balance between different poles: The two poles are first, complexity (of applying ethical reasoning) and second, simplicity so that also non-philosophers can apply them. Thus, it is also a balance that needs to be found between theory foundation and practical "ready to use" tools. These tools should also be acceptable by experts of philosophy. Last but not least, while these tools shall be helpful, they must not be easily instrumentalised. They shall not serve the purpose of window dressing of decision-makers.

4 Translational ethics: making tools

Borchers, a philosopher researching decision-making and the role of ethical tools therein, pronounces that ethical tools have to be developed together by academics and decision-makers (Borchers 2016). We agree that bridges have to be built between the academic ethical and practical health discourse to work together on ethical normative guidance and also ethical tools. This way it can be best assured that ethical concepts are well used and understood in terms of what they could mean in practice. Ethicists and decision-makers in environment and health have to understand each other. On the one hand, ethicists have to understand what the technical and empirical problem is when making difficult and ethically relevant choices in environment and health. On the other hand, decision-makers have to understand what ethical concepts mean: what their scope is, what they imply, how to develop arguments and judgements involving moral norms and values.

For this reason, we would like to emphasise that translational aspects between these two paradigms – philosophical ethics and environment and health – need to take place and need to be facilitated. Only in an interdisciplinary discourse, which we would like to call translational ethics (Van Duin et al. 2015), with members of both paradigms, would the development of a meaningful tool be successful. Not only can philosophers develop ethical tools for environment and health, or the other way around, environment and health scientists and decision-makers can also develop ethical tools for their paradigm.

5 Proposal for an ethical toolbox for environment and health

Having said that, ethical tool development needs an interdisciplinary approach, we would like to make a first proposal for a tool. However, such a proposed tool still needs further development and validation in wider interdisciplinary discourses and trial phases in practice.

Our proposed ethical tool for environment and health is a list of ethical norms in forms of ethical principles (see Table 10.1) that can be broken down to normative questions that then, again, can be used like a checklist, or, as we prefer to call it, an "aide memoire" that can be a starting point for ethical analysis and reflection (Schröder-Bäck et al. 2014). The first seven principles are as presented also in Schröder-Bäck et al. (Schröder-Bäck et al. 2014). Additional principles are "prudence/precaution" and "honesty" from Malone and Zölzer (Malone and Zölzer 2016), who reflected on and suggested norms and values for environment and health. Additional to this, an ethical tool of principles in the format of an "aide memoire" is a suggestion of how to apply these principles.

6 An "aide memoire" of principles and normative questions as an ethical tool

The following principles are guiding norms when exploring the moral dimensions of an environment and health challenge. The principles are presented systematically and not in a certain hierarchical order. Indeed, there is no predefined weight to each of the principles. What role they play in making arguments and judgements is to be determined in the process of ethical justification and depends on the context and specificities of the situation. Here, in the formulation of the questions that are listed below in this "aide memoire," the ethical principles are specified as normative questions, directing the attention to concrete potential moral pitfalls of environment and health. In the specification we speak of an

Table 10.1 Ethical principles for environment and health as basis for the "aide memoire" tool

1	Beneficence
2	Non-maleficence
3	Respect for autonomy
4	Justice
5	Health maximisation
6	Efficiency
7	Proportionality
8	Prudence/precaution
9	Honesty

"intervention" (rather than a policy or any other term). "Intervention" is to be understood as a placeholder for a planned action or inaction in the context of environment and health. For example, the iodine tablets distribution programme in Aachen, or the development of a guideline on evacuation in case of a nuclear power plant accident.

Beneficence and non-maleficence

The first principles to be mentioned are "beneficence" (do good) and "non-maleficence" (do no harm). They both reflect the longstanding health ethics tradition that is founded in the Hippocratic ethos that health professionals shall do good to their individual patient or client and shall avoid doing harm. Thus, the specified questions relating to these principles in the context of environment and health are:

- Is the environment and health intervention promoting the health of and doing good for all persons affected by this intervention?
- Will no avoidable harm be done to individuals by the proposed intervention?

Respect for autonomy

The bioethicists Tom Beauchamp and James Childress (2001) recognised that this Hippocratian normative perspective is not sufficient for the context of modern biomedicine and added two further principles. First, there is "respect for autonomy:" Given that relevant normative dimensions of health are not only "good" and "harm," and, even more, it is difficult to say what good and harm is in the health and environment context, the will of individuals has to play a role. Beauchamp and Childress illustrate this with the example of aggressive therapies, which might add to the life expectancy, but do not lead to gains in quality of life. Here, they argue, the norm that the will and decision-making capacity of patients and citizens are to be taken into account as well is very relevant. Indeed, the will of the patient can overrule the other two principles that demand the health professional to do good and avoid harm. From this norm to respect the will and decision-making capacity of patients and citizens, the following questions could lead the environment and health professional to consider:

- Is the environment and health intervention refraining from coercion and manipulation, but rather supporting the choice of citizens?
- Are citizens well informed about the intervention?
- Is "informed consent" to take part in the intervention considered?
- Does the intervention raise the ability to exercise autonomy?
- Is self-responsibility not only demanded, but possible for every person?
- Are privacy and personal data respected?
- Is the self-respect of individuals or of populations supported and respected?
- If the intervention is paternalistic, is this justifiable?

Justice

As Beauchamp and Childress convincingly argued, the other principle that has to be added to the Hippocratic ethos to reflect a relevant ethical normative scope is the principle of justice. Justice asks if the benefits and burdens of an intervention are distributed in a fair way. It furthermore asks if (sub-)populations, and especially vulnerable populations, are not treated unfairly (e.g. are stigmatised or discriminated against). For the context of environment and health, specific questions of environmental justice could be specified:

- Is the proposed intervention not putting sub-populations at risk of being excluded from public goods and benefits?
- Is no one stigmatised, discriminated against, or excluded as a consequence of the proposed environment and health intervention?
- Does the intervention not enlarge social and health inequities, but rather works against inequities?
- Does the intervention consider and support vulnerable sub-populations?
- Does the intervention rather promote than endanger fair (and *real*) equality of opportunity and participation in social action?
- Does the intervention refrain from eroding senses of social cohesion and solidarity?
- Are aspects of procedural justice – such as transparency, participation – respected? Are all stakeholders heard and no (critical) stakeholders excluded on purpose?

Health maximisation

These four principles of bioethics, as mentioned earlier – and their context sensitive specifications in form of questions – are relevant for environment and health as well (Zölzer 2015). However, we believe that more principles should be included in an environment and health "aide memoire." There is the principle of "health maximisation" that carries the normative aspect that good has to be done to a population, as the principle of "beneficence" did for the individual level. Health shall be maximised, and then be also fairly distributed at the same time, which already shows the necessary normative intertwining of the norms of health maximisation and justice. From the principle of "health maximisation," one could derive ethical questions such as:

- Is the environment and health intervention indeed suitable for improving population health (health in a wider sense, including the avoidance of fear, panic etc.)?
- Is the intervention evidence-based and effective (and more so than alternatives)?
- Does it have a positive sustainable, long-term effect on the public's health?

Efficiency

When speaking of "maximisation" and "effectiveness," we can and should also emphasise the moral dimension of "efficiency." In the context of public and environment and health, resources are scarce, and thus one has to also consider opportunity costs of actions. Choosing one intervention might also mean to choose it over another intervention, or that resources are not available for other interventions that also have the potential to do good or work against health inequities. As such, efficiency is also a moral norm that is of relevance, and it could be broken down into questions such as:

- Is the proposed environment and health intervention cost-effective?
- Is the intervention more efficient than alternative interventions?

Proportionality

Another principle that has also been proposed for other public health ethical contexts is "proportionality." Learning from interventions in the past (which took the "sledgehammer to crack a nut" and thereby infringed on aspects of autonomy), we would like to formulate the following question:

- Is the environment and health intervention the least infringing of all possible alternatives?

Prudence/precaution

Malone and Zölzer (2016) added "prudence/ precaution" and "honesty" as meaningful normative additions to an environment and health ethical framework (in the context of radiation protection in diagnostic radiology). "Prudence," which they seem to use identically to "precaution," to them means that "where an action potentially causes a serious irreversible harm, measures to protect against it must be taken even if the causal relationships involved are not fully established scientifically" (Malone and Zölzer 2016: 3). A question for the "aide memoire" that could be inferred from this principle is:

- Are sufficient measures being taken to protect against potential – but unlikely – harm being caused by the intervention?

Honesty

"Honesty" is the last principle for discussion within the development of an ethical toolbox in the form of an "aide memoire" for the context of environment and health. To Malone and Zölzer (2016) this means that transparency, truthfulness and accountability are given when developing and implementing interventions.

This seems to be particularly relevant for public and environment and health, given that actors are often professionals in public institutions where trust is essential to maintain credibility and the functioning of public structures. Trust, again, can only be achieved when abiding to honesty. The following questions could thus be formulated:

- Are the actors proposing or implementing an environment and health intervention, and its implications, in a truthful and transparent manner?
- Are benefits and risks discussed and presented to the public in a transparent way?

7 How to apply the "aide memoire"

We also want to offer some guidance on how one can apply the principles and normative questions as laid out previously in the "aide memoire." Thus, decision-makers of an environment and health institution could consider following these steps to identify whether a proposed intervention contains moral issues, and to work towards finding the best justifiable solution or way forward (indeed, we believe that every proposed intervention shall be assessed in such a way, even if it is not evident that there are ethical issues):

1. Consider the intervention at stake, go through the "aide memoire" and ask the proposed questions: What moral issues related to this intervention do the questions raise? Which ethical principles are at stake? Are they in conflict with each other? Using the language of the norms and values: What is the problem or even the dilemma?
2. Check for alternatives: Are alternative solutions feasible with fewer moral issues?
3. Weigh and balance: Are all conflicting principles still of equal value? Or can one make trade-offs between principles, accepting that the importance of pursuing one principle at the cost of another is unavoidable (given that no alternative, ethically better acceptable interventions are available)?
4. Determine integrity: What does one conclude from the weighing? Can one personally accept the conclusion drawn?
5. Act and convince: Act according to one's own judgement and convince colleagues and others also based on ethical reasoning. Disclose what ethical principles are affected – supported or infringed – by the proposed intervention and how you would balance actions and decisions in the potential conflict to solve the moral challenge or dilemma.

8 Tools in practice and education

This is but one proposal of an ethical toolbox for environment and health: combining principles broken down to operational and specific questions and with a suggestion, how one can use these principles and normative questions, and to come to a judgement on actions and decisions. These steps are relevant for justification processes of intervention implementation. However, we do not suggest that this is a tool sufficient for all contexts of environment and health. Indeed, in some contexts, some of the norms and values mentioned in this aide memoire are not relevant at all, while others might be missing. Stakeholders of environment and health might rather prefer other approaches and tools (not based on questions, or not with predefined principles etc.). Thus, this proposal of an ethical tool is only the base for future discussion and development.

Despite such a tool running the risk of being too simplistic, we are convinced that it is better to use such a tool than ignoring ethical questions completely, or making intuitive decisions only. Rather, at least this minimal ethical reflection is important for justification of decisions and actions. Importantly, justification is most relevant in the context of public institutions and actors: One has to be able to convince and explain why one has chosen or will choose an intervention (over another), and here questions of effectiveness are not the only questions at stake, as moral values also play a role.

Our experience of university training in health sciences and/or public health is that ethical training needs more integration, but little time is available to integrate ethics into the current curricula. Thus, we suggest teaching tools in short time slots, rather than having no ethical training in bachelor and master programmes at all. However, it would be preferable, of course, to have more time available in which one can also explain ethical theories of justice and autonomy, the theories of consequentialism and so forth, in more depth. Introducing virtue theories would also enrich the understanding of the moral landscape for our future health professionals and decision-makers in environment and health.

9 Conclusion

The concept of an "ethical tool" seems promising. An ethical tool can make it easier for persons to address and solve a decision conflict and support open discussion. Thus, from a practical point of view, an ethical tool has a positive connotation. On the other hand, philosophical purists might disagree and say that philosophical reflection about practical and moral problems cannot be simplified, and that such tools lead to simplistic mechanisms that give the appearance of easy solutions. However, easy solutions and easy answers do not exist in ethics, otherwise, a question would not even appear for ethical reflection.

Against this tension, we personally conclude that ethical tools cannot be more than *starting points* for ethical reflection. We need more debate and research about what ethical support decision-makers want and need, and how philosophers can be helpful in improving environment and health practice.

Note

1 *Germans in Aachen Get Free Iodine Amid Belgium Nuclear Fears*. www.bbc.com/news/world-europe-41121761.

References

Aceijas C., Brall C., Schröder-Bäck P., Otok R., Maeckelberghe E., Stjernberg L., Strech D., Tulchinsky T. (2012) 'Teaching Ethics in Schools of Public Health in the European Region – Results of a Screening Survey', *Public Health Reviews*, 34(1), 146–55.

Beauchamp T. L., Childress J. F. (2001) *Principles of Biomedical Ethics*. 5th ed. New York, NY: Oxford University Press.

Beekman V., Brom F. W. A. (2007) 'Ethical Tools to Support Systematic Public Deliberations About Ethical Aspects of Agricultural Biotechnologies', *Journal of Agricultural and Environmental Ethics*, 20, 3–12.

Borchers D. (2016) 'Ethiktools', in: *Ethik in den Gesundheitswissenschaften – Eine Einführung*, edited by Schröder-Bäck P., Kuhn J., 136–46. Weinheim: Beltz-Juventa.

Darragh M., Milmoe McCarrick P. (1998) 'Public Health Ethics: Health by the Numbers', *Kennedy Institute of Ethics Journal*, 8, 339–58.

Gaare Bernheim R. (2003) 'Public Health Ethics: The Voices of Practitioners', *The Journal of Law, Medicine, and Ethics*, 31(4) (Special Suppl), 104–9.

Jennings B. (2003) 'Introduction: A Strategy for Discussing Ethical Issues in Public Health', in: *Ethics and Public Health: Model Curriculum*, edited by Jennings B., Kahn J., Mastroianni A., Parker L. S., 1–12. Washington, DC: Association of Schools of Public Health.

Kass N. (2001) 'An Ethics Framework for Public Health', *American Journal of Public Health*, 91(11), 1776–82.

Malone J., Zölzer F. (2016) 'Pragmatic Ethical Basis for Radiation Protection in Diagnostic Radiology', *British Journal of Radiology*, 89. doi:10.1259/bjr.20150713.

Schröder-Bäck P., Duncan P., Sherlaw W., Brall C., Czabanowska K. (2014) 'Teaching Seven Principles for Public Health Ethics: Towards a Curriculum for a Short Course on Ethics in Public Health Programmes', *BMC Medical Ethics*, 15, 73.

Van Duin C., Brall C., Scholtes B., Schröder-Bäck P. (2015) 'Ethics for Public Health Practice – Translating Norms and Values', *European Journal of Public Health*, 26(Suppl 1), 42.

Zölzer F. (2015) 'Evacuation in Case of a Nuclear Power Plant Accident – Discussion of Some Ethical Questions', *Kontakt – Journal of Nursing and Social Sciences Related to Health and Illness*, 17, e177–e182.

11 Cost-benefit and cost-effectiveness considerations in the assessment of environmental health risks

Ethical aspects

Friedo Zölzer and Husseim Stuck

1 Introduction

Decision making on topics of environmental health should be based on well-established facts and widely shared values. Both are not easy to come by. It is difficult to demonstrate beyond argument a causal link between certain environmental factors and certain effects on human health, because in most practical situations there is more than one factor at work, and in addition, the effects of small doses of toxins or radiation are notoriously controversial. But even if we agreed on risk estimates for a particular environmental exposure, that would still not tell us what to do, for instance which protection measures to take or not to take. These kinds of decisions necessarily involve value judgements, and here again we encounter a variety of positions among those involved, which have only begun to be explicitly discussed in recent years.

Take radiation protection as an example. The basic idea in the first few decades after the discovery of X-rays and radioactivity was that radiation effects occurred only if a certain threshold dose was exceeded, and protection would be entirely adequate if doses were limited to a level below this threshold. But gradually in the second half of the 20th century, it became clear that even small doses of radiation carried a certain risk, i.e. a probability of cancer induction, which made it impossible to define a "safe" dose. The only thing which could be done in this situation was to agree on certain principles which would help us determine which radiation exposure could be considered "acceptable" or "tolerable" and which would have to be considered "unacceptable". The choice of words here clearly indicates that this is not a matter of science (alone), but one of value judgement, in other words of ethics.

The first two principles promoted by the International Commission of Radiological Protection (ICRP) call for justification and optimisation of exposure. Justification means that "any decision that alters the radiation exposure situation should do more good than harm" (ICRP 2007, paragraph 203), whereas optimisation calls for exposures to be kept "as low as reasonably achievable" (ibid.). That all sounds plausible and easily applicable, apart from the fact that it does not tell us how to compare good and harm in practice. What if the harm is the possible cancer death of some of the exposed individuals after a certain latency period, whereas the good is some financial gain for the electricity provider, or to say it less provocatively, the production of energy for thousands of people? Similarly, the exhortation to act reasonably will find widespread approval, but when people are asked to explain what this actually means for them, opinions will vary widely. The optimisation principle has been supplemented with the recommendation to take "into account economic and societal factors" (ibid.), which again sounds helpful, but does not provide distinct advice when it comes to practical decision making. How exactly should economical and societal factors be taken into account if they are to be weighed against human health, or even lives?

The ICRP, for some time at least, favoured a particular approach to decision making which translates all good and harm into monetary value and considers net profit or loss as the final criterion of what is right and wrong. This method is called cost-benefit analysis and has of course been applied to many issues, not just those of radiation protection. Originally, ICRP focused very much on this and other quantitative methods (ICRP 1973), but later recognised that "operational procedures, good practices, and qualitative approaches" could and should also play a role for the optimisation process (ICRP 2006, paragraph 2). In the following, we will review some of the basic assumptions of cost-benefit analysis and its main problems from the perspective of ethics, and that will explain – to some extent we hope – why the Commission is not so committed anymore to its use in general.

Related to cost-benefit analysis, but quite distinct from it, is cost-effectiveness analysis. It does not claim that all good and harm can be monetised, nor that right and wrong can be decided by assessing net profit or loss. It rather provides information on actual (or potential) expenditure for measures improving health and security, and thus supports decision making in situations where different courses of action are possible. The ICRP has discussed it as a method to identify the best option to reach a certain aim, where the aim itself has been set by other means (ICRP 1989; ICRP 2006). Cost-effectiveness analysis can be used for comparisons not only within a field, such as radiation protection, but also between fields, such as radiation vs. chemical protection, as will be seen later.

We look at radiation protection as an example of a field where both cost-benefit and cost-effectiveness analysis have been applied, but the main aim of this paper is not to critique the recommendations of the ICRP regarding its use of the two methods. More generally, we are interested in the ethical values underlying one or the other, and we hope to show that although both apply some kind of "dollars per life" calculation, they are fundamentally different in terms of those values.

2 Cost-benefit analysis

Over the past few decades, Cost-benefit Analysis has had its ups and downs, but overall it seems to have gathered momentum and, in spite of much criticism and its abandonment in certain areas, it is still very much *en vogue*. In the United States of America (US), for instance, it has been applied for questions of water quality, land conversion, and waste deposition since the 1960s.

The National Environmental Policy Act of 1969 first required its application for regulatory programmes. On several occasions over the last few decades, the White House has issued Executive Orders expressly recommending cost-benefit-analysis in the areas of governance, economy, environment, and health (Sagoff 2009; CEG 2015).

Cost-benefit analysis is based on assumptions and premises characteristic of utilitarian ethics. Central to it is the notion of "human preference". "Cost" is that which reduces the chances of realising preferences, "benefit" is that which contributes to furthering them. When considering whether or not to accept a project or a policy, cost-benefit analysis assesses whether the project's or policy's net impact on the realisation of human preferences is positive or negative, and it also allows comparison of different projects or policies in terms of net impact so that the best option can be identified.

One approach to evaluating costs and benefits are Contingent Valuation Methods. They share an overarching principle, namely the inference of the monetary value of non-marketed goods and services from information regarding people's preferences. Two such methods often used are Willingness To Pay (WTP) and Willingness To Accept (WTA). Both demand the agents to state their preferences concerning intangible, or non-marketed goods and services, and use that information to derive a price for what originally had none (Pearce, Atkinson, and Mourato 2006).

It is generally accepted that the risk of death is not marketed as such, but that different degrees of risk can be marketed instead. Thus people are not directly asked the amount of money at which they value life, but it is assumed that they make certain choices which reflect a certain value that they attribute to their lives (Kelman 1981). Empirical evidence is sought for people's WTP for a decrease in the probability of a risk, or people's WTA a sort of compensation for the worsening of the situation as compared to the status quo. From the monetary value which is placed on a marginal change in the likelihood of death, the "Value of a Statistical Life" (VSL) is then derived (Pearce, Atkinson, and Mourato 2006). To give a simple example: people might be asked how much they would be willing to pay in order to improve road safety and reduce the risk of accidental death, say by 1 in 10 000. If among 10 000 respondents the answer was 300 USD on average, one would conclude that together they were ready to contribute 3 million USD to save one life, which then equates to the Value of a Statistical Life.

The ICRP in those publications recommending the use of cost-benefit analysis in radiation protection also referred to the "value of life", but it did not mention (at least not explicitly) Willingness to Pay or Willingness to Accept. Rather it suggested that "various economic models, including the Human Capital Approach" could be used (ICRP 2006, paragraph A17). The Human Capital Approach equates the "value of a human life" with the market value of the output produced by an individual over an expected lifetime. Without referring to human preferences in the broad sense, it focuses exclusively on the economic dimension of human life. The ICRP did recognise that "there have always been some reservations about the use of the concept from an ethical point of view" (ICRP 2006, paragraph A9), but this is – as far as we can see – the closest the Commission ever got to a critical appraisal of cost-benefit analysis in terms of ethics. Generally, the assumption in all relevant ICRP documents seems to be that the assignment of a monetary value to human life is unproblematic, even if cost-benefit analysis is not the answer to everything.

A very important discussion regarding the monetary value of human life revolves around the question of whether or not the assessment made in one setting applies to others as well, e.g. whether a value derived for road accidents can be used in the context of environmental pollution and *vice versa*. The term used here is "transferability". Currently, government agencies in many countries have decided on a monetary value for human life and apply the same figure to a number of different settings without the slightest hesitation. Recent case studies, however, invite policy makers to rethink such assumptions and provide evidence of non-transferability (Pearce, Atkinson, and Mourato 2006). Table 11.1 presents "Values of a Statistical Life" from different contexts, i.e. different areas of competence of US government agencies, different health risks, different countries, etc. This kind of compilation has to be regarded critically, of course, as different methods to calculate the monetary value of human life may yield different quantities, and the discrepancies noted should be considered mainly as highlighting the complexity of this assessment.

As is obvious from this compilation, which does not claim to be representative but just serves to show the range of values suggested in the literature, WTP studies do not always and everywhere suggest the same (or a similar) "Value of a Statistical Life". A number of factors have been identified that influence the results of WTP studies. Only a few will be discussed here.

First of all, the *type of risk* plays a role. Compare the results for different food hazards in the US in Table 11.1. The lowest and highest values are at least one order of magnitude apart. When one looks at the policy values of government agencies in the US, the variation is much smaller, because each of them represents the result of a meta-analysis of different studies. The discrepancies between the agencies have been further reduced over the last decade. Note that the policy value of the Environmental Protection Agency (EPA) for air pollution in 2005 was not based on WTP surveys in that field, but on a whole range of mostly unrelated studies. Similarly, the recommendation of the Nuclear Regulatory Commission (NRC) in 1995 did not stem from an assessment of WTP for the reduction of radiation risks, but from a review of data provided by different government agencies.

A more complete overview of the range of "Values of a Statistical Life" is given in Figure 11.1. From this frequency distribution, it is clear that the lowest and the highest estimates are at least two orders of magnitude apart.

Second, the *country and/or average income* has an influence. See the results of air pollution studies in Table 11.1. There is a clear correlation between VSL and Gross Domestic Product (GDP) per capita, ranging from about 0.04 million USD in Bangladesh to 4.67 million USD in Japan (Miller 2000). Even within Europe, there are large differences: a recent WHO/OECD study listed values between 0.84

Table 11.1 Value of a statistical life according to different contingent valuation studies as well as policy values of US government agencies

Risk	*Value of a Statistical Life*	*Author*
Road traffic (US; median of 10 different studies 1972–1998)	4.30 million USD	Anderson and Treich (2011)
Road traffic (Sweden; median of 5 different studies 1995–2004)	4.00 million USD	Anderson and Treich (2011)
Road traffic (Thailand, mean of two WTP surveys in Bangkok, 2003)	1.17 million USD	Vassanadumrongdee and Matsuoka (2005)
Road traffic (US, policy value of the Department of Transportation, 2003)	3.00 million USD	Robinson (2007)
Road traffic (US, policy value of the Department of Transportation, 2016)	9.40 million USD	Viscusi and Masterman (2017)
Air pollution (Thailand, mean of two WTP surveys in Bangkok, 2003)	1.03 million USD	Vassanadumrongdee and Matsuoka (2005)
Air pollution (Brazil, WTP survey in Sao Paulo 2003, suggested value for policy analysis)	1.04 million USD	Arigoni Ortiz, Markandya, and Hunt (2009)
Air pollution (France, WTP survey in and around Marseille 2000/2001)	1.91 million USD	Chanel and Luchini (2008)
Air pollution (US; policy value of the Environmental Protection Agency, 2005)	6.45 million USD	Robinson (2007)
Environmental hazards (US; policy value of the Environmental Protection Agency, 2016)	9.70 million USD	Viscusi and Masterman (2017)
Trihalomethanes in drinking water (US; WTP study 1985)	0.31 million USD	Carson and Mitchel (2000)
Pesticides in food, adult (US; WTP study 2007, pooled model)	7.50 million USD	Hammitt and Haninger (2010)
Pesticide in food, child (US; WTP study 2007, pooled model)	12.4 million USD	Hammitt and Haninger (2010)
Food hazards (US; policy value of the Food and Drug Administration, 2003)	5.00 million USD	Robinson (2007)
Food hazards (US; policy value of the Food and Drug Administration, 2015)	9.30 million USD	Harris and Roach (2017)
Radiation exposure (France, WTP survey among professionals, 1997)	0.49 million USD	Schneider et al. (2000)
Radiation exposure (South Korea, WTP survey among professionals, 2000)	3.57 million USD	Choi, Lee, and Lee (2001)
Radiation exposure (US; Nuclear Regulation Commission)	3.84 million USD	NRC (1995)
Radiation exposure (US; Nuclear Regulation Commission)	9.00 million USD	NRC (2015)

(Values are stated here as reported by the authors; note that considering inflation 1 USD (1995) = 1.55 USD (2015) and 1 USD (2005) = 1.21 USD (2015)).

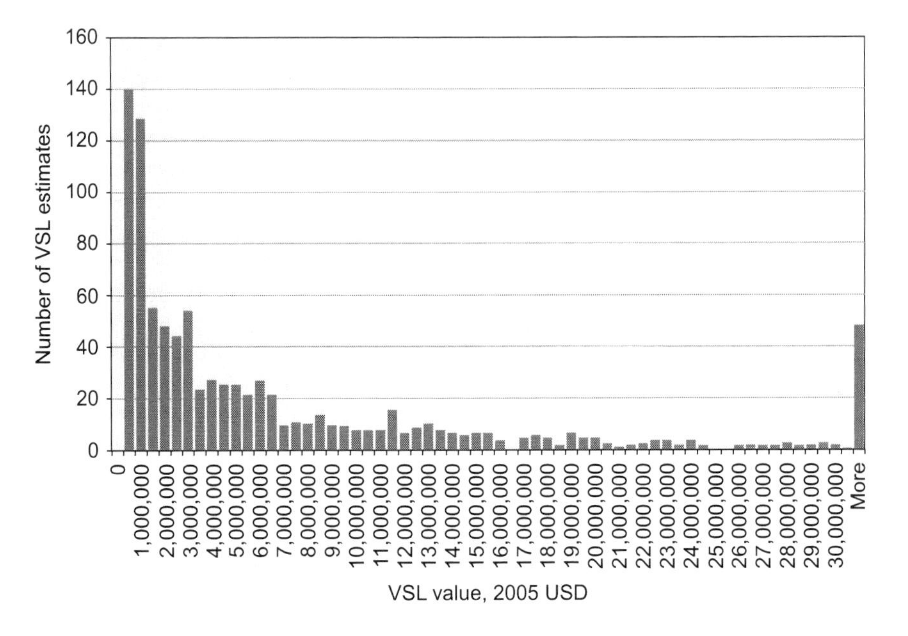

Figure 11.1 Frequency distribution of VSL values from 900 WTP studies undertaken mostly in OECD countries

(modified from Lindhjem et al. 2011)

USD for the Republic of Moldova and 8.41 million USD for Luxemburg (WHO and OECD 2015). Income affects the Value of a Statistical Life because individuals who are poor simply do not think of themselves as being able to spend money for risk reduction. It has been observed that people with "unusually strong constraints on their choices", most of all people with very limited financial resources, will exhibit a high amount of indifference to "take the bundled good" when questioned (Kelman 1981: 37). The fact that poor people show a lower WTP than rich people, resulting in a lower Value of a Statistical Life, has been one of the main arguments put forward against this kind of contingent valuation (Sunstein 2004).

Third, *age* makes a difference. Compare the results for pesticides in food in Table 11.1. In the past, much of the research addressing risks was centred on accidents, especially road and workplace casualties, where the people affected happen to share similar characteristics such as average age. Environmental degradation, however, may disproportionately affect children and elderly people. In the case of children, both their higher sensitivity to certain environmental factors (such as carcinogenic chemicals and radiation, or allergens), and their longer life expectancy has to be taken into consideration. For elderly people, factors causing health problems with a long latency period (such as cancer) are less of a problem than those affecting the cardiovascular system. Policies aiming at an improved air quality, for instance, apart from having long-term benefits for children, will have their greatest short-term effect on the morbidity and mortality of the elderly, or seen from another perspective, not implementing such policies might result in "harvesting" the older generation (Pope et al. 1995). In the context of cost-benefit analysis, the question is whether someone who is 80 years of age has the same WTP for a reduction in risk as a person who is 30 years of age, which is then expressed in a different "Value of a Statistical Life". The above-mentioned "Human Capital Approach" suggests a similar influence of age, because obviously the output produced by an individual over the remaining lifetime is smaller for people at retirement age than for those in their twenties.

Finally, the *level of risk* has an influence. Once it has been reduced – say, through the implementation of certain policies – the WTP for a further reduction is often smaller. This is important to keep in mind especially for VSL estimates in developed countries, where policies addressing life risks do not always have a dramatic effect on overall life chances. These countries have already reached a relatively high standard of health and safety, and therefore further reducing risk results in no more than a small change in the total number of lives saved in comparison to what would be expected in developing countries. The "Value of a Statistical Life" can thus under certain circumstances be dependent on the overall level of risk – which again has led some authors to suggest that it is an altogether inappropriate concept, as one would expect the value of a life to be the same for all (Pearce, Atkinson, and Mourato 2006). Some argue that the problems can be overcome by using the "Value of a Statistical Life-Year" (VSLY) instead. Here Willingness To Pay or Willingness To Accept do not relate to an overall risk of death, but a risk of reducing life expectancy. Typically, the value of a statistical life-year is 80 000 USD where the value of a statistical life is 1 million USD (Hammitt 2008).

The fact that the impact of risk-reducing policies depends on all the factors just mentioned (and others which we will not discuss here), makes the attribution of a monetary value to human life and its inclusion in Cost-Benefit Analysis a complex task (Pearce, Atkinson, and Mourato 2006). More fundamental to this discussion than methodological issues, however, is the question of whether human life can at all be judged in terms of "cost" and "benefit" (Ackerman 2008). In the view of those critical of this approach, the value of intangible goods in general is such that they are "not for sale". An early critic of cost-benefit analysis put it this way:

> The very statement that something is not for sale affirms, enhances, and protects a thing's value in a number of ways. To begin with, the statement is a way of showing that a thing is valued for its own sake, whereas selling a thing for money demonstrates that it was valued only instrumentally. Furthermore, to say that something cannot be transferred in that way places it in the exceptional category – which requires the person interested in obtaining that thing to be able to offer something else that is exceptional, rather than

allowing him the easier alternative of obtaining the thing for money that could have been obtained in an infinity of ways.

(Kelman 1981: 39)

3 Cost-effectiveness analysis

At first sight, cost-effectiveness analysis seems very similar to cost-benefit analysis. In a way, both put a dollar (or euro) value on an individual life. But whereas cost-benefit analysis typically uses the contingent evaluation methods briefly described previously to derive the "Value of a Statistical Life", cost-effectiveness analysis is interested in actual or planned expenditure by the public authorities and uses these to calculate "Costs for life saved". In a way, therefore, it assesses the "Willingness to Pay" not of individuals, but of the society as a whole, or more practically speaking the decision makers in charge (be it legislators or regulators). It aims at comparing the relative costs and outcomes of two or more environmental health interventions, e.g. regulations of radiation protection or chemical protection. Similarly to what was briefly mentioned in the context of cost-benefit analysis, measures used can not only be "cost per life saved", but also "costs per life-year saved", or "cost per quality-adjusted life-year (QALY) saved". In the latter case, the health conditions of individuals affected are taken into account, as it is clear that a year of life spent in good health must be valued differently from a year of life spent with disabilities or on the verge of death (Kamm 2015; Russell and Sinha 2016).

To give an example of a "cost per life saved" calculation: consider 10 000 people living in a radioactively contaminated area, exposed to 20 mSv per year at the moment, gradually decreasing over the next 60 years to 5 mSv per year due to radioactive decay. The expected number of radiation-induced fatal cancer cases, assuming a linear non-threshold dose-effect relationship and applying the nominal risk coefficient recommended by ICRP of 5×10^{-2} Sv^{-1}, can be estimated to be about 300. Let us suppose that remediation work would reduce the dose rate to (initially) 5 mSv per year, so that the expected number of radiation induced fatal cancer cases would be reduced to 75, i.e. 225 lives would be saved. If, just for the sake of this example, we assume that the cost of remediation (reconstructing houses, removing top soil, bringing in non-contaminated food) is 900 million €, the resulting cost per life saved is 4 000 000 €.

Such estimates have been produced for the protection against many different environmental health risks, as well as for various measures of transport safety, of workplace security, of health care etc., and in some cases for different areas of the world. We will look at examples later. Before we do so, however, it should be mentioned that there are of course a number of factors that make cost-effectiveness analysis less straightforward than it may seem from the short description given. Some are the same as with cost-benefit analysis, such as the often controversial nature of risk estimates, especially when it comes to small doses of environmental agents, or the notorious methodological differences between studies, which certainly limit comparability. Also, some of the life-saving interventions referred to as follows have actually been implemented, some have been partially implemented, some have been proposed and are about to be implemented, some have been proposed and will never be implemented.

In practice, authorities have to use cost-effectiveness analysis within the confines of limited resources. Different decision rules have been suggested, the simplest being (a) to choose interventions in ascending order of cost per life saved until the budget is exhausted, or (b) to finance interventions as long as a certain threshold level of cost per life saved is not exceeded. The latter possibility, however, is not different in principle from cost-benefit analysis, as the threshold level is usually "inspired" by Contingent Valuation Studies, i.e. it reflects the "willingness to pay" of the individuals potentially affected (Svensson and Hultkrantz 2017). In either case, decisions would be taken on purely economic grounds, whereas societal factors such as the distribution of risks might have to be taken into consideration as well.

In the following, we will primarily have a look at cost-effectiveness of radiation and chemical protection measures. These data were compiled in response to a question raised by the organisers of the First European Radiation Protection week (2016) in Oxford, where the title of one of the sections was "Protection from chemical and ionising radiation risks – is the balance correct?" More specifically, the question to be looked at was whether we spend comparable amounts of money to reduce radiation and chemical risks.

As can be seen in Tables 11.2 and 11.3, the cost per life saved calculated for different interventions against radiation hazards ranged from 10 000 to 110 million €. Of course, we selected only a small number of studies, emphasising the extremes, but the figures do show that the money spent for one kind of intervention may, if put into protection measures against another hazard, save 10 000 times more lives. The most frequently occurring values (in order to avoid the term "median", which seems inappropriate for the small selection of values presented here) are around 1 million € or a bit more. For interventions against chemical

Table 11.2 Cost per life saved for radiation protection interventions

Intervention	*Cost per life saved*	*Author*
Measures against indoor radon	10 000–50 000 €	Swedish RP Institute (1993)
Average of 13 radiation protection interventions	900 000 €	Ramsberg and Sjöberg (1996)
Swedish Radiation Protection Policy	3.5 million €	Swedish RP Institute (1992)
Standards against radionuclides in uranium mines	8 million €	Viscusi (2000)
Cover/move uranium mill tailings	110 million €	Viscusi (2000)

(Values are stated here as reported by the authors; note that considering inflation 1 € (1995) = 1.45 € (2015) and 1 € (2000) = 1.35 € (2015); the exchange rate varied between 0.75 USD/€ in 1995, 1.08 USD/€ in 2000, 0.75 USD/€ in 2010, and 0.90 in 2015).

Table 11.3 Cost per life saved for chemical protection interventions

Intervention	*Cost per life saved*	*Author*
Regulating trihalomethane in drinking water	500 000 €	Viscusi (2000)
Cleaning up arsenic-contaminated sites	2 million €	Forslund et al. (2010)
Average of 5 interventions against pollutants in the environment	7 million €	Ramsberg and Sjöberg (1996)
Retrieval system for petrol gases at pumps for motor vehicles	25 million €	Sjöberg and Ogander (1994)
Regulating 1,2-dichloro-propane in drinking water	1.7 billion €	Viscusi (2000)

(Values are stated here as reported by the authors; note that considering inflation 1 € (1995) = 1.45 € (2015), 1 € (2000) = 1.35 € (2015) and 1 € (2010) = 1.08 € (2015); the exchange rate varied between 0.75 USD/€ in 1995, 1.08 USD/€ in 2000, 0.75 USD/€ in 2010, and 0.90 in 2015)

hazards it seems that both the minimum and maximum are somewhat higher, namely 500 000 and 1.7 billion €. Similar to the case of radiation, however, for the same money that saves one life in the worst case, one could save 3–4000 lives. Although both minimum and maximum are about an order of magnitude higher than for radiation protection, the most frequently occurring values do not seem to be quite that far off, perhaps a few million euros. But again: the selection is small and a bit arbitrary.

One value in each table stems from the study of Ramsberg and Sjöberg (1996), who summarised data from different sources regarding cost per life saved in Sweden. A little later, the same authors also published a detailed compilation on cost per life-year saved (not cost per life saved!) (Ramsberg and Sjöberg, 1997), which was in the order of 30 000 € for radiation protection[1] and 20 000 € for toxin control.[2] These values can be compared with those of Tengs et al. (1995) for the US. Here, both radiation protection and toxin control came to around 3 million dollars per life-year saved,[3] which was a hundred times higher than in the Swedish study. The reason for this discrepancy is not known. Ramsberg and Sjöberg (1997) suggest it could be a matter of the limited number of studies available, which probably neither in Sweden nor in the US were representative of all possible interventions against radiation or chemical hazards. For the present context, it is important to note that in both compilations the highest values were separated from the lowest by several orders of magnitude, as was the case for cost per life saved (see earlier).

Thus, it can be stated that the costs per life saved are comparable overall for measures reducing radiation and measures reducing chemical risks, while there is a very wide span between the lowest and highest estimates for either radiation protection or chemical protection. This finding raises questions of justice, as will be discussed next.

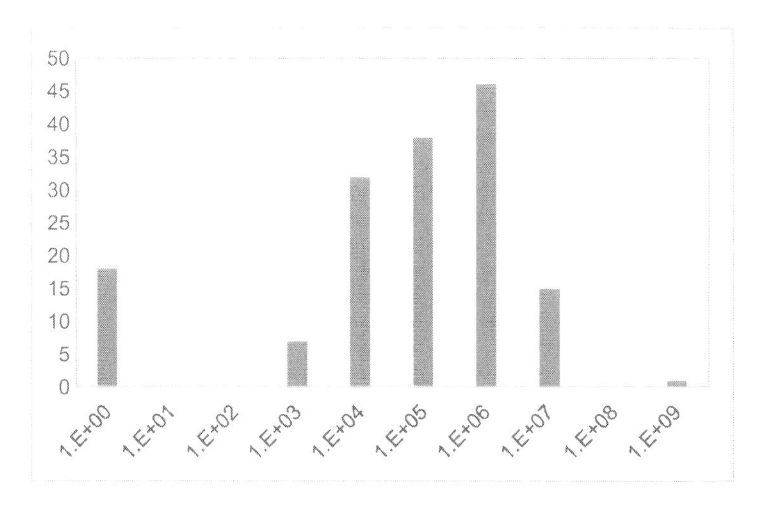

Figure 11.2 Distribution of cost per life saved for 157 different interventions in Sweden (x-axis: order of magnitude of cost per life saved in euros; y-axis: number of interventions, redrawn from Ramsberg and Sjöberg 1996)

Now, if we look more broadly at life-saving interventions, i.e. beyond radiation and chemicals, we find similar variations of cost-effectiveness estimates. The comparison of 157 life-saving interventions in Sweden (Ramsberg and Sjöberg 1996) which has already been mentioned above, resulted in the distribution shown in Figure 11.2. The average cost per life saved is around 26 million € taking all studies together, but when the outlier at a billion euros is taken out, the average is 3.7 million €, which is close to the median of 4.7 million. So here, for all 157 interventions taken together, we have a similar variation and a similar average as for radiation or chemical protection alone.

Again if we briefly look at cost per life-year, the later study of Ramsberg and Sjöberg (1997) shows a variation from 0 to 100 million €, with a median of 17 000 €, which is very close to what they found for radiation or chemical protection alone. In the much larger study of Tengs et al. (1995), the cost per life-year ranges between 0 and 99 billion dollars, with an overall median of 48 000 dollars, which does not seem to be too far off, but comes even closer to the Swedish value if the exceptionally high estimates for cost per life-year in radiation protection and toxin control are excluded (as Ramsberg and Sjöberg 1997, observe.) The higher values for radiation protection and toxin control could also, to some extent at least, reflect the long latency periods for carcinogenic factors. In other words, radiation and chemical protection may save the same number of people (per million dollars) as other security measures, but they do not save as many life-years because radiation and chemicals do not kill immediately. Whatever the reasons for the discrepancy found in the American study (Tengs et al. 1995), the purpose

Table 11.4 Cost per life saved for interventions in developing countries

Intervention	*Cost per life saved*	*Author*
Improving perinatal care in developing countries	20–80 €	Hanmer, Lensink, and White (2003); Paul and Singh (2004)
Removing hexavalent chromium from Indian wells	120 €	Hanrahan, Fuller, and Singh (2007)
Nutrition communication in Mali	200 €	Ross (1997)
Remediation of lead contaminated sites in Zambia	300 €	Hanrahan, Fuller, and Singh (2007)
Vaccination to avoid diarrheal disease in Vietnam	1000 €	Fischer et al. (2005)

(Values are stated here as reported by the authors; note that considering inflation 1 € (1995) = 1.45 € (2015), 1 € (2000) = 1.35 € (2015) and 1 € (2010) = 1.08 € (2015); the exchange rate varied between 0.75 USD/€ in 1995, 1.08 USD/€ in 2000, 0.75 USD/€ in 2010, and 0.90 in 2015)

of this short review of data for a broad variety of risk factors was to show that similarly large variations for radiation or chemical protection are seen as with many other interventions.

In terms of costs per life saved for the same kind of intervention in different countries, we do not know of any study addressing this question systematically. Our assumption is that differences would depend on nothing else but the prices of work and material, whereas people's perception of their situation would not play a role (as they do for the Contingent Valuation Methods discussed earlier). We did find information, however, about the costs per life saved for basic public health measures around the world which are quite different from the costs per life saved calculated for the reduction of technological risks. Table 11.4 again shows a somewhat arbitrary set of data, actually deliberately selected to show how cheap lifesaving interactions in developing countries can be. Values are a factor of 1000 smaller than the typical costs per life saved in radiation and chemical protection in developed countries. As these factors usually affect children, the discrepancy in terms of costs per life-year (instead of costs per life saved) will be even more dramatic. In the case of the last study in the table, the one by Fischer et al. (2005), who give both measures, it is estimated that the cost per disability-adjusted life-year averted is about 30 €, i.e. about 3% of the cost per life saved.

4 Comparison of cost-benefit and cost-effectiveness analysis in terms of ethics

In this last section, we will highlight certain ethical aspects that relate to either cost-benefit or cost-effectiveness analysis. We will do so on the basis of a recent publication of the International Commission on Radiological Protection (ICRP 2018), which reviewed the ethical foundations of the system of radiological protection. The document endeavours to show that certain "core values" have been at the basis of that system throughout its evolution, and it discusses their importance for the practice of radiological protection. The "core values" are:

- Beneficence/Non-maleficence: *Do good, and avoid doing harm*
- Prudence: *Recognise and follow the most reasonable course of action, even when full knowledge of its consequences is not available*
- Justice: *Distribute benefits and risks fairly*
- Dignity: *Treat individuals with unconditional respect, and recognise the capacity to deliberate, decide and act without constraint*

The "core values", of course, have some similarity with the "Principles of Biomedical Ethics" by Beauchamp and Childress (1979), which are probably the most widely referred to ethical principles in the medical context. Moreover, Beauchamp and Childress (2013) claim that their framework is compatible with "common morality" which is "not relative to cultures or individuals, because it transcends both", and this cross-cultural validity was also an important consideration for the ICRP – not surprisingly for an organisation which is meant to set standards for government regulations world-wide.

In terms of the general applicability of the "Principles of Biomedical Ethics", which were developed mainly as a guide for decision making in clinical situations, there has, for instance, been some discussion in the literature about their usefulness in the context of public health. In order to cover specific aspects of that field, some authors have argued that the Beauchamp and Childress approach should be supplemented with a number of additional principles or core values, such as precaution, solidarity, effectiveness, and others (Coughlin 2008; Schröder-Bäck et al. 2014). Similarly, for environmental health (which can be understood to form part of public health) it has been suggested that the "Principles of Biomedical Ethics" should be considered as a basis, but that there are related principles or values which are needed to cover issues specific to the field, namely dignity as a corollary to respect for autonomy, solidarity as a corollary to beneficence, precaution as a corollary of non-maleficence and sustainability as a corollary of justice (Zölzer 2017).

The ICRP report does not rely completely on Beauchamp and Childress, either. Their system has "beneficence" and "non-maleficence" as two independent values, whereas ICRP combines them into one, emphasising the necessity of balancing good and harm. This reflects the first principle of radiological protection – justification: "Any decision that alters the radiation exposure situation should do more good than harm".

"Prudence" is not mentioned as an independent value by Beauchamp and Childress. It is, however, of great importance for radiological protection (as well as for the protection against chemical risks), where sometimes action has to be taken without exact knowledge of the risks involved, for instance at low doses. In such cases, the second principle of radiological protection applies – optimisation: "The likelihood of exposure, the number of people exposed, and the magnitude of their individual doses shall be kept as low as reasonably achievable, taking into account economic and societal factors" (ICRP 2007, paragraph 203). Here the underlying assumption is that even small doses of radiation carry a certain risk, with a similar risk per dose as observed at higher doses, and that this approach is based on "prudence". Although ICRP also refers to "precaution" (more details in ICRP 2018), this is not the only consideration guiding optimisation; "economic and societal factors" are to be considered as well. So "prudence", at least as used by ICRP, is a broader concept than "precaution", because it looks at the risks of the individual, but also at the benefits for the larger whole. We will briefly come back to this later.

Beauchamp and Childress list "respect for autonomy" instead of "dignity". This has been attributed to their Western cultural background, which assigns decision making in a clinical situation to the patient and the patient only, whereas the approach may be different elsewhere in the world (but that is a different discussion). "Dignity" is a more fundamental concept, basic not only to autonomous decision making, but also to non-discrimination, for instance, and this is what the ICRP document is referring to in particular.

Together with "justice", which is common to biomedical ethics and ethics of radiological protection, "dignity" forms the basis of the third principle of radiological protection – dose limitation: "The total dose to any individual from regulated sources in planned exposure situations . . . should not exceed the limits specified" (ICRP 2007, paragraph 203). The main purpose here is a fair distribution of risks, and the avoidance of treating a person as a mere means to an end, which could happen if one individual would be exposed to a relatively high risk in order to save many from a relatively low one.

We will now take a look at cost-benefit and cost-effectiveness analysis, and the values underlying them. Both refer to "economic and societal factors", but they do so in different ways, placing their emphasis on different ethical principles, as it would seem.

Cost-benefit analysis tries to express both good and harm in monetary values, in order to be able to judge whether net-benefit is achieved. It is thus primarily concerned with beneficence and non-maleficence, focusing on the overall outcome so much that it sometimes neglects justice. This is the case, for instance, where it collates the consequences of decision making for different groups or individuals, not taking into consideration the fact that the good may be obtained by some, but the harm by others. An example of this could be a certain waste disposal scenario, which might benefit many, especially those who are able to afford living in cleaner and greener neighbourhoods, but might have health deteriorating effects for those who have to be content with cheaper housing closer to the disposal site. Attempts have been made to include such considerations into cost-benefit analysis, but this is not the rule (Atkinson and Mourato 2008; Cranor and Finkel 2018). The concept of social justice developed by John Rawls in his "Justice as Fairness" suggests that inequalities are only acceptable if they are "to the greatest benefit to the least advantaged" (Rawls 1971: 13) which is clearly not the case in our scenario (Pinkerton et al. 2002). (Social) justice is closely related to the fourth core value, dignity. With it, cost-benefit analysis is hardest to reconcile in our view. Most people, if they were asked directly, would probably agree that it is impossible to reduce a human life to a monetary value. This is particularly obvious with the Human Capital Approach mentioned by the ICRP in its earliest recommendations concerning cost-benefit analysis, because it considers nothing but the economic output produced by an individual. Reservations also apply to the Contingent Valuation Methods. They appear to respect people's own appraisal of health risks, but the fact that the "Value of a Statistical Life" is influenced by factors such as country, income, and age raises doubts about the compatibility of this approach with the concept of all humans being born with equal dignity.

Cost-effectiveness analysis, on the other hand, is very much focused on justice, especially justice as a fair distribution between people affected by similar risks. It does not advise for or against an action as such, but compares the monetary aspects of different possible actions supposed to reduce the same or similar types of risk. Thus, one could say that it is not primarily concerned with beneficence and non-maleficence, although of course indirectly it is, in so far as it helps to secure an effective use of resources. It also does not suggest that monetary criteria are sufficient to decide about the right or wrong of an action and admits that there must be other criteria which play a role in decision making. Consider, for instance, the fact that with the same money which would be sufficient to save just one life in the case of a uranium sludge depository, thousands of lives could be saved when spending it on measures against radon. But it may not be considered acceptable (or politically opportune) for plenty of other reasons to leave the waste deposits as they are, for instance because people living in the vicinity are worried, the economy of the area will be negatively affected, tourism will not develop, etc. Not all of these factors lend themselves to being considered in a rational analysis, obviously, but some have to be accepted as "extra-rational", which does not mean that they should not be taken into account (Pinkerton et al. 2002). The concerns regarding dignity raised in the context of cost-benefit analysis do not apply here, as there is no attempt to measure both human lives and economic gains or losses in monetary terms, but it just compares lives with lives, and dollars with dollars.

Cost-benefit analysis and cost-effectiveness analysis are quite similar as far as prudence is concerned. Both make cautious but reasonable assumptions about risks that are not really known, such as the risks caused by low doses of radiation and chemicals. They calculate risks according to the best available mathematical models, which, as mentioned earlier, are not based on epidemiological evidence alone, but involve extrapolations. When it comes to "economic and societal factors", the two methods differ again on how these are taken into account.

In summary, it seems to us that from an ethical perspective cost-benefit analysis is fundamentally flawed, or at least suffers from serious drawbacks. It fails to comply with important aspects of justice and is incompatible with most people's understanding of human dignity, which is especially obvious when one looks at the different values of a statistical life derived for different types of risk, in different countries, with different age groups, etc. By contrast, cost-effectiveness analysis does not have these problems. It is compatible with all ethical values or principles considered here. The differences in costs per life saved, which become obvious with the comparison of different interventions, do not point to a problem with the method itself, but highlight a challenge with decision making on public spending, namely that the same amount of money could save a hundred or thousand times more lives if directed to one problem instead of another.

Notes

1 From their Tables I and II, it seems that the median for 13 interventions was 1 400 € per life-year saved, but seven of those concerned indoor radon, which entails relatively low costs as mentioned above (our Table 11.2). If these are pooled, the seven remaining values come to around 30 000 €.
2 This value, given in their Table III, is actually a quote from Hellqvist et al. (1982), which is not available to us, so we cannot judge how biased the underlying selection of 19 studies may be.
3 The median for radiation protection is based on 26 interventions listed in their Appendix A under "radiation control" and "radon control." The authors claim that the median for "toxin control" is based on 144 interventions, but this group apparently includes those for radiation protection. In their Appendix A, 93 interventions of chemical protection as such are listed. Nevertheless, the median for these alone is not much different from that for the whole group; around 2 million dollars.

References

Ackerman F. (2008) *Critique of Cost-Benefit Analysis, and Alternative Approaches to Decision-Making*. Available at www.ase.tufts.edu/gdae/Pubs/rp/Ack_UK_CBAcritique.pdf. Date Accessed: 20 November 2017.

Anderson H., Treich N. (2011) 'The Value of a Statistical Life', in: *A Handbook of Transport Economics*, edited by De Palma A., Lindsey R., Quinet E., Vickerman R. Cheltenham: Edward Elgar.

Arigoni Ortiz R., Markandya A., Hunt A. (2009) 'Willingness to Pay for Mortality Risk Reduction Associated With Air Pollution in São Paulo', *Revista Brasileira de Economia*, 63, 3–22.

Atkinson G., Mourato S. (2008) 'Environmental Cost-benefit Analysis', *Annual Review of Environment and Resources*, 33, 317–44.

Beauchamp T. L., Childress J. F. (1979[1], 2013[7]) *Principles of Biomedical Ethics*. Oxford: Oxford University Press.

Carson R. T., Mitchell R. C. (2000) 'Public Preferences Toward Risk: The Case of Trihalomethanes', in: *Handbook of Contingent Valuation*, edited by Alberini A., Bjornstad D., Kahn J. R. Northampton, MA: Edward Elgar.

CEG = Center for Effective Government (2015) *Cost-Benefit Analysis*. Available at www.foreffectivegov.org/node/3470. Date Accessed: 20 November 2017.

Chanel O., Luchini S. (2008) 'Monetary Values for Air Pollution Risk of Death: A Contingent Valuation Survey', *GREQAM Groupement de Recherche en Economie Quantitative d'Aix-Marseille* (Document de Travail no. 2008–5). Available at https://halshs.archives-ouvertes.fr/halshs-00272776/document. Date Accessed: 20 November 2017.

Choi K. S., Lee K. J., Lee B. W. (2001) 'Determining the Value of Reductions in Radiation Risk Using the Contingent Valuation Method', *Annals of Nuclear Energy*, 28, 1431–45.

Coughlin S. S. (2008) 'How Many Principles for Public Health Ethics', *Open Public Health Journal*, 1, 8–16.

Cranor C. F., Finkel A. M. (2018) 'Toward the Usable Recognition of Individual Benefits and Costs in Regulatory Analysis and Governance', *Regulation & Governance*, 12, 131–49.

Fischer T. K., Anh D. D., Antil L., Cat N. D., Kilgore P. E., Thiem V. D., Rheingans R., Tho le H., Glass R. I., Bresee J. S. (2005) 'Health Care Costs of Diarrheal Disease and Estimates of the Cost-effectiveness of Rotavirus Vaccination in Vietnam', *The Journal of Infectious Diseases*, 192, 1720–6.

Forslund J., Samakovlis E., Johansson M. V., Barregard L. (2010) 'Does Remediation Save Lives? – On the Cost of Cleaning Up Arsenic-contaminated Sites in Sweden', *Science of the Total Environment*, 408, 3085–91.

Hammitt J. K. (2008) 'Valuing "Lives Saved" vs. "Life-years Saved"', *Eurohealth*, 14, 34–7.

Hammitt J. K., Haninger K. (2010) 'Valuing Fatal Risks to Children and Adults: Effects of Disease, Latency, and Risk Aversion', *The Journal of Risk and Uncertainty*, 40, 57–83.

Hanmer L., Lensink R., White H. (2003) 'Infant and Child Mortality in Developing Countries: Analysing the Data for Robust Determinants', *Journal of Development Studies*, 40, 101–18.

Hanrahan D., Fuller R., Singh A. (2007) *Cost Effectiveness and Health Impact of Remediation of Highly Polluted Sites in the Developing World*. Available at www.blacksmithinstitute.org/files/FileUpload/files/Polluted%20Places/costEff1.pdf. Date Accessed: 20 November 2017.

Harris J. M., Roach B. (2017) *Environmental and Natural Resource Economics: A Contemporary Approach*. New York, NY: Taylor & Francis.

Hellqvist B., Juås B., Karlsson C., Mattsson B., Thompson S. (1982) *Värdering av Risken för Personskador. En Jämförande Studie av Implicta och Explicita Värden*, 2nd Ed. Göteborg, Sweden: Nationalekonomiska Institutionen vid Göteborgs Universitet.

ICRP = International Commission on Radiological Protection (1973) 'Implications of the Commission Recommendations that Doses be Kept as Low as Readily Achievable', *ICRP Publication 22*. Oxford, UK: Pergamon Press.

ICRP = International Commission on Radiological Protection (1989) 'Optimization and Decision-Making in Radiological Protection', *ICRP Publication* 55. Ann. ICRP 20/1.

ICRP = International Commission on Radiological Protection (2006) 'The Optimisation of Radiological Protection'. *ICRP 101*. Ann. ICRP 36, 65–104.

ICRP = International Commission on Radiological Protection (2007) 'The 2007 Recommendations of the International Commission on Radiological Protection', *ICRP Publication 103*. Ann. ICRP 37.

ICRP = International Commission on Radiological Protection (2018) 'Ethical Foundations of the System of Radiological Protection', *ICRP Publication 138*. Ann. ICRP 47.

Kamm F. M. (2015) 'Cost Effectiveness Analysis and Fairness', *Journal of Practical Ethics*, 3, 1–14.

Kelman S. (1981) 'Cost-Benefit Analysis: An Ethical Critique', *Regulation*, 5, 33–40.

Lindhjem H., Navrud S., Braathen N. A., Biausque V. (2011) 'Valuing Mortality Risk Reductions From Environmental, Transport, and Health Policies: A Global Meta-Analysis of Stated Preference Studies', *Risk Analysis*, 31, 1381–407.

Miller T. R. (2000) 'Variations between Countries in Values of Statistical Life', *Journal of Transport, Economics and Policy*, 34, 169–88.

NRC = United States Nuclear Regulatory Commission (1995) *Reassessment of NRC's Dollar Per Person-Rem Conversion Factor Policy*. NUREG-1530, Initial. Available at www.nrc.gov/docs/ML0634/ML063470485.pdf.

NRC = United States Nuclear Regulatory Commission (2015) *Reassessment of NRC's Dollar Per Person-Rem Conversion Factor Policy*. NUREG-1530, Revision 1. Available at www.nrc.gov/docs/ML1523/ML15237A211.pdf.

Paul V. K., Singh M. (2004) 'Regionalized Perinatal Care in Developing Countries', *Seminars in Neonatology*, 9, 117–24.

Pearce D., Atkinson G., Mourato S. (2006) *Cost-Benefit Analysis and the Environment: Recent Developments*. Paris: OECD Publishing.

Pinkerton S. D., Johnson-Masotti A. P., Derse A., Layde P. M. (2002) 'Ethical Issues in Cost-effectiveness Analysis', *Evaluation and Program Planning*, 25, 71–83.

Pope C., Thun M., Namboodri M., Dockery D., Evans J., Speizer F., Health C. (1995) 'Particulate Air Pollution as a Predictor of Mortality in a Prospective Study of US Adults', *American Journal of Respiratory and Critical Care Medicine*, 151, 669–74.

Ramsberg J., Sjöberg L. (1996) 'The Cost-Effectiveness of Lifesaving Interventions in Sweden', *Rhizikon – Risk Research Report*, No. 24, Center for Risk Research, Stockholm, Sweden, 271–90.

Ramsberg J., Sjöberg L. (1997) 'The Cost-effectiveness of Lifesaving Interventions in Sweden', *Risk Analysis*, 17, 467–78.

Rawls, J. (1971) A Theory of Justice. Harvard University Press, Cambridge, MA, USA.

Robinson L. A. (2007) 'How US Government Agencies Value Mortality Risk Reductions', *Review of Environmental Economics and Policy*, 1, 283–99.

Ross J. (1997) 'Cost-Effectiveness of the Nutrition Communication Project in Mali', *SARA Project, Washington, DC, USA*. Available at http://citeseerx.ist.psu.edu/viewdoc/download?doi=10.1.1.558.5703&rep=rep1&type=pdf. Date Accessed: 20 November 2017.

Russell L. B., Sinha A. (2016) 'Strengthening Cost-Effectiveness Analysis for Public Health Policy', *American Journal of Preventive Medicine*, 50, S6–S12.

Sagoff M. (2009) 'Regulatory Review and Cost-Benefit Analysis', *Philosophy & Public Policy Quarterly*, 29, 21–6.

Schneider T., Schieber C., Eeckhoudt L., Godfroid P. (2000) 'A Model to Establish the Monetary Value of the Man-sievert for Public Exposure', in: *IRPA-10, Proceedings of the 10th International Congress of the International Radiation Protection Association on Harmonization of Radiation, Human Life and the Ecosystem, No. P-9-114*. Hiroshima: Japan Health Physics Society.

Schröder-Bäck P., Duncan P., Sherlaw W., Brall C., Czabanowska K. (2014) 'Teaching Seven Principles for Public Health Ethics: Towards a Curriculum for a Short Course on Ethics in Public Health Programmes', *BMC Medical Ethics*, 15, 73–82.

Sjöberg L., Ogander T. (1994) 'Att rädda liv – Kostnader och effekter (Saving Lives: Costs and Effects)', *Ds 1994:14 Finansdepartementet*, Stockholm, Sweden.

Sunstein C. R. (2004) 'Are Poor People Worth Less than Rich People? Disaggregating the Value of Statistical Lives', *John M. Olin Program in Law and Economics Working Paper No. 207*. Available at http://chicagounbound.uchicago.edu/law_and_economics/63/. Date Accessed: 20 November 2017.

Svensson M., Hultkrantz L. (2017) 'A Comparison of Cost-benefit and Cost-effectiveness Analysis in Practice: Divergent Policy Practices in Sweden', *Nordic Journal of Health Economics*, 5, 41–53.

Swedish Radiation Protection Institute = Statens strålskyddsinstitut (1992) 'Vad får skydd mot strålning och andra risker kosta? (What Protection Costs Will Be Incurred for Radiation and Other Risks?)', *SSI Rapport No. 92-10*, Stockholm, Sweden.

Swedish Radiation Protection Institute = Statens strålskyddsinstitut (1993) 'Radon – En Rapport över Laget (Radon – A Situation Report)', *SSI Rapport No. 93-10*, Stockholm, Sweden.

Tengs T. O., Adams M. E., Pliskin J. S., Safran D. G., Siegel J. E., Weinstein M. C., Graham J. D. (1995) 'Five-hundred Life-saving Interventions and Their Cost-effectiveness', *Risk Analysis*, 15, 369–90.

Vassanadumrongdee S., Matsuoka S. (2005) 'Risk Perceptions and Value of a Statistical Life for Air Pollution and Traffic Accidents: Evidence From Bangkok, Thailand', *Journal of Risk and Uncertainty*, 30, 261–87.

Viscusi W. K. (2000) 'Risk Equity', *Journal of Legal Studies*, 29, 843–71.

Viscusi W. K., Masterman C. L. (2017) 'Income Elasticities and Global Values of a Statistical Life', *Journal of Benefit-Cost Analysis*, 8, 226–50.

WHO Regional Office for Europe, OECD (2015) *Economic Cost of the Health Impact of Air Pollution in Europe: Clean Air, Health and Wealth*. Copenhagen: WHO Regional Office for Europe. Available at www.euro.who.int/__data/assets/pdf_file/0004/276772/Economic-cost-health-impact-air-pollution-en.pdf.

Zölzer F. (2017) 'A Common Morality Approach to Environmental Health Ethics', in: *Ethics of Environmental Health*, edited by Zölzer F., Meskens G., 51–68, Oxford: Routledge.

12 The need for consistency in dealing with individual sensitivity to workplace hazards

Chris J. Kalman

1 Introduction

I am a career occupational physician in the UK. The speciality focuses on the fitness of the individual for their work, and of the work for the individual. Principle considerations include adaptations and modifications in the workplace triggered by disability or the need for rehabilitation back to work, as well as the important area of occupational illness or disease associated with exposure at work. Both these issues appear to be particularly relevant in relation to consideration of individual sensitivity to occupational hazards to health.

My own employment has centred on the hazards of ionising radiations, in the medical support to UK's Naval submarine nuclear propulsion programme, as a chief medical officer of a nuclear power electricity generating utility, and now in the National Health Service, an organisation which of course causes much more radiation doses to individual people than the other two. One of the joys of occupational medicine is that we may have more time to speak to patients/clients than many other clinical specialities and, over the years, I have probably spent more time than most talking to workers alone or in groups in relation to their feelings about radiation and its hazards. I have also spent countless hours providing information and training about those hazards.

The first ISEEH in 2011 was initially branded as a meeting on the ethics of radiation protection. I dusted off data and slides to present an issue which had dominated my life a number of years earlier, dealing with the ethical responsibility owed by researchers to workers involved in epidemiological and other types of study in relation to workplace hazards. It is still easy to recall the absolute anguish caused to workers, and their families, by failures to meet that responsibility. Workers who have agreed to participate in studies must deserve the courtesy of receiving the results of the work in a controlled manner, rather than from the banner newspaper or television headlines, that often follow press releases of high profile radiation studies. I have to say how much I enjoyed that first ISEEH meeting with its distinct groupings of radiation and philosophy. I was struck however by how little we knew of each other's specialities. My previous contact with philosophers and ethicists had been minimal with little awareness of their science; or is it their art? Similarly however, discussion could also demonstrate the limited radiation science knowledge in the other group.

Historically, the UK has made some significant contribution to occupational medicine, such as the first identification of occupational cancer by Percival Pott in 1775, and the massive contribution made by Charles Thackrah with his treaty on "the effects of arts, trades and professions on health and longevity" in 1832. In the following years, there were some more dubious ethical activities around the certification of children as meeting the minimum age for work as chimney sweeps or in factories, but we appear to have moved on from there. In recent years, particularly since the foundation of the Faculty of Occupational Medicine of the Royal College of Physicians, the speciality has championed the need for specific ethical guidance for occupational health practice, first published in 1980, and frequently updated since (Faculty of Occupational Medicine 2012). The research aspects mentioned earlier were included in the 2006 edition, though as yet individual sensitivity is not an aspect that features.

2 Individual sensitivity to ionising radiations

Differing individual sensitivities to ionising radiations have been discussed and indeed demonstrated for very many years. The fact that there were differences between patients in their response to ionising radiotherapy has long been demonstrated in the clinic. The classical example is in relation to skin damage from treatment for breast cancer, where appropriate testing would allow the possibility to increase doses to the less sensitive to enhance the chance of cure, as well as reducing doses to the more sensitive to reduce the probability or avoid distressing side effects. For occupational physicians however, there was scope to take some comfort from the possibility that there would be major differences in mechanisms leading to cell killing of both cancer and normal cells at acute doses of 10s of gray (Gy) in the clinic, and the possible induction of cancer from chronic annual exposures of doses orders of magnitude less in the millisieverts (mSv) range accrued in the workplace or from the natural environment. It is sometimes easier and simpler to consider deterministic and stochastic effects as radiation killing cells or leaving them damaged in some way. Logic determines that you don't cause cancer in cells that have been killed, and therefore it is possible to at least postulate very real differences in outcomes from different mechanisms of sensitivity at different doses. It is clear however, that life evolved at far higher natural background radiation levels than even the highest areas we know of today. We know that ionising radiations produce double strand DNA breaks, probably the crucial lesion for cancer induction, and that there are complex systems for repair of radiation damage, many of which are based on genetic factors. Radiation sensitivity to cancer in certain well known single gene syndromes like Ataxia Telangiectasia is well established. Therefore, even before considering newer radiation biology, such as genomic instability, and bystander effects, common sense would have suggested that the heterogeneity in the human population would exhibit, to some extent, heterogeneity in radiation sensitivity. These issues were last evaluated in detail by the International Commission on Radiation Protection (ICRP) in 2005 (ICRP 2007, 56), and at that time the body concluded "genetic susceptibility to radiation induced cancer involving strongly expressed genes is rare."

Research has progressed significantly since the last ICRP conclusions. The stimulus for the ISEEH14 presentation was the publication in the UK of an expert review of human radiation sensitivity (UK Health Protection Agency 2013). So what does this report tell us? In summary: that there is known genetic radiation sensitivity, but it goes on to question the ethics of genetic testing of workers, indicating that for some well-known genes, such as ATM, genetic tests are available and could in principle be applied in occupational protection. They note that there are more syndromes known with demonstrable increased radiosensitivity, and that cellular studies appear to indicate that the spectrum of radiosensitivity is broader at low dose rates.

Public health is of course increasingly aware of environmental and lifestyle factors which are associated with health outcomes in general, and cancers in particular. This report indicates that the risk of cancer from radiation "to some extent" relates to factors that apply to cancer in general, and raises the potential of lifestyle factors to be important in occupational risk from ionising radiation. They note that in animal studies, radiosensitivity to cancer induction is often related to spontaneous incidence.

Finally, the report indicates that, in certain situations, risks of specific cancers could be much higher in certain human sub groups. Here there is focus on the proposal that radiation-induced leukaemia could occur almost entirely in those members of the population who carry clonal expanded lymphocytes with preleukaemic translocations.

Even before this report, I believe that it was clear that regulators in various countries were beginning to think about radiation sensitivity in their systems of radiation protection. Given the media profile, public concern and research focus of ionising radiation as a topic, it would appear inevitable that regulation will be driven forward in this area, with the potential for setting precedents which would therefore have to be considered relevant in all areas of occupational and environmental risk.

3 Individual sensitivity to occupational hazards

As doctors, physicists and regulators or philosophers and ethicists, we must recognise that individual sensitivity is not purely an ionising radiation matter. While there have been some regulator discussion documents on the subject (UK Health and Safety Executive 2007), it is not an issue which is routinely addressed, nor is it one which currently features much if at all in regulatory controls for occupational hazards.

Comparing available non-radiation research with the UK Human radiation sensitivity report provides many interesting examples. Looking first at genetic sensitivity, this is of course well-established in relation to sunlight, which like ionising radiation is ubiquitous in our lives and in the environment. In the occupational area, genetic factors have been linked to a wide range of diseases, with end points including bladder cancer from aromatic amines, dust diseases such as silicosis, acute toxicity from pesticides, hearing loss from noise exposure and chronic disease toxicity from beryllium (Schulte and Howard 2011). In the period immediately before ISEEH14, there was a new report on the interactions of specific genotypes and lung function following occupational exposure to a wide range of occupational exposures to vapours, dusts and fumes (Mehta et al. 2014). There are established genetic links increasing sensitivity to infections that may be acquired occupationally (Martchenko et al. 2012), and even in relation to stress and psychological health (Karg et al. 2011). It is conventional to consider workplace hazards in a table of physical, chemical, psychological and biological factors, and there is now clear evidence for some importance of individual genetic sensitivity in health effects in all these areas.

With regard to lifestyle, the principle link identified in the UK paper was a more than additive risk between radon exposure and smoking in relation to lung cancer induction. This of course mimics the well-established multiplicative risk between asbestos and smoking for the same end point. Intuitively, in complex systems of cancer induction which may require several mutations and non-genetic effects, and where there are lifestyle factors which are already well established, it is clear that there may be synergisms between these lifestyle and occupational factors, both in increasing risk and indeed in protection from risk. In malignant cell transformation experiments it was always interesting to note how many cells would be transformed compared with actual cancers in whole animals irradiated at similar doses. This does clearly raise the potential for consideration of lifestyle factors in relation to fitness to work in a variety of situations.

Looking for non-radiation risks which could be much higher in certain human sub groups, in my current employment you need to look no further than Natural Rubber Latex (NRL). With the vast increase in NRL glove use based on the developing HIV epidemic, the true risks of Type I immediate hypersensitivity and anaphylaxis from NRL were increasingly recognised as a very real life-threatening occupational hazard and significant risk to healthcare staff and others. This risk however is almost exclusively borne by a strongly atopic group of people who often have pre-existing and multiple allergies.

In summary, ionising radiations are not unique in relation to individual sensitivity. It appears likely however, that the profile of ionising radiations will drive the development of radiation protection regulation to include some consideration of sensitivity. At present it seems that this activity is being undertaken in isolation. There is of course a history of radiation taking the lead in development of regulation, with the promulgation of concepts such as the principle of optimisation and "as low as reasonably achievable (ALARA)" (ICRP 1977, 3) which are now adopted with different titles in the regulation of other hazards, particularly carcinogens. I question however if it is desirable for radiation to take action in isolation within this individual sensitivity field. For me, the answer must be no. There is a need for a major piece of work addressing the issue aimed at establishing some principles of consensus which we can explain to workers, the people who truly matter, which are equally applicable to noise, dust, ionising radiations and the rest. Despite some significant proposals and evaluations of the issues and factors, there has been no real effort at consensus development as yet.

4 How might regulation work?

If sensitive populations are to be protected, this can be achieved either by special standards for individuals within that group (differentiated protection), or strict general standards to protect all (unified protection) (Hansson 2009). The most extreme form of differentiated protection would of course be the actual exclusion of sensitive individuals from various roles in the workplace to ensure they are not exposed.

It is at least possible to think of the potential for differentiated protection in the occupational situation, where work and hence exposure can be controlled. It is much more difficult to consider how it could operate in relation to environmental exposures from hazards released from industry. Here there is little or no control of the exposed population, and even methods of estimating exposure are far less exact.

The issue is even more complicated in relation to hazards where there is natural exposure. I suppose ionising radiations are the archetypical example here. A very significant amount of occupational exposure results from natural background in the workplace, there is a wide variation in natural background doses, and these exceed the doses resulting from radioactive discharges from industry or health provision. I am pretty sure that outside the relevant scientific community, natural background radiation is a concept viewed with a good deal of scientism; indeed I too needed conversion. My "St Paul" moment came many years ago, when in the Royal Navy, I was promoted and moved from a running submarine to a squadron support post. I required enhanced radiation protection training and was sent to what was then the Royal Naval College at Greenwich. The course was mostly attended by graduate health physicists who knew nothing about submarines. One morning, based on my practical experience, I was asked to demonstrate to the students how to perform an alpha background air sample. On board, this was something done regularly, and within our thick metal submarine walls not a lot was expected to happen. Here, however, in a prestigious historical building designed by Sir Christopher Wren, the lights on the scaler flashed like a Christmas tree. Natural background is real. If we are to regulate for individual sensitivity, then there surely must be consistency as to how the hazard is regarded in different situations.

5 Ethical factors

In the ISEEH 14 presentation, I made it clear that I was not proposing any detailed personal view on what the solution for regulation including individual sensitivity should look like. About the same time I wrote an editorial for the Journal of Occupational Medicine (Kalman 2015), on the subject, where there was significant discussion at the drafting stage on the desirability of including a proposed solution. One thing my involvement with ISEEH has taught me however, is that such proposals would be entirely the wrong approach. The way forward must be a meeting of minds of relevant expertise and stakeholders, with time to explore all relevant considerations and aimed at consensus building. It is however appropriate in a paper such as this to attempt to raise some of these factors, as well as looking at how they have been addressed in regulation to date.

Looking in the first instance more at ethics than science, in a leading article introducing Mehta's 2014 paper, Nelson and Kelsey (2014, 229–230) ended by saying: "Traditionally we strive to protect the most susceptible to exposure as a matter of principle. This principle should not be abandoned." It is questioned however, if this is indeed what regulators have done, or indeed whether this is the current consensus. Looking at the simple hazard of noise, one of the few situations where there have been considerations of sensitivity in regulation, it is clear that variations in sensitivity were increasingly recognized from the early 1970s. The adoption of action levels in regulation in the late '80s that recognized these would not protect all exposure, provides an example of the alternative policy.

In the past, the issue of sensitivity has been examined significantly in relation to the employment of women and exposure to teratogens in the workplace. Particularly in the U.S. there has been a dichotomy between issues such as civil rights prohibiting discrimination in employment on grounds of gender, and so called foetal protection policies. In 1991, the US Supreme Court ruled that "unless pregnant employees differ in their ability or inability to work, they must be treated the same as other employees for all employment related purposes" (US Supreme Court 1991). These sorts of consideration have led to the need for specific regulatory standards for the unborn child, such as the significant difference between UK statutory controls for ionising radiations between 1985 and 1999, moving from consideration of women of child-bearing age to treatment of the foetus as a member of the general public in terms of dose limitation. It is clearly possible that over time we will identify other temporary considerations such as medical treatment or illness and capability, which are relevant to individual sensitivity. This is of course already a vital part of occupational medicine in terms of modifications or restrictions at work in relation to immunosuppression from drug therapy or in relation to manual handling capability. I suppose that manual handling controls and limits provide a prevalent example of differentiated protection already commonplace internationally. There is also the potential for gender rights issues to again come to the fore, in areas where there is proven differences in sensitivity between males and females. Into the future, another major challenge for occupational health will be the ageing population. Pensions for workers fortunate enough to live in countries that pay them will be paid later and later, as human life expectancy continues to grow. Workers will work for longer and longer, though it is clear they may "have greater sensitivity" to many of the hazards, compared with their younger co-workers.

There seems little doubt that a substantial proportion of sensitivity is based on genetics. There are however in existence very differing views on genetic testing in the workplace. The International Labour Organisation continues to indicate that genetic screening in the workplace should be prohibited, or at least limited to cases explicitly authorised by national legislation (International Labour Organisation 1997). The U.S. prohibits discrimination on the basis of genetic information, and indicates employers are not able to enquire about genetic testing until after the job offer has been made (U.S. Legislation 2008). In Europe the advisory group to the European Commission has been less dogmatic, concluding that workers and their representatives should be involved in deciding when and how genetic testing in the workplace is done (European Commission 2003). In terms of ethics it is also probably worth recording the potential for resistant sub groups, and what, if any, regulatory systems could or should be put in place for them. While the width of the dose response curves will vary, it seems likely that there will be a band of general sensitivity in the middle, with sensitive and resistant sub groups on either side.

National systems dealing with disability also have some parallels here. Firstly, it may be that the condition relating to the sensitivity may itself trigger its categorisation as a disability. In the UK the term is defined as a health effect that causes a substantial effect on the individual's day to day living. This I suppose could well be the case for a person with significant increased sensitivity to an environmental factor whether it is natural or manmade. Particularly in relation to genetic syndromes there may well be other aspects to the condition which trigger disability separate from considerations of a specific sensitivity. Even if the condition itself is not considered a disability, there are parallels between how increased sensitivity and disability could be considered. In the UK (UK Legislation 2010) there is a statutory duty for employers to consider reasonable modifications in the workplace to allow workers covered by the legislation to take up or to maintain employment. However, like the U.S. situation regarding genetic testing (above), questions regarding disability can only take place after the offer of employment has been made. It is however possible for an employer to designate roles where *not* having a particular health condition is considered an intrinsic part of the job, allowing a simple decision that the individual is not fit for the post.

Consideration of the issue in isolation can, of course, make policy that affects other important ethical principles. In an earlier section, I mentioned that the risk of Type 1 anaphylaxis to NRL is borne solely by the strongly atopic. The vast increase in NRL glove use required to protect healthcare workers after the diagnosis of HIV determined the need for re-consideration of regulatory controls. In some countries this has prompted ever increasing efforts to continue to improve and reduce still further the potential for sensitisation using hypoallergenic gloves. In the UK, however, the decision was taken to take steps to eliminate NRL gloves, based on the system of hierarchy of controls, and the availability of a "suitable" alternative. This appears to raise the issue of sustainability, with a natural agriculture product being substituted with non-sustainable alternatives from the petrochemical industry. It is clear that many large organic molecules like latex occurring in the natural environment will cause allergy, including life-threatening anaphylaxis, in part of the human population. There would be real issues of sustainability if all these naturally grown products were required to be substituted in this way. In relation to food, most, if not all, primary starches are in this category, it being true for wheat, rye, oats, barley, rice and nuts, with actual local incidence relating to the amount eaten in that part of the world. Should we consider this as individual sensitivity in terms of the ethics of environmental health and seek to control exposure?

The issues of synergy between lifestyle factors and sensitivity to occupational hazards appear to add a further major need for ethical consideration of the matter. Clinical medicine has long been advising patients on the modification of lifestyle in relation to risks from underlying health conditions; similarly health promotion is now a recognised profession looking at modifying population and individual risk. In the main this has centred on advice rather than compulsion, though there is increasing regulatory control in relation to the purchase of known hazards, and limits on exposure to others, as is the case in smoking. In the workplace, controls on activity such as smoking are commonplace, where the activity causes increased hazard at work, such as an increase in risks relating to fire hazards. Requirements not to undertake an activity at all, including at home, based on workplace considerations are unknown to me. It seems clear to me that a wide perspective of existing ethical principles will be required in relation to any consensus on sensitivity regulation and lifestyle.

6 Practicality

In any discussion of factors, it is not possible to ignore monetary cost. Amendments to the systems of regulation and control based on individual sensitivity, including aspects of lifestyle would inevitably cost, both for the operation of the system itself, and in relation to its operation in industry and life in general. What can society afford? A system based on higher expenditure in a higher risk or bigger sensitive sub group could have some logic, but this would probably be lost on an individual at intermediate risk, or higher risk of a less life-threatening hazard in a small sensitive sub group.

How these issues are resolved I will leave to others, but as one involved professionally in talking to workers about hazard and risk, my plea would be for consistency and principles which apply to various hazards and indeed to the same hazard in different situations or practices. While workplace costs are borne by the employer, natural exposure and environmental considerations may fall to society or indeed the exposed individuals themselves, in situations like remediation to houses to reduce radon levels. In current radiation protection, a brief examination of estimates of the cost of saving a man Sv of dose currently demonstrates massive differences between considerations of discharges from nuclear power, discharges from nuclear medicine and control of natural background. These are difficult to explain or justify to workers.

The plea for clarity extends beyond considerations of cost into the actual basis of the system of regulation adopted. Radiation physics, extended into biology, and now the new biology is complex. However, the current straight line dose response through the origin for stochastic effects is a spectacularly simple system for protection. Importantly it can be explained to workers in a matter of minutes. It allows the idea of collective dose, and coupled with the concepts of whole body dose equivalence, and committed dose means that it is comparatively easy to practice radiation protection on a daily basis.

Most national statutory systems of health and safety regulation include requirements for workers to be trained, not only in to how to protect themselves at work, but also in relation to the hazard and risk they face. I have always felt that this latter aspect was crucial, and when done correctly provides a massive input to the individual's safety. During my naval career, I had one role where my job included advice at government ministry level. On my first day I was met by a senior civil servant who told me: "In the ministry there are some people like you, who know, then there are others whose job it is to turn the words of those who know into words which are intelligible by politicians. I am one of those." We can debate as to whether the public are likely to understand more or less than politicians, but the point is crucial, and our systems of regulation must be able to be understood by the workers they seek to protect. With millions of workers currently exposed to hazards where there is some evidence of individual sensitivity, those deciding the way forward must also recognise that they do not have a blank sheet of paper, and that new systems must build on what is currently understood.

7 Scientific factors

We can then turn to the consideration of science, biology, physics and toxicology. It is comparatively easy to determine if somebody is pregnant, but other sensitive sub groups may be much more difficult to identify. It is probably the difficulty in taking forward meaningful tests, which has held back the issue of regulation based on sensitivity to date. The UK report however tells us that testing for some genetic radiation sub groups is available and could be done now. There are however a number of interesting issues around the identification of at risk groups. What if we identify a group for which we have a test, but we know there is a group at greater risk where there is no accurate test available? What if we regulate in relation to known sensitivities, only to find that at a later date there are groups even more sensitive? There are the hugely important issues of both sensitivity and specificity, with important implications for false positives and false negatives.

Of major concern will be the strength of the association, and hence the actual risk faced by the individuals concerned. The possibilities extend from a single gene defect with the almost certain consequence of the effect if exposure takes place, to a small factor in a multifactorial pathway, requiring other exposures or factors including lifestyle issues, contributing a slight risk to the population. These factors may well affect the regulatory system chosen. It may be considered appropriate to exclude from exposure small groups at high risk, whereas lower risk to large sub groups could argue for changes in population controls and limits. Over time our knowledge will in all probability develop. It seems to me important not to legislate and state principles based on the simple large risks we may know, which, in the future, it will be impossible to follow as small multifactorial issues are identified.

Scientific evaluation of the mechanism of sensitivity is vital, leading to a consideration of a dose response for the effect. It is interesting to remember how young this science is. The assumption of a threshold for almost all toxins was the basis for almost all regulation until the middle of the 1970s and radiation's adoption of

ALARA. This sort of thresholdless risk is now assumed for many hazards, particularly carcinogens, but clearly is not really compatible with regulatory systems based on absolute safety. In radiation protection we already recognise that there may be different dose response relationships for different effects or end points. It certainly seems credible if sensitivity is based around issues of failure to repair, rather than in relation to the primary insult, that sensitivity will have a different dose relationship to that primary effect, with thresholds, quadratics, straight lines and even protection on the list. Radiation, like a number of human hazards, does demonstrate adapted responses. These issues are not easy, but it seems hard to understand how a system of protection, including consideration of sensitive sub groups, can be put in place without a full understanding of these dose responses.

8 Conclusion

In conclusion, I would restate that individual sensitivity to workplace hazards is a fact of life. Sat in the clinic, I see workers who have been exposed to way beyond the hand arm vibration action levels for many years, although apparently immune to the effects of such exposure. On the other hand, we see individuals essentially minimally exposed at or around the action level over a short period of time, who have developed symptoms. It is not a radiation specific consideration, and extends into other physical, chemical, biological and even psychological workplace exposure.

There is clear and growing evidence for individual sensitivity to ionising radiations. Given the well-established infrastructure around the development of radiation protection systems, coupled with the media and public profile of this hazard, I suspect we will see some plans to incorporate sensitivity considerations into radiation protection in the fairly near future. My plea at ISEEH was for this not to happen. The issue is too important to be left to a single hazard to lead or determine policy. This may set precedents that are not compatible with a solution based on the issue as a whole. In my view there is a need for a major piece of work, at least for the EU, if not the world, involving regulators, toxicologists, specialists in ethics, worker representatives and employers to examine the issue as a whole. Stakeholder discussion and the development of consensus, based on common view of the data and knowledge provides the best way for the issue to be resolved appropriately. With such a document in place, its implementation for various hazards could proceed based on the actual sensitivities identified. I would hope that there would be room for occupational medicine input at that table.

References

European Commission (27 July 2003). Reference European Group on Ethics in Science and New Technologies. Opinion 18. Ethical Aspects of Genetic Testing in the Workplace.

Faculty of Occupational Medicine of the Royal College of Physicians (2012) *Ethics Guidance for Occupational Health Practice*. Available at: www.fom.ac.uk

Hansson S. O. (2009) 'Should We Protect the Most Sensitive People?', *Journal of Radiological Protection*, 29(2), 2011–18.

Holtzman N. A. (2003) 'Ethical Aspects of Genetic Testing in the Workplace', *Community Genet* 2003 6(3), 136–8.

International Commission on Radiation Protection (1977) 'ICRP Publication 26 Recommendations of ICRP', *Ann. ICRP*, 1(3), 3.

International Commission on Radiation Protection (2007) '2007 Recommendations of the ICRP', *Ann. ICRP*, 37(2–4), 56.

International Labour Organisation (1997) 'Protection of Workers' Personal Data', *ILO Code of Practice 1997*.

Kalman C. (2015) 'Individual Sensitivity to Occupational Hazards', *Occupational Medicine*, 65, 2–3.

Karg K., Burnmeister M., Sheddon K., Sen S. (2011) 'The Serotonin Transporter Variant (5 – HTTLRP) Stress and Depression Meta- Analysis Revisited. Evidence of Genetic Modification', *Archives of General Psychiatry*, 68(5), 444–54.

Martchenko M., Candille S. I., Tang H., Cohen S. N. (2012) 'Human Genetic Variation Altering Antrax Toxin Sensitivity', *Proceedings of the National Academy of Sciences of the United States of America*, 109(8), 2972–7.

Mehta A. J., Thun G. A., Imboden M. et al. (2014) 'Interactions Between SERPINA 1 PiMZ Genotype, Occupational Exposure and Lung Function Decline', *OEM*, 71(4), 229–30.

Nelson H. H., Kelsey K. T. (2014) 'Genetic Susceptibility in the Workplace: A Scientific and Ethical Challenge', *OEM*, 71, 229–30.

Schulte P., Howard J. (2011) 'Genetic Susceptibility in the Setting of Occupational Health Standards', *Annual Review of Public Health*, 32, 149–59.

UK Health and Safety Executive (2007, August) 'HSE Horizon Scanning Intelligence: Group Genetic Testing in the Workplace', *HSE SRO14*.

UK Health Protection Agency (2013) HPA RCE-21, *Human Radiosensensitivity*, March 2013.

UK Legislation (2010) *The Equality Act 2010*. Available at: legislation.gov.uk

US Legislation (2008) *The Genetic Nondiscrimination Act of 2008*. (Pub, L.110–233, 122 Stat. 881, enacted May 21 2008).

US Supreme Court (1991) *Automobile Workers v Johnson Controls 499 US 187 (1991)*.

Index